CLINICAL EPIDEMIOLOGY & EVIDENCE-BASED MEDICINE

Fundamental Principles of Clinical Reasoning & Research

DAVID L. KATZ
Yale University School of Medicine

Errata

Please note: An error resulted in an omission on the title page. The title page should acknowledge Laura Greci, MD, senior resident in internal and preventive medicine at Griffin Hospital in Derby, CT, and Haq Nawaz, MD, MPH, associate director, preventive medicine residency program, Griffin Hospital, Derby, CT, as collaborating authors.

Sage Publications
International Educational and Professional Publisher
Thousand Oaks ▪ London ▪ New Delhi

For information:

 Sage Publications, Inc.
2455 Teller Road
Thousand Oaks, California 91320
E-mail: order@sagepub.com

Sage Publications Ltd.
6 Bonhill Street
London EC2A 4PU
United Kingdom

Sage Publications India Pvt. Ltd.
M-32 Market
Greater Kailash I
New Delhi 110 048 India

Printed in the United States of America

Library of Congress Cataloging-in-Publication Data

Katz, David L.
    Clinical epidemiology and evidence-based medicine: Fundamental principles of clinical reasoning and research / by David L. Katz.
        p.   cm.
    ISBN 0-7619-1938-4 (cloth: acid-free paper)
    ISBN 0-7619-1939-2 (pbk.: acid-free paper)
    1. Clinical epidemiology.   2. Evidence-based medicine.   I. Title.
    RA652.2.C55   K38   2001
    614.4—dc21   2001001275

This book is printed on acid-free paper.

01   02   03   04   05   06   7   6   5   4   3   2   1

Acquiring Editor:	C. Deborah Laughton
Editorial Assistant:	Veronica Novak
Production Editor:	Sanford Robinson
Editorial Assistant:	Cindy Bear
Typesetter:	Technical Typesetting, Inc.
Indexer:	L. Pilar Wyman
Cover Designer:	Ravi Balasuriya

I dedicate this book to my wife, Catherine: the reason why.

Contents

Preface   ix
Acknowledgments   xxi

Section I

Principles of Clinical Reasoning

**1. Of Patients and Populations: Population-Based Data in
Clinical Practice**   **5**

**2. Test Performance: Disease Probability, Test
Interpretation and Diagnosis**   **13**
    Test Performance   13
    Disease Probability   25
    Test Interpretation   31

**3. Quantitative Aspects of Clinical Thinking: Predictive
Values and Bayes' Theorem**   **45**
    Application   50
    Alternative Applications   56
    Odds and Probabilities: Bayes' Theorem
      and Likelihood Ratios   57
    Implications of Bayes' Theorem for Diagnostic Testing   60
    Conceptual Factors Influencing Probability Estimates   62
    Bayes' Theorem and the Sequence of Testing   64

4. Fundamentals of Screening: The Art and Science of
   Looking for Trouble   69
   Screening Defined   70
   Screening Criteria   70
   Statistical Considerations Pertinent to Screening   73
   Sequential Testing   77
   Statistics, Screening and Monetary Costs   79
   Statistics, Screening and Human Costs   84
   Screening Pros and Cons   87

5. Measuring and Conveying Risk   91
   Measuring Risk to the Individual Patient   92
   Risk Factors   96
   Measuring Risk in Clinical Investigation   96
   Measuring Risk Modification   97

Section II

Principles of Clinical Research

6. Hypothesis Testing 1: Principles   107
   Association   110
   Variation   112
   Measuring Central Tendency: The Mean   113
   Measuring Dispersion: Variance and Standard Deviation 114
   Testing Hypotheses: The Signal to Noise Ratio   116
   Types of Clinical Data   116
   Characterizing Associations: Univariate, Bivariate,
      and Multivariate Methods   119
   Eliminating Alternative Explanations: The Threat
      of Confounding and Bias   120

7. Hypothesis Testing 2: Mechanics   127
   Parametric Methods   128
   Nonparametric Methods   134
   Odds Ratios and Risk Ratios   139
   Other Methods of Hypothesis Testing   141
   Hypothesis Testing and the Stipulation of Outcome   142

8. Study Design   **147**

    Case-control Studies   151
    Cohort Studies   155
    Retrospective Cohort Studies   155
    Prospective Cohort Studies   156
    Randomized Clinical Trials   158
    Meta-Analysis   160
    Active Control Equivalence Studies (ACES)   163
    Crossover Trials   164
    Factorial Trial Designs   164
    Other Study Designs   165
    Sampling   166
    Assessing Study Validity   167
    The Strength of Evidence   169
    Constructively Deconstructing the Medical Literature   170

9. Interpreting Statistics in the Medical Literature   **181**

    Statistical Significance   182
    One-tailed and Two-tailed Tests of Significance   185
    Type I and Type II error   188
    p-values   190
    Sample Size   191
    Confidence Intervals   194
    Other Considerations   195

Section III

From Research to Reasoning: The Application of Evidence in Clinical Practice

10. Decision Analysis   **203**

11. Diagnosis   **211**

12. Management   **219**

Appendices

Appendix A: Getting at the Evidence   **225**
    Appendix A.1: Accessing the Medical Literature:
        How to Get There from Here   225
    Appendix A.2: A Walking Tour of Medline   241
    Appendix A.3: Publication Bias: The Limits
        of Accessible Evidence   245
Appendix B: Considering Cost In Clinical Practice:
    The Constraint of Resource Limitations   **249**
Appendix C: Clinically Useful Measures Derived
    from the 2 × 2 Contingency Table   **257**

Glossary   **261**
Text Sources   **279**
    Books   279
    Users' Guides to the Medical Literature   280
    Other Articles   282
Epilogue   **283**
Index   **285**
About the Author   **295**

Preface

Evidence has securely claimed its place among the dominant concepts in modern medical practice. To the extent possible, clinicians are expected to base their decisions (or recommendations) on the best available evidence. Physicians may see this as one possible silver lining in the dark cloud of managed care. Insurers competing for clientele and revenue have increasingly made it a practice to include in benefits packages only those items for which there is convincing proof of benefit. Moreover, these items must provide their benefit at reasonable and acceptable cost. Thus, when applying evidence to the practice of medicine the benefit of the evidence must be measurable and definable, the cost must be measurable, and, perhaps the subtlest challenge of all, evidence itself must be defined and measured.

Despite current efforts to bridge the gap between medicine and public health through the Medicine-Public Health Initiative,[1,2] the philosophical divide between a discipline devoted to the concerns of populations and one devoted to the advocacy of an individual seems impassable. However, the consistent application of evidence to clinical decision making is the bridge between the concerns of clinical practice and the goals of public health.

Evidence-based practice is population-based practice. Evidence applied clinically is derived from the medical literature, where the standards of evidence, and therefore practice, continuously evolve. But what is reported in the literature is not the experience of an individual patient (other than in case reports, a modest although time-honored and often important source of evidence, or in n-of-1 experiments), and certainly not the experience of our individual patient, but rather the experience of a population of patients. Therefore the practice of evidence-based medicine requires the application of population-based data to the care of an individual patient whose experiences will be different in ways both discernible and not, from the collective experience reported in the literature. All evidence-based decisions made on behalf of (or preferably, with) individual patients are extrapolation or interpolation from the prior experience of other patients. Clinical medicine is evidence-based only if it is population-based.

This may or may not seem a provocative concept, but consider the alternative. To base clinical decisions for an individual on the individual alone, the outcome of an intervention would need to be known in advance. In other words, medicine would need to borrow from astrology or some other system of predicting future events. The choice of an initial antihypertensive drug for a hypertensive patient cannot be based, before the drug is prescribed, on the response of the patient in question. Nor can the benefits to the patient be known in advance. The drug is chosen based on the published results of antihypertensive therapy in other patients. The particular drug is selected based on how closely the characteristics of our patient match those of others who have benefited from specific therapies. Once the drug is selected, while the therapeutic effect on the surrogate measure (e.g., blood pressure) is detectable, any outcome benefit to our patient (e.g., stroke prevention) remains unknowable. We can never identify the stroke we have prevented in an individual. The strokes we prevent by prescribing antihypertensives, the myocardial infarctions we prevent by prescribing aspirin or statins, are statistical events. We know the rate at which such conditions occur in particular populations, and research demonstrates how these rates can be changed. By applying the intervention to our patient, we expect the risk of the event to decline comparably. But unless an intervention eliminates the risk of a clinical event entirely (few, if any, do), our patient may suffer the event despite intervention. Alternatively, our patient may have appeared to be at risk, but would have never suffered the event even without intervention. We can never know. We never base what we do for an individual on the outcomes particular to that individual. We base what we do on the experience of populations, and the probability that our patient will share that experience. Astute medical care is predicated on the capacity to identify similarities between a single patient and the particular population whose collective experience is most likely to inform and anticipate the single patient's experience. In his Poetics, Aristotle considers this "eye for resemblances," or "intuitive perception of the similarity in dissimilars," a mark of genius.[3] If so, it is a genius the clinician frequently has cause to invoke.

The science of applying the principles of population-based (epidemiologic) evidence to the management of individual patients has come to be known as *clinical epidemiology*. While epidemiology characterizes the impact of health related conditions on populations, clinical epidemiology applies such data to individual patient care. Clinicians are traditionally uncomfortable with the notion of catering to populations rather than individual patients. Clinical epidemiology asserts that the two are effectively the same, or at least inextricably conjoined. Individual patient care is informed by the interpretation of population-based data. When populations are well served by the health care they receive, the individual members of those populations are (generally) well served. When individuals are well served by the clinical care they receive, in the aggregate, the pattern of that care becomes (usually) the sound practice of health care delivery to populations.

Implicit in the concept of evidence being the derivative of a populations experience is the need to relate that experience back to the individual patient. The inapplicability of some evidence to some patients is self-evident. Studies of prostate cancer are irrelevant to our female patients; studies of cervical cancer are irrelevant to our male patients. Yet beyond the obvious exclusions is a vast sea of gray. If our patient is older than, younger than, sicker than, healthier than, ethnically different from, taller, shorter, simply different from the subjects of a study, do the results pertain? As our individual patient will never be entirely like the subjects in a study (unless they were a subject, and even then their individual experience might or might not reflect the collective experience), can the results of a study ever be truly pertinent? Clinical epidemiology is a sextant, or in more modern but equally nautical terms, the geographical positioning system (GPS), on a vast sea of medical uncertainty. And, to extend the metaphor, the skills of piloting can be acquired and increase the reliability with which a particular destination (i.e., diagnosis, therapeutic outcome) is achieved. Yet each crossing will be unique, often with previously unencountered challenges and hazards. No degree of evidence will fully chart the expanse of idiosyncrasy in human health and disease. Thus, to work skillfully with evidence is to acknowledge its limits. Judgment must be prepared to cross those seas as yet uncharted by evidence.

It is expected that some of the material in this text, particularly the more statistically involved, will diverge from what we would accept as intuitive. However, comfort can be taken from the fact that we are all *de facto* clinical epidemiologists. As clinicians, we decide which information pertains to a particular patient every day of practice: who does and does not get prescribed an antibiotic (and if so, which one); who does and does not get treated with insulin, metformin, a sulfonylurea, a thiazolidinedione; who does and does not get advised to be x-rayed, injected, phlebotomized, cannulated, or instrumented. Cognizant or not of the subtleties as they play out, in each such decision we are comparing our patient to others that have come before; others in our own practice, relying as we tend to do (though we tell one another we should not) on the compelling lessons of personal anecdote, or others whose experience has been more formally conveyed, in the tables and graphs of a peer-reviewed article. While the choices we ultimately make in clinical testing and management are a product of our interaction with patients, our shared and disparate values, beliefs, and preferences, the decisions that delineate those choices are largely the product of clinical epidemiology.

Because we all practice clinical epidemiology, an understanding of this tool (or array of tools) we use is incumbent upon us all. If every clinical decision derives in whole or in part (and it does) from the tacit comparison of our patient to a population of patients, then the skill with which that comparison is made is fundamental to the skill with which medicine is practiced. Integral to that comparison is the capacity to recognize the defining characteristics of both patients and populations as the basis for defining the bounds of similarity and dissimilarity. The physician's capacity to evaluate the context in which "evidence" was gathered is equally important. The ability to evaluate the quality as well as the pertinence of evidence is essential. Of course, finding the best available evidence when one is uncertain about a clinical decision is prerequisite to its interpretation.

Viewed with the cool glare of reductionism, the practice of evidence-based medicine requires a discrete and modest skill set. One must be able to find the available evidence. One must be able to evaluate the relevance and quality of evidence. And one must be able to interpret evidence presented in terms pertinent to populations so that the same data may inform patient care decisions. These skills, like any others, can be learned and mastered. The various tools of our trade—stethoscopes and sphygmomanometers—were handed to us along with the lessons that made us competent in their use. While the tools of evidence-based practice have become enjoined among the more highly valued items in our proverbial black bags, most of us have had no formal instruction in their use. Consequently, many of us are likely using these tools less effectively than we might.

While ***clinical choices*** (for both testing and treatment) are predicated on, at a minimum, the knowledge, judgment, values, preconceived notions, experiences, preferences and fears of both clinician and patient, ***clinical decision-making*** is greatly influenced by three considerations: **probability**, **risk**, and **alternative**. Probability is fundamental to such decisions, as we evaluate and treat patients only for a given condition or conditions it seems they might have. We do not order CT scans of every patient's brain, yet we do order some. The distinction is derived from our estimate of the probability of finding relevant pathology. A clinical decision cannot be reached without a semiquantitative estimate of probability. A patient either seems likely enough, or not likely enough, to need a particular test or treatment, to result in our recommending it. This is a truism for any test applied only to some patients.

Some low probability diagnoses are pursued because they pose such high risk. Here, too, the natural tendencies of our minds are in alignment with clinical epidemiology. We admit some patients to the hospital to "rule out MI" even though we believe the probability of myocardial infarction (MI) to be low, because the risk associated with undetected MI is high. We have all been taught to do a lumbar puncture (LP) whenever we wonder "should I do an LP?" because of the devastating consequences of missing meningitis.

Finally, we factor in alternatives: alternative treatments, alternative tests, alternative diagnoses. When chest pain seems atypical for angina, but no alternative explanation is at hand, we are more apt to treat the pain as angina. When pneumonia is present to explain shortness of breath, we will be less inclined to work up pulmonary embolism (PE), despite pleuritic chest pain and tachycardia. When we have excluded the impossible we are apt to focus on what remains, however improbable.[4] By a process to which we are, for the most part, comfortably incognizant, we make every decision factoring in considerations of probability, risk, and alternatives.

But an unconscious process is a process that cannot be optimally regulated. By knowing that our decisions are borne on our musings over probability, risk, and alternative, these parameters should become of sufficient interest to us to warrant conscious monitoring. Each of these parameters is population-based. There is no probability of genuine relevance to an individual: there is the rate of occurrence in populations, and the degree of concordance between individual and population characteristics. There is no true individual risk; for an individual, an event occurs (100% risk) or does not (0% risk). There, is however, the comparability of the patient to groups in whom the event rate in question is higher or lower. The alternatives available for an individual patient are those options and interventions applied under similar circumstances to other patients, with varying degrees of success.

Similar principles underlie the research that constitutes the evidence base (or its greater portion) for clinical practice. As is detailed later in the text, studies are constructed in an effort to establish the collective experience of a few (the study subjects) as representative of the many. While the clinician looks for correspondence between patient and study participants, the investigator must consider the relevance of the study to the larger population of potential future patients. Just as the probability of outcomes, good and bad, guides clinical management, the probabilities of outcomes, good and bad, false and true, are estimated and factored into the statistical stipulations and design of a study. The appropriateness of a particular methodology depends as much on alternatives as does the appropriateness of a clinical intervention. As is expressed by the conventional safeguards against false-positive and false-negative error (see Chapter 9) and the application of progressively stringent standards of human subject protection,[5,6,7,8] thorough consideration of risk is intrinsic to the research process. Even less rigorous means of conveying evidence, such as case reports and case series, depend for their interest and relevance on probability, alternative, and risk. Such reports are meaningful only when the putative association is apparent and convincing; the clinical need nontrivial; the risks of application acceptable; alternative explanations unlikely; and the pertinence to our patients probable. Probability, alternative, and risk influence one another within the disciplines of clinical practice and clinical research, and these disciplines in turn interact. The needs, insights and frustrations of practice are an important source of hypotheses and attendant methods in clinical research. The evidence generated by such studies naturally serves to inform clinical practice. These interactions are displayed in Table 1.

Ultimately, then, while judicious practice depends on evidence, the derivation of evidence depends on many of the same principles as judicious practice. The thoughtful and diligent practitioner remains abreast of the literature to apply the best practice an evolving evidence base supports. The diligent and thoughtful investigator exploits evolving methodologies to generate evidence most conducive to advances in science and practice. The highest standards of evidence-based practice are achieved not only when evidence is well applied, but also when that evidence is

TABLE 1	The Influence of Probability, Risk, and Alternatives on Clinical Research and Clinical Reasoning, and the Salient Interactions		
Discipline	Factor Interactions[1,2]	Factor	Discipline Interactions
Clinical Research		**Probability:** The estimated probability of a meaningful association between putative cause (exposure, intervention) and effect (measure of outcome) is the basis for generating and/or testing particular hypotheses.	Needs for new treatments and technologies, and insights derived from clinical anecdote, are sources of hypotheses that serve as the basis for clinical studies. Clinical experience is often the basis for initial probability and risk estimates in the generation and testing of research hypotheses.
		Risk: Research design is constrained and/or influenced by intervention risks, the risks of non-intervention (placebo) when treatment is available, and the risks of false-positive or false-negative outcomes.	
		Alternative: Hypotheses are generated and tested when a particular causal association is deemed more probable, important, or testable than alternatives. Among the conditions for the establishment of causality in research is the exclusion (to the extent possible) of alternative explanations of the apparent association.	

[1] In research, higher risk is justified by greater probability of a particular outcome and the relative lack of acceptable alternatives. The probability of demonstrating any particular causal association will vary inversely with the relative probability of alternative explanations for the outcome of interest.

[2] In clinical practice, conditions that are highly probable will be priority considerations even if low risk. Lower probability considerations will become prioritized when they represent high risk potential. The relative probability of any outcome or conclusion will vary inversely with the plausibility, relative probability, and abundance of alternative explanations.

Note: Dashed arrows indicate interactions among the factors within one discipline. Bold arrows indicate interactions between disciplines.

TABLE 1 (continued.)

Discipline	Factor Interactions[1,2]	Factor	Discipline Interactions
Clinical Reasoning		**Probability:** The estimated probability of a particular condition (or conditions) in a given patient is an important basis for generating a differential diagnosis and conducting and interpreting pertinent diagnostic tests. The estimated probability of a response (or range of responses) to a given intervention (or to non-intervention) is similarly an important basis for the selection of management strategies.	The published results of studies become the evidence base (or a critical component of it) underlying clinical practice. Outcomes and the patterns of disease and risk factors in populations become the basis for probability and risk estimates in practice.
		Risk: Clinical practice is constrained and/or influenced by intervention risks, the risks of non-intervention when treatment is available, and the risks of false-positive or false-negative results of diagnostic testing.	
		Alternative: A particular diagnosis is made when one condition is deemed more probable, important, or treatable than alternatives. Among the conditions for the establishment of a diagnosis is the exclusion (to the extent possible) of alternative explanations for the patient's condition.	

well produced. Part of the burden for the responsible cultivation of higher standards and better outcomes in medicine falls, naturally, to researchers and those that screen and publish their findings. But application is ultimately the responsibility of the clinician, who is obligated to consider not only the pertinence of particular evidence to his or her practice but the adequacy and reliability of the evidence itself. At every step, from the design of a study to clinical counseling, probability, alternative, and risk must be addressed. For evidence to be well applied the correspondence of this one patient to those that came before must be considered, the compatibility of prior knowledge with current need revisited.

We cannot, therefore, practice clinical medicine and avoid population-based principles. We cannot practice clinical medicine and avoid the practice of clinical epidemiology. But the discipline of evidence-based practice/clinical epidemiology (the terms might be used interchangeably) is not one in which most of us have had any formal initiation. All of the art and all of the science of medicine depend on how artfully and scientifically we as practitioners reach our decisions. The art of clinical decision-making is judgment, an even more difficult concept to grapple with than evidence. As the quality and scope of evidence to support clinical interventions is, and will likely always remain, limited in comparison to the demands of clinical practice, the practice of evidence-based medicine requires an appreciation for the limits of evidence, and the arbiters of practice at and beyond its perimeters. Judgment fortified by the highest standards of decision-making science is a force to be reckoned with, enabling us each to extract the best possible results from a process to which we are naturally inclined. Ultimately that is the validation of evidence-based practice, or population-based practice, or clinical epidemiology—the outcomes to which such concepts contribute. Rigorous reasoning is the means, desirable outcomes the ends.

〳 FOR WHOM IƧ THIƧ BOOK INTENDED?

This book is about concepts, or rather the methodology of arriving at robust clinical decisions that binds together an array of concepts. This book is not about the facts, or current fund of medical knowledge, on which such decisions rest. The life span of medical facts is short and shortening further all of the time. Fortunately the methods for extracting optimal performance from the prevailing facts of the day are enduring. The intent here is to provide a basic mastery of such methods, that is, the capacity to harness the power of our intrinsic heuristics (decision-making pathways) and apply it to a constantly evolving body of knowledge. The medical literature and clinical vignettes will be referenced as required to demonstrate applications of the methods described. But the message is in the methods rather than their application to any particular study or article or case.

The intended audience for this text is anyone who makes, or will make, clinical decisions. Worth noting are a number of excellent texts on the subjects of clinical epidemiology and evidence-based medicine already available, many of which I have used liberally as sources (see Text Sources). Compared to most of these, this text is intended to be more clinician-friendly and assumes less prior knowledge. Every effort has been made to present material in a simple and uncluttered manner. Most tables in the text, for example, should be interpretable at a glance.

One of the important distinctions I have made while writing this text is to endeavor to teach less and clarify more. The contention on which this text is based is that clinicians are intuitive clinical epidemiologists, and therefore don't really need to learn to function as such. This text is designed to help reveal the influence and application of this intuition. By doing so, it should illuminate the processes of converting evidence to decisions, research to practice. The more we understand the ways in which we approach evidence and make decisions, the more reliably we can control these processes, and their attendant outcomes.

While a fair amount of statistics is included, the use of a calculator in clinical practice is certainly not intended. Rather, as quantitative principles already underlie clinical reasoning, one is well advised to have a basic familiarity with those principles. Fundamentals of practice truly hang in the balance. A positive or negative test result is at times highly reliable, at other times highly unreliable. A bit of number crunching demonstrates how different clinical conclusions can, and should, be under different circumstances. The numbers need not be recalled for the importance of the concepts to be retained.

The consistent application of the basic principles of clinical epidemiology infuses with the strengths of science the decision making that presupposes all else in clinical practice, including its outcomes. That science and evidence are limited and are dependent upon judgment for their application is implicit in the text everywhere it is not explicit. Also implicit throughout the text is that the medical decisions reached by clinicians serve only to provide patients—the ultimate decision makers—with good information upon which to base their decisions.

I am grateful to the many accomplished clinicians and clinical epidemiologists whose contributions I have drawn on so heavily, both in the drafting of this text and in my own clinical and research efforts. I acknowledge with appreciation and humility that in drafting this text I have followed where many luminaries have led. That said, if I have wandered off the trails blazed by the leaders of this field, I can blame no one but myself. Any misstep—ambiguity, miscalculation, or distortion—is of course my responsibility. While hoping that none is found, I apologize and offer my sincere regret in advance on the chance that any is.

With a great reverence for the unique burdens and privileges of clinical practice, I submit the principles of this text in the belief and hope that they will enhance your ability to obtain the best possible outcomes for your patients.

※ REFERENCES

1. Reiser SJ. Medicine and public health. Pursuing a common destiny. *JAMA.* 1999;276:1429–1430.
2. Reiser SJ. Topics for our times: The medicine/public health initiative. *Am J Public Health.* 1997;87:1098–1099.
3. Barnes J (ed). *The Complete Works of Aristotle.* Vol. 2. Princeton, NJ: Princeton University Press; 1984:2335.
4. Conan Doyle A. The sign of four. In: Conan Doyle A. *The Complete Sherlock Holmes.* New York: Doubleday; 1930:87–138.
5. Amdur RJ. Improving the protection of human research subjects. *Acad Med.* 2000;75:718–720.
6. Bragadottir H. Children's rights in clinical research. *J Nurs Scholarsh.* 2000;32:179–184.
7. Beasley JW. Primary care research and protection for human subjects. *JAMA.* 1999;281:1697–1698.
8. High DM, Doole MM. Ethical and legal issues in conducting research involving elderly subjects. *Behav Sci Law.* 1995;13:319–335.

Acknowledgments

I am grateful to Dr. Ralph Horwitz, chairman of medicine at the Yale School of Medicine, for setting the standard so many of us strive (without much hope of success) to meet.

I sincerely appreciate the vision of Dan Ruth, and the guidance and support of C. Deborah Laughton, at Sage. The transition from idea to book is a relay race, in which their laps were very well run indeed.

I acknowledge with thanks the contributions of my collaborators, Dr. Laura Greci, a senior resident in preventive medicine/internal medicine at Griffin Hospital in Derby, CT, and Dr. Haq Nawaz, associate director of the same preventive medicine residency.

I am grateful to my parents, Dr. Donald Katz and Susan Katz, for never (well, hardly ever. . .) discouraging me when, as a child, I incessantly asked, "why?" To my Dad, I also add appreciation for the walks at Horse Heaven; I do my best thinking there.

I am deeply indebted to Jennifer Ballard, administrator of the Yale Prevention Research Center, who makes me wonder every day how I managed before!

I am grateful to my children, Rebecca, Corinda, Valerie, Natalia, and Gabriel, for their patience and unconditional love, seemingly unattenuated by the countless times I have turned from them to the computer, and turned down their invitations to play.

Above all, I am grateful to my wife, Catherine, my best editor as well as my best friend, for the love and the coffee and the kind words as much as for the ruthlessly honest (and always constructive) criticism.

Section I

PRINCIPLES OF
CLINICAL REASONING

This section is *not* an effort to encourage the use of statistics in clinical decision-making. Rather, it is intended to disclose and characterize the statistical aspects of decision-making as it is already occurring. For if clinical decisions are already governed in part by quantitative principles, it follows that the process of reaching them is more controllable, more predictable, and more reliable if the process is understood.

The case that statistical principles influence our decision-making efforts can be made with virtually any clinical scenario. Consider, for example, the patient presenting with fever and headache. Not all such patients undergo lumbar puncture. Yet some patients do. How is the decision reached? First, by acquiring as much pertinent information as possible to support inferences regarding **probability**, **alternative**, and **risk**. These three parameters influence (and perhaps even dominate) clinical decisions.

In all patients with fever and headache, there is a finite probability of meningitis. While none of us could comfortably commit to a precise numerical estimate of probability in a given patient, we all manage to decide whether meningitis (or any diagnosis) is **probable enough to warrant intervention** (either diagnostic or therapeutic). *Probable enough* implies a quantitative threshold. And while the placement of that threshold varies widely among clinicians, each of us must place it somewhere; failure to do so is failure to decide.

What makes a condition *probable enough*? Until or unless a differential diagnosis list is shortened to a single item, the probability of any diagnosis on the list is in part mediated by all of the competing probabilities. In a patient with migraines, a headache mimicking prior migraines makes meningitis less likely, but certainly not impossible. Automatically, unthinkingly, we establish estimates of **relative probability** in deciding whether or not a condition is *probable enough*. And in the unusual advent of a single-item differential, wisdom attributed to Sherlock Holmes applies: when the impossible has been excluded, whatever is left, however improbable, must be true.[1] At times, *probable enough* need not be very probable at all.

This is particularly true when risk is high. But as all clinical decisions carry risk, whether they dictate action or inaction, probability must be estimated across the range of alternatives. Intervention for each diagnos-

---

[1] Conan Doyle, A. The sign of four. In: Conan Doyle, A. *The Complete Sherlock Holmes.* New York: Doubleday; 1930:87–158.

tic consideration carries risk. Intervention for the wrong diagnosis carries risk without the potential for benefit. Lack of intervention for the correct diagnosis carries risk, perhaps compounded by the risk of inappropriate intervention.

To establish the risk estimates for each consideration for a single unremarkable clinical encounter is a daunting prospect for even the most mathematically inclined among us, **yet we all do so**. Decisions could not otherwise be reached. To generate such risk estimates consciously is unthinkable, but we unthinkingly do so with each patient encounter. Somehow, the relative probabilities and risks of multiple permutations are converted into decisions. Orders are written. Tests are done. Treatment is administered. And often, because this ungoverned process serves us well, patients respond.

But patients don't always respond. And while adverse outcomes despite optimal decisions will always occur, certain adverse outcomes are doubtless attributable to less than optimal decisions. To the extent that the powerful heuristics of our decision-making operate of their own accord, we have little means to enhance the process or its products. An understanding of the process is prerequisite to its improvement.

Clinicians all apply statistical principles in generating semiquantitative estimates of probability and risk across a spectrum of alternatives. The process is intrinsic and unavoidable. But to the extent that we subject patients to the process without understanding it, we engage in an act of faith rather than science. And we demand less understanding of the performance characteristics of our minds than we do of far less potent technologies.

Thus, the application of statistics to clinical decision-making is simply an elucidation of the discrete principles already at work in the clinician's mind. The content of this section characterizes the statistical principles we unavoidably, but for the most part unintentionally and unthinkingly, already apply. An understanding of these principles is essential to assess, control, and refine the decision-making process on which clinical outcomes depend.

Of Patients
and Populations

Population-Based Data in Clinical Practice

INTRODUCTION

The process of medical evaluation is unavoidably dependent on semiquantitative estimates of disease probability in individual patients. Such estimates are in turn dependent on the prior experience of populations and our familiarity and interpretation of this prior experience. This chapter demonstrates both the need and the intrinsic capacity for clinicians to generate quantitative estimates of disease probability and the dependence of these estimates on population experience.

Consider that a patient presents to your office. How likely is it that the patient has coronary disease? Naturally, you can't answer the question. You have virtually no information about the patient. Yet you have probably already begun the process of generating an estimate. If you are a pediatrician, patients in your practice are unlikely to have coronary disease. Therefore, this patient presenting to you is unlikely to have coronary disease. Similarly, if you are a specialist (other than a cardiologist) to whom patients are referred after passing through the filter of primary care, it is also unlikely that the patient has coronary disease.

But if you are an internist or family practitioner, you may have already started to consider the probability of coronary disease. If you practice in the US, many of your adult patients will have coronary disease; so, too, might the patient in question. If you practice in certain other countries, the probability of coronary disease may be so low that you need hardly ever consider it; therefore, you would not consider it in this patient.

Of note, even at this very preliminary stage of evaluation, is the role of **bias** or, more bluntly, **prejudice** in clinical decision making. We base our decision on experience, either our own or that of others. Making inferences about an individual based on the prior experience one has had with others in the same population is the essence of prejudice, or prejudging. This term is not meant to have negative connotations in clinical practice. Prejudice—a tendency to judge the probability of a diagnosis in an individual based on the probability of that condition in the population the patient comes from—is appropriate and essential. It would be foolish to consider coronary disease routinely in individual patients from a population in which coronary disease almost never occurred. *Almost never* is not *never*, so an individual patient *might* have coronary disease; it would just be highly improbable in such a population. The prejudice borne of experience, and familiarity with the population in question, would influence clinical judgment and decisions in an appropriate way.

So one immediately begins to formulate an impression of probability based on the characteristics of other patients one has seen. But we want more information. In this case, we would like to know whether or not the patient has chest pain suggestive of angina. We would like to know the patient's age and gender; whether or not the patient is hypertensive or diabetic; whether the patient smokes, is sedentary, has hyperlipidemia; whether the patient has a family history of heart disease; whether the patient is obese. The way we conduct our histories and physicals is proof that we want to know these things. But as we progress from one question to another in what at times is an almost mechanical process, we often fail to ask ourselves, "why?" Why do the answers to such questions matter? How many such questions do we need to ask? How can we tell when we have enough information from the history to progress to the physical? How do we know when enough information has been gleaned from the exam?

Our ability to reach conclusions is proof that we can find answers to the above questions. But if we do so through a process to which we are inattentive, the process may fail. A process so fundamental to our performance as clinicians is a process we should feel compelled to understand and master.

The reason that we ask the questions we do is not the one that seems most self-evident. We do not question our patients so that we can know what condition they have. This statement will likely seem heretical, but it is not intended to be. How often do we know with complete certainty the explanation for symptoms in a patient? What we are after, at least much of the time, is the establishment of a sufficiently familiar pattern to invoke our prejudices with security, a sufficiently familiar narrative to predict the conclusion with confidence. In attempting to determine how probable coronary disease is in the patient in question, we ask questions that sequentially allow us to place the patient in the context of populations in which coronary disease is more or less probable. If the patient has chest pain typical of angina pectoris and happens to be a 70-year-old male smoker with diabetes, hypertension, hyperlipidemia, and a family history of heart disease, we can now answer the question with considerable confidence; the probability of coronary disease is high.[1] We have not seen, and do not know, the patient in question. And the patient may not, in fact, have coronary disease. But this patient is clearly very much like others who, in what we have seen or been taught, do have coronary disease. Thus, population-based practice is unavoidable. It infiltrates the process of clinical decision making at every step. Our inferences about an individual patient are derived from the historical experience of other patients whom we believe to be much like our own.

If the process of relating past experience—the experience of populations to the individual patients under our current care—happens of its own accord, why make a fuss about it? Is there intrinsic value in coming to know a process that tends to proceed spontaneously? We naturally conduct our histories so that we can characterize our patients and determine what clinically meaningful conditions they might or might not have. Is there value in transplanting the process to the purview of conscious oversight?

There is. The history and physical can be considered a process of sequential hypothesis testing. Each question asked tests hypotheses about the population from which the patient might come. Once this is acknowledged, there comes a point in the history when additional questions (and answers) cannot dissuade us from a particular conclusion. In the case under consideration, a point in the history would be reached when coronary disease would seem sufficiently probable to warrant further investigation. Even if the answers to subsequent questions were negative, lowering the probability of coronary disease, our suspicion, based on both probability and risk, might be great enough to warrant commitment to a workup. Recognizing this semiquantitative element in our decision making is essential to manage the result. For example, if the patient seemed very likely to have coronary disease, would we abandon that belief if the ECG were normal? Probably not. What if a stress test were normal? Would we proceed from a routine to a nuclear stress test or refer the patient for cardiac catheterization? The answer would depend on how robust the clinical suspicion of coronary disease was, compared with the negative results of any testing done. In such a scenario, would the clinical impression or the results of testing rule the day?

To decide, we would need to be able to compare the reliability of the clinical test results with that of the judgment that resulted in the testing in the first place. Of course, we do this all the time. But we do it quite variably. You will probably agree that permutations of the above scenario presented to 100 different physicians might well result in 100 slightly different plans. And while some of that variability might be legitimized in the allowance for medicine's art, some would simply be the result of deficient science, of failing to apply rigorous methods to the decision-making process. If a negative stress test makes angina pectoris less likely, we need to know *how much* less likely in order to decide whether or not further testing is required. But we also need to know how much less likely *relative to what*? What was the probability with which we started? This vaguely characterized concept, the clinical impression, is prerequisite to every clinical decision, whether in pursuit of diagnosis, prognosis, or treatment. Yet in routine practice, it defies definition. While we expect to know how reliably a stress test performs in identifying angina pectoris, do we demand the same of the medical evaluation on which the decision to order the stress test rests? In general, we do not. And we most certainly should.

Our questioning generally cannot lead us to certain conclusions about the individual patients under our care. In the process of sequentially testing hypotheses about the patient, we are in essence endeavoring to define as narrowly as possible the population of which the patient is representative. Once that goal is achieved, epidemiology can offer us a fairly stable estimate of the probability of the particular condition under consideration. That estimate is the **prevalence** of the condition in the population on which we've settled. Prevalence, the proportion of a specified population with a particular condition at a particular point in time, is related to the probability of disease in an individual member of that population. **Incidence**, the number of new cases of a particular condition in a defined population during a given period of time (typically a year) is related to the risk of that condition in an individual member of that population.

Clinical epidemiology allows us, then, to convert the population data of the epidemiologist into a concept of practical utility for patient care. The analogue of prevalence for the individual patient is the **prior probability**, the probability of the condition in question *prior to* any subsequent testing that might be indicated to further evaluate our impression(s). In essence, there is a discrete probability of a condition prior to every question posed during the history that is modified by each answer to become an estimate of the **posterior probability**, the probability resulting from, or following, a test. Each such posterior probability becomes the prior probability estimate in advance of the next question. The questions should be tailored to the continuously revised probability estimate, so that the pertinent hypotheses are tested. There is, of course, no such thing as a comprehensive H&P; we cannot ask all questions of possible clinical significance in the course of an interview. The same pertains to the physical; a comprehensive physical exam is as unachievable as a comprehensive history. The exam is tailored to test the hypotheses generated through the history. Each relevant aspect of the exam completed serves in turn to modify the probability of whatever condition or conditions are under consideration. Thus the physical exam, like the history, is sequential hypothesis testing and sequential conversion of prior probability to posterior probability, then back to prior probability in advance of the next maneuver.

This construct may seem artificial, yet it is the mere application of principles we already accept as fundamental to the medical workup. We could not legitimately order an echocardiogram, stress test, MRI, or V/Q scan with no advance knowledge of how reliably each performs. We should know in advance of any test we order how secure we will be with the result if positive or negative and what the implications for clinical management will be of each possible outcome. Yet by far the most potent "technology" to which our patients are subject is our decision making, the antecedent to all other medical technology. No other technology will be applied unless so guided by the "results" of our clinical evaluation. How reasonable is it to ignore the performance characteristics of the process that underlies all use of technology, then require that the performance characteristics of the secondary technologies be known? We may know how reliably a CAT scan performs, yet we generally do not know in any systematic way how reliably we determine the need for the CAT scan. And as will be demonstrated in Chapters 2 and 3, the performance of the CAT scan, or any other technology, is dependent on the context in which it is obtained. Just as a 5mm PPD reaction is positive for TB in a high-risk patient but negative in a low-risk patient,[2,3] a positive test when the probability of the condition is very low cannot mean the same thing as it does when the probability is high.

This can be demonstrated by use of an extreme, and therefore absurd, example. If a pregnancy test is accurate *almost all of the time* (e.g., 99% accurate), a presupposition rarely met by tests we use routinely, and it returns positive when ordered for a male patient, we know it must be wrong. Not because the test has suddenly lost our trust but because the prior probability of the condition (pregnancy) in the patient (a male) is 0. If a prior probability of 0 invalidates the positive result of a highly accurate test, a prior probability of 1 (100%) similarly invalidates the results of a negative test, no matter how reliably the test generally performs. These extremes help clarify that the range of prior probabilities between 0 and 1 must also influence how we interpret a test. If a prior probability is very close to 0, we should require a much higher standard of technological evidence before we conclude with confidence that a condition has been *ruled in*. If a prior probability is very close to 1, we will similarly require a high standard of evidence to conclude that disease can be *ruled out*.

But the implications of this construct run deeper still. If a prior probability between 0 and 1 can be established and the performance characteristics of the relevant technologies are known, then the ability of each diagnostic test to change our probability enough to alter clinical management can be determined in advance. Certainly, a test not reliable enough to alter a very high or low prior probability estimate is of little clinical utility. But worse, if the principles of clinical epidemiology are overlooked, the test is potentially harmful. A positive test, if interpreted identically in all patients regardless of whether their probability of disease is high or low, will provide misinformation as often as information. Dissociated from the principles of clinical epidemiology, medical technology, whether invasive or noninvasive, poses very real threats to patient care.

SUMMARY/TAKE-AWAY MESSAGES

The care of the individual patient is directed toward the best achievable outcome for that individual. But the future outcome for an individual patient is unknown and cannot be ascertained. Rather, the probability of both diagnosis and treatment response is based on the prior experience of similar patients. The reliability of the **prior probability** estimate is based on the confidence with which disease **prevalence** in the population is known, the appropriateness of the particular diagnosis under consideration, and the degree of correspondence between the patient and the population. The results of diagnostic testing must be interpreted in light of the prior probability estimate and not used to replace it. When test results are incompatible with patient characteristics, even highly accurate tests may be more apt to be wrong than right. The reliability of the diagnostic process is substantially dependent on the prior probability estimate as well as on the judicious selection and performance characteristics of the diagnostic tests themselves. Measures of test performance, their quantitative interaction with estimates of disease probability, and the implications for diagnosis are considered in Chapter 2.

REFERENCES

1. Cannon CP. Diagnosis and management of patients with unstable angina. *Curr Probl Cardiol*. 1999;24:681–744.
2. Mackin LA. Screening for tuberculosis in the primary care setting. *Lippincotts Prim Care Pract*. 1998;2:599–610.
3. Starkey RD. Tuberculin testing: Placement and interpretation. *AAOHN J*. 1995;43:371–375.

Test Performance

Disease Probability, Test Interpretation and Diagnosis

Few, if any, diagnostic tests perform perfectly. Instead, tests are accurate or inaccurate, reliable or unreliable, to varying degrees, under varying clinical circumstances. Tests yield positive or negative, correct or incorrect results in patterns that are dependent on patient characteristics, and substantially predictable. The reliability of the diagnostic process is dependent in part on an appreciation for the quantitative impact of test performance on disease probability. The probability of a particular diagnosis depends on underlying estimates of disease probability prior to testing, the performance of selected tests, and the assumptions imposed to facilitate test interpretation. This chapter explores the quantitative aspects of the diagnostic process.

⑆ TEST PERFORMANCE

The performance of tests used to titrate the probability of any particular diagnosis can be cast in terms familiar to most of us. **Sensitivity** is the ability of a test to detect disease when it is present. **Specificity** is the ability of a test to exclude disease when it is absent.

While ostensibly simple, these concepts underlie much of the reasoning in clinical epidemiology and therefore merit more rigorous treatment.

Each term is used in medicine much as it is used in the vernacular. Consider the use of sensitivity in the vernacular, such as *sensitive* skin. Skin that is sensitive will feel the lightest touch of the wind. If the wind blows, sensitive skin will feel it. But we know nothing about how such skin will feel when the wind does not blow.

The denominator for sensitivity is the presence of the condition in question (e.g., disease). Sensitivity can tell us nothing about the test's performance in patients who are condition (disease) free. In terms of a population, the denominator for sensitivity is the **prevalence**, the proportion of the population with the condition. Of those with the condition, some will test positive (true positives), and some will test negative (false negatives). Sensitivity is the proportion of disease positives in whom the test is positive. If a test is negative in a patient with disease, it is a false-negative result. Thus, sensitivity (the true-positive rate) and the rate of false-negative error are complementary and add to 1.

Specificity pertains to the proportion of the population that is free of disease. In comparable terms, the denominator for specificity, all disease-free individuals, is 1 – prevalence. A test is specific when it reacts only to the singular condition under investigation. The proportion of those free of disease identified as disease free is the specificity. Specificity pertains only to the denominator of those who are negative for the condition. Those who are disease free but have a positive test result are false positives. The specificity (the rate of true negatives) plus the false-positive error rate are complementary and add to 1. Note that among those with disease there are true positives and false negatives; sensitivity defines the rate at which true positives are identified. Among those free of disease, there are true negatives and false positives. Specificity defines the rate at which true negatives are identified. In both cases, recalling the denominator is helpful. Specificity is relative to those free of disease, and sensitivity to those with disease. Only those with disease are subject to being false negatives; only those who are disease free are subject to being false positives.

Just as the *P* wave orients one to the basic interpretation of an electrocardiogram, the denominator orients one to the fundamental interpretation of epidemiologic (clinical or otherwise) principles. To consider how sensitivity and specificity measure the performance of a test, the denominator to which each pertains is the first item to recall. In clinical epidemiology, start with the denominator, the portion of the statement that indicates "in those with..." some particular characteristic. The numerator, the occurrence of events within the denominator population, will tend to follow quite readily (see 2 × 2 table, Appendix C).

The relationships between sensitivity, specificity, false-negative error, false-positive error, and prevalence can best be demonstrated with use of a 2 × 2 contingency table. By convention, such tables set true disease status across the top and test status along the side. The cells are labeled *a* through *d*, beginning in the upper left and proceeding left to right through each row. Such a table is shown in Box 2.1.

As depicted in the 2 × 2 table, the entire study population, or *n*, is $a + b + c + d$. The population with disease is $(a + c)$. The population that is disease free is $(b + d)$. Sensitivity is the proportion of those with disease (the denominator; $a + c$), in whom the test is positive (the numerator; *a*). Therefore, sensitivity is $a/(a + c)$. Specificity is the proportion of those without disease (the denominator; $b + d$), in whom the test is negative (the numerator; *d*). **False-negative error** can occur only when disease is truly present. It is the proportion of those with disease $(a + c)$ in whom test results are incorrectly negative (*c*). **False-positive error** can occur only when disease is truly absent. It is the proportion of those without disease $(b + d)$ in whom test results are incorrectly positive (*b*).

Sensitivity and specificity are performance characteristics pertinent to every diagnostic test. To interpret the results of a test, its performance characteristics, as well as the context in which it is operating, must be known.

Consider a common clinical scenario, such as the need to evaluate a patient with chest pain for evidence of ischemia. Prior to ordering any test, we will have asked a series of questions and performed a physical exam. If the pain sounds atypical, we may begin thinking that the probability of angina is low. But if we find the patient to have multiple cardiac risk factors, we are likely to revise our estimate of the probability of angina upward. If the physical exam fails to reveal any support for an alternative diagnosis, we will again revise upward our impression of angina. Conversely, if we find the pain to be reproducible with palpation, we will revise our estimate downward. The knowledge gained from the history and physical alters the context in which we select and interpret our subsequent diagnostic tests and should therefore influence our confidence in the results obtained.

Box 2.1

The 2 × 2 contingency table and its applications to the performance of diagnostic studies.

Disease

		+		–
	+	a		b
Test				
	–	c		d

Cells:
a = true positives; disease present, test positive
b = false positives; disease absent, test positive
c = false negatives; disease present, test negative
d = true negatives; disease absent, test negative

Rows:
$(a + b)$ = all test positives
$(c + d)$ = all test negatives

Columns:
$(a + c)$ = all disease positives
$(b + d)$ = all disease negatives

Pertinent formulas:

Disease free population $(1 - \text{prevalence}) =$	$b + d$
Disease positive population (prevalence) $=$	$a + c$
Prevalence $=$	$(a + c)$
Prior probability = "prevalence rate" $=$	$(a + c)/n$
Sample population $= n =$	$a + b + c + d$
Sensitivity $=$	$a/(a + c)$
Specificity $=$	$d/(b + d)$

Altering Test Performance

Consider that we have evaluated a patient with chest pain and concluded, on the basis of the history and physical exam, that the probability of ischemia is moderate, say, 20%. While a specific numerical probability may seem contrived and uncomfortable, the notion that disease is improbable, probable, or highly probable is not. Applying a numerical estimate to such impressions facilitates demonstration of how important test performance is in the diagnostic process. In this scenario, we will want to conduct diagnostic tests to confirm or exclude a diagnosis of ischemic heart disease. The performance characteristics of the test or tests we choose will influence the reliability with which we can make a final diagnosis and develop an appropriate plan of management.

Scenario 2.1a

Consider that we test for ischemia by use of an ECG with a sensitivity of 70% and a specificity of 60%.[1] We can determine the influence of testing results on the probability of disease by using a 2 × 2 table in which the prior probability estimate becomes the prevalence in a hypothetical population of n patients. Box 2.2 is such a table, in which $n = 100$.

In a population of 100, a prior probability of 20% translates into a prevalence of 20. Therefore the disease positive cells, a and c, must add up to 20. The remaining patients, (1 − prevalence), are all in the disease-free cells, b and d. Therefore, b and d add up to 80. Sensitivity is the

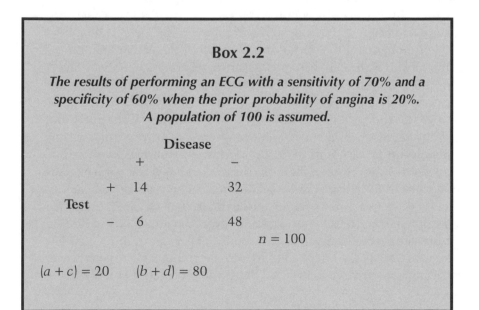

Box 2.2

The results of performing an ECG with a sensitivity of 70% and a specificity of 60% when the prior probability of angina is 20%. A population of 100 is assumed.

	Disease	
	+	−
Test +	14	32
Test −	6	48

$n = 100$

$(a + c) = 20$ $(b + d) = 80$

capacity of a test to detect disease when it is truly present. An ECG with a sensitivity of 70% will detect 70% of those with disease. Thus, cell *a* will be 14 (70% of the 20 patients with disease). Cell *c* is those patients with disease in whom test results are negative, or the false negatives. In this case, there are 6 such cases.

In this example, 80 patients are disease free. Given a specificity of 60%, 48 of the 80 patients without disease will be correctly identified by the cardiogram as being free of ischemia. Thus, cell *d* is 48. The remainder of the 80 disease-free subjects will be incorrectly identified as having disease. Cell *b*, the false positives, is 32.

What do we know after this exercise? We don't know for sure whether or not our patient has ischemia. We are still engaged in the process of narrowing the population characteristics we can apply to our patient. We have decided our patient is from a population in which the probability of ischemia is moderate. If the cardiogram is negative in such a patient, the patient then comes from an even more narrowly defined population: those in whom clinical evidence suggests moderate probability of coronary ischemia and in whom the ECG is negative for ischemia. Clearly, in such patients, the probability of ischemia is lower. How much lower? The contingency table allows us to answer.

The population we are now interested in is those patients with a prior probability of ischemia of 20%, who subsequently have a nonischemic cardiogram. In Box 2.2, this group is represented by cells *c* and *d*. Again, it is helpful to begin with the denominator. To answer the question, how probable is ischemia if the cardiogram is negative, the denominator is all patients in whom the cardiogram is negative, whether correctly or incorrectly. In Box 2.2, there is a total of 54 patients in whom the cardiogram is negative. Only 6 of these have disease. Thus, the probability of disease in this group, the posterior probability, is 6/54, or 11%. Conversely, the probability that ischemia is truly absent given a negative cardiogram in this population is 48/54, or 89%. This measure, true negatives (cell *d*) over all negative test results (the sum of cells *c* and *d*) is the **negative predictive value** (NPV). The negative predictive value reveals the probability of being disease free given a negative test result. The remaining negative test results are false negatives (cell *c*) and reveal the probability of disease being present despite a negative test result. The proportion of misleading negative tests is (1 − NPV). In this case, the proportion (or percentage) of misleading negative tests is 11%. Thus, the probability of ischemia is

11% with a negative cardiogram, down from 20% before the cardiogram. (The term proportion misleading negatives (PMN) is clinically useful, but not currently in use. The term is coined here, and its use recommended. See 2 × 2 table in Appendix C.) In other words, the negative cardiogram has reduced the prior probability of 20% to a posterior probability of 11%. One final way of evaluating the negative cardiogram is by use of what may be termed the **false-negative index** (FNI), the ratio of false- to true-negative test results. The FNI for Box 2.2 is the false negatives ($c = 6$) over the true negatives ($d = 48$). The FNI for Box 2.2 is therefore 0.125. (The false-negative index is a newly coined term; see 2 × 2 table in Appendix C.) For every true-negative test result, there will be 0.125 false negatives, or 1 false negative for 8 true negatives. A FNI below 1 indicates that there will be more true than false negatives; conversely, a FNI above 1 indicates that more negative test results will be false than true.

What if the cardiogram is positive? We again want to know the probability that ischemia is present or absent. Now, the denominator is those from our population in whom the cardiogram is positive. In Box 2.2, test results are positive in cell a (true positives; 14) and in cell b (false positives; 32). Therefore, the denominator is ($a + b$), or 46. The probability of ischemia in this group is $a/(a + b)$, which is 14/46, or 30%. This is the probability of disease in those with a positive test result, or the **positive predictive value** (PPV). The remainder of those with a positive test result are false positives. The proportion misleading positives (PMP) is (1–specificity), or $b/(b + d)$. In Box 2.2, the PMP is 70%. (The term proportion misleading positives (PMP) is coined here, and its use is recommended. See 2 × 2 table in Appendix C.) In other words, 70% of those from the population with a 20% prior probability of ischemia in whom the cardiogram is positive are nonetheless disease free. Another way to look at this is the **false-positive index** (FPI), the ratio of false positives ($b = 32$) to true positives ($a = 14$). (The false-positive index is a newly coined term. See 2 × 2 table in Appendix C.) In this case the FPI is approximately 2.3; for every 1 true-positive test, there will be 2.3 false positives. A FPI below 1 indicates that there will be more true than false positives; conversely, a FPI above 1 indicates that more positive test results will be false than true. Thus, a positive cardiogram in scenario 2.1a, does not allow us to diagnose ischemia with confidence. Ischemia remains improbable despite a positive cardiogram.

Scenario 2.1b

Consider that we again test for ischemia by use of an ECG in a patient with a 20% prior probability of disease. Assume now, however, that the sensitivity of the cardiogram is reduced to 40%, perhaps because of abnormalities in the patient's resting cardiogram, and that the specificity of the cardiogram is reduced to 30%. This scenario reveals an important aspect of diagnostic tests often overlooked: the performance characteristics of almost any test are dependent to varying degrees on the population to which they are applied.[2] While the ECG may be a fairly good test for acute cardiac ischemia, the test may perform much less reliably in a population with left bundle branch block. An x-ray may be accurate in the diagnosis of pneumonia, but not in a patient with lung cancer. Therefore, patient/population characteristics not only influence the probability of disease (prior probability) but also the accuracy with which diagnostic tests perform. In this scenario, the prior probability of angina is held constant, while the accuracy of the cardiogram is altered.

In a population of 100, a prior probability of 20% translates into a prevalence of 20; therefore the disease-positive cells, a and c, must add to 20 as shown in Box 2.3. The remaining patients, (1 − prevalence), are all in the disease-free cells, b and d. Therefore, b and d add to 80. Sensitivity

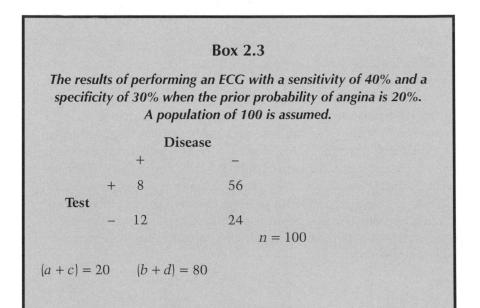

Box 2.3

The results of performing an ECG with a sensitivity of 40% and a specificity of 30% when the prior probability of angina is 20%. A population of 100 is assumed.

	Disease	
	+	**−**
Test +	8	56
−	12	24

$n = 100$

$(a + c) = 20$ $(b + d) = 80$

is the capacity of a test to detect disease when it is truly present. An ECG with a sensitivity of 40% will detect 40% of those with disease. Thus, cell *a* will be 8 (40% of the 20 patients with disease). Cell *c* is the number of patients with disease in whom test results are negative, or the false negatives. In this case, there are 12 such cases.

In this example, 80 patients are disease free. Given a specificity of 30%, 24 of the 80 patients without disease will be correctly identified by the cardiogram as being free of ischemia. Thus, cell *d* is 24. The remainder of the 80 disease-free subjects will be incorrectly identified as having disease. Cell *b*, the false-positives, is 56.

We are still engaged in the process of narrowing the population characteristics we can apply to our patient. We have decided our patient is from a population in which the probability of ischemia is moderate. If the cardiogram is negative in such a patient, the patient then comes from an even more narrowly defined population: those in whom clinical evidence suggests moderate probability of coronary ischemia and in whom the ECG is negative for ischemia. Clearly, in such patients the posterior probability of ischemia should be lower. How much lower? The contingency table allows us to answer. The population we are now interested in is those patients with a prior probability of ischemia of 20% who subsequently have a nonischemic cardiogram. In Box 2.3, this is cells *c* and *d*. Again, it is helpful to begin with the denominator. To answer the question "How probable is ischemia if the cardiogram is negative," the denominator is all patients in whom the cardiogram is negative, whether correctly or incorrectly. In Box 2.3, there is a total of 36 patients in whom the cardiogram is negative. Of these, 12 have disease. Thus, the probability of disease in this group, the posterior probability, is 12/36, or 33%. Conversely, the probability that ischemia is truly absent given a negative cardiogram in this population is 24/36, or 67%. This measure, true negatives (cell *d*) over all negative test results (the sum of cells *c* and *d*) is the negative predictive value (NPV). The remaining negative test results are false negatives (cell *c*) and reveal the probability of disease being present despite a negative test result (proportion misleading negatives). In this case, the proportion misleading negatives is 33%. Thus, the probability of ischemia is 33% despite a negative cardiogram, up from 20% before the cardiogram. In other words, the negative cardiogram has raised the prior probability of 20% to a posterior probability of 33%! The poor performance characteristics of the test in this patient (i.e., this population of patients) result in a paradox: the probability of disease is actually higher after a negative test than it was before any testing was done. This is because under the conditions and assumptions imposed, the test is wrong more often than it is right (see below). The FNI for Box 2.3 is the false negatives ($c = 12$) over the true negatives ($d = 24$). The FNI for Box 2.3 is therefore 0.5. For every true-negative test result, there will be 0.5 false negatives.

What if the cardiogram is positive? We again want to know the probability that ischemia is present or absent. Now, the denominator is those from our population in whom the cardiogram is positive. In Box 2.3 test results are positive in cell a (true positives; 8) and in cell b (false positives; 56). Therefore, the denominator is $(a + b)$, or 64. The probability of ischemia in this group is $a/(a + b)$, which is 8/64, or 12.5%. This is the probability of disease in those with a positive test result, or the positive predictive value (PPV). Thus, a positive cardiogram in scenario 2.1b actually lowers the posterior probability of disease. The remainder of those with a positive test result are false positives. The proportion misleading positives, $1 - PPV$, is 87.5%. In other words, 87.5% of those from the population with a 20% prior probability of ischemia in whom the cardiogram is positive are nonetheless disease free. In this case, the false-positive index (FPI), the ratio of false positives ($b = 56$) to true positives ($a = 8$), is 7; for every 1 true-positive test, there will be 7 false positives. An FPI below 1 indicates that there will be more true than false positives. An FPI above 1 indicates the converse, that more positive test results will be false than true.

Scenario 2.1b demonstrates that a test with poor performance characteristics will not only fail to help reach an accurate diagnosis but is actually apt to do harm. An ischemic cardiogram in this patient would tend to make us think that the probability of ischemia had gone up when in fact it would have gone down. A nonischemic cardiogram would naturally make us believe that ischemia could be more securely excluded, but the probability of ischemia in this scenario is actually higher after a negative cardiogram than before testing. The performance characteristics of tests are therefore of vital importance to the diagnostic process. Naturally, a test performing this poorly would not be used. Yet many diagnostic tests are employed with little consideration given to their performance characteristics. This scenario, extreme though it may be, points out the potential hazards.

Scenario 2.1c

Consider that we again test for ischemia using an ECG in a patient with a 20% prior probability of disease. Assume now, however, that the sensitivity of the cardiogram is raised to 90%, perhaps because the patient has a perfectly normal baseline cardiogram, and that the specificity of the cardiogram is also raised to 90%. In this scenario, the prior probability of ischemia is held constant, while the accuracy of the cardiogram is altered.

In a population of 100, a prior probability of 20% translates into a prevalence of 20. Therefore the disease-positive cells, *a* and *c*, must add to 20 as shown in Box 2.4. The remaining patients, (1 – prevalence), are all in the disease-free cells, *b* and *d*. Therefore, *b* and *d* add to 80. An ECG with a sensitivity of 90% will detect 90% of those with disease. Thus, cell *a* will be 18 (90% of the 20 patients with disease). Cell *c* is the number of patients with disease in whom test results are negative, or the false negatives. In this case, there are 2 such cases.

In this example, 80 patients are disease free. Given a specificity of 90%, 72 of the 80 patients without disease will be correctly identified by the cardiogram as being free of ischemia. Thus, cell *d* is 72. The remainder of the 80 disease-free subjects will be incorrectly identified as having disease. Cell *b*, the false-positives, is 8.

If the cardiogram is negative, the population we are now interested in is those patients with a prior probability of ischemia of 20% who subsequently have a nonischemic cardiogram. In Box 2.4, this is cells *c* and *d*. Again, it is helpful to begin with the denominator. In Box 2.4, there

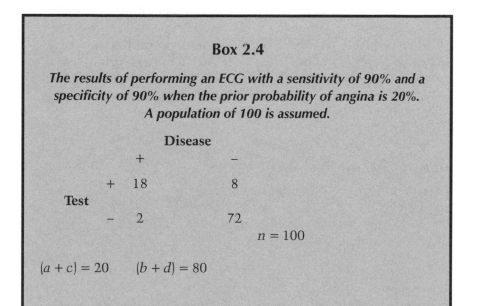

Box 2.4

The results of performing an ECG with a sensitivity of 90% and a specificity of 90% when the prior probability of angina is 20%. A population of 100 is assumed.

	Disease	
	+	**–**
Test **+**	18	8
–	2	72

$n = 100$

$(a + c) = 20$ $(b + d) = 80$

is a total of 74 patients in whom the cardiogram is negative. Of these, 2 have disease. Thus, the probability of disease in this group, the posterior probability, is 2/74, or 2.7%. Conversely, the probability that ischemia is truly absent given a negative cardiogram, the NPV, in this population is 72/74, or 97.3%. In this case, the PMN is 2.7%. Thus, the probability of ischemia is 2.7% with a negative cardiogram, down from 20% before the cardiogram. In other words, the negative cardiogram has reduced the prior probability of 20% to a posterior probability of 2.7%. The FNI for Box 2.4 is 0.028. For every true-negative test result, there will be 0.028 false negatives.

What if the cardiogram is positive? The denominator is those from our population in whom the cardiogram is positive. In Box 2.4 test results are positive in cell a (true positives; 18) and in cell b (false positives; 8). Therefore, the denominator is $(a + b)$, or 26. The positive predictive value (PPV), the probability of ischemia in this group, is $a/(a + b)$, which from Box 2.4 is 18/26, or 69%. Thus, a positive cardiogram in scenario 2.1c considerably raises the posterior probability of disease. In Box 2.4, the PMP is 31%. In other words, 31% of those from the population with a 20% prior probability of ischemia in whom the cardiogram is positive are nonetheless disease free. In this case, the (FPI), the ratio of false positives $(b = 8)$ to true positives $(a = 18)$, is 0.44; for every 1 true-positive test, there will be 0.44 false positives.

Scenario 2.1c demonstrates that a test with good performance characteristics can substantially alter the accuracy with which a disease is diagnosed or excluded. In this scenario, an ischemic cardiogram raised the probability of disease from 20% to almost 70%. A negative cardiogram lowered the probability of ischemia from 20% to 2.7%. When there is considerable diagnostic uncertainty a test that performs well can be tremendously helpful.

Summary: Altering Test Performance

Accurate tests are more helpful in reaching correct diagnoses than inaccurate tests. This concept is hardly earth-shattering, but it conceals surprising subtleties. The performance characteristics of any diagnostic test, its sensitivity (ability to detect disease when disease is present) and specificity (ability to exclude disease when disease is absent) are based on the characteristics of the populations in which the test itself was tested. To the extent that an individual patient differs from the test population used to validate the test, test performance may vary. Even when patient characteristics are not thought to threaten test performance, the standards for testing should vary based on the degree of clinical uncertainty. Test performance is uninfluenced by disease prevalence, but diagnostic accuracy (predictive value) is influenced by disease prevalence. Sensitivity and specificity of a test should be good enough to enhance meaningfully one's certainty that disease is present or absent before that test is ordered. As shown above, a test that performs poorly, either in general or in a particular patient, may actually increase, rather than diminish, diagnostic uncertainty. Worse, if the test is simply believed it may result in the inappropriate exclusion of disease or in an inappropriate diagnosis. The implications of this section are that test performance should be known with some confidence **before** a test is ordered, as should the prior probability of disease. To enhance or refute a very strong suspicion of disease (a high prior probability), a test will need to be highly accurate, especially with regard to negative results. To reduce or reverse a very low suspicion of disease (a low prior probability), a test will similarly need to be highly accurate but this time especially with regard to positive results. Tests with operating characteristics common to clinical experience—sensitivity and specificity in the 75%–90% range—are best utilized when a considerable degree of diagnostic uncertainty (i.e., prior probability close to 50%) exists.

〃 DISEASE PROBABILITY

What if it is the degree of diagnostic uncertainty (the prior probability) that varies, while the performance characteristics of the test remain constant? This situation also has marked effects on disease probability and the reliability of testing, and is often overlooked in the diagnostic process.

Scenario 2.2a

On the basis of history and physical we conclude that the probability of angina is low. For purposes of demonstration, a "low" probability will be set at 10%.

An ECG will be ordered in such a patient and will either reveal evidence of ischemia or not. To know how these results can be interpreted, the reliability of the cardiogram must be known. Consider that the sensitivity of a resting cardiogram is approximately 70% and the specificity approximately 60%.[3] Box 2.5 demonstrates the results of performing an ECG when the prior probability of angina is 10%. If a population of 100 is assumed, a prior probability of 10% translates into a prevalence of 10. Therefore the disease-positive cells, *a* and *c*, must add to 10. The remaining patients, (1 − prevalence), are all in the disease-free cells, *b* and *d*. Therefore, *b* and *d* add to 90. An ECG with a sensitivity of 70% will detect 70% of those with disease. Thus, cell *a* will be 7 (70% of the 10 patients with disease). Cell *c* is those patients with disease in whom test results are negative, or the false negatives. In this case, there are 3 such cases.

In this example, 90 patients are disease free. Given a specificity of 60%, 54 of the 90 patients without disease will be correctly identified by the cardiogram as being free of ischemia. Thus, cell *d* is 54. The remainder of the 90 disease-free subjects will be incorrectly identified as having disease. Cell *b*, the false-positives, is 36.

The population we are now interested in is those patients with a prior probability of ischemia of 10% who subsequently have a nonischemic cardiogram. In Box 2.5, this is cells *c* and *d*. Again, it is helpful to begin with the denominator. To answer the question, how probable is ischemia if the cardiogram is negative, the denominator is all patients in whom the cardiogram is negative, whether correctly or incorrectly. In Box 2.5, there

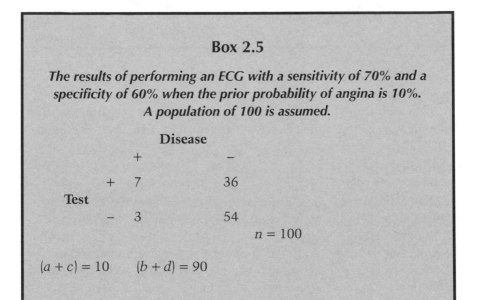

Box 2.5

The results of performing an ECG with a sensitivity of 70% and a specificity of 60% when the prior probability of angina is 10%. A population of 100 is assumed.

	Disease	
	+	−
Test +	7	36
−	3	54
		n = 100

$(a + c) = 10$ $(b + d) = 90$

is a total of 57 patients in whom the cardiogram is negative. Only 3 of these have disease. Thus, the probability of disease in this group, the posterior probability, is 3/57, or 5%. Conversely, the probability that ischemia is truly absent given a negative cardiogram, the NPV, in this population is 54/57, or 95%. The remaining negative test results are false negatives (cell *c*). In this case, the PMN is 5% (i.e., of 100 negative test results, on average 95 will be correct, while 5 will be incorrect). Thus, the probability of ischemia is 5% with a negative cardiogram, down from 10% before the cardiogram. In other words, the negative cardiogram has reduced the prior probability of 10% to a posterior probability of 5%. The FNI for Box 2.5 is the false negatives (*c* = 3) over the true negatives (*d* = 54), therefore 0.06. For every true-negative test result, there will be 0.06 false negatives.

What if the cardiogram is positive? In Box 2.5, test results are positive in cell *a* (true positives; 7) and in cell *b* (false positives; 36). Therefore, the denominator is (*a* + *b*), or 43. The probability of ischemia in this group, the PPV, is *a*/(*a* + *b*), which from Box 2.5 is 7/43, or 16%. The remainder of those with a positive test result are false positives. In Box 2.5, the PMP is 36/43, or 84%. In other words, 84% of those from the population with a 10% prior probability of ischemia in whom the cardiogram is positive are nonetheless disease free. The FPI is approximately 5, so for every 1 true-positive test there will be 5 false positives. Thus, a positive cardiogram in scenario 2.2a does not allow us to diagnose ischemia with confidence. Ischemia remains improbable despite a positive cardiogram.

Scenario 2.2b

Consider another patient in whom, after history and physical exam, the probability of ischemia is estimated at 80%. A cardiogram, with the same performance characteristics already noted (sensitivity of 70%, specificity of 60%) is obtained. The results are shown in Box 2.6.

If a population of 100 is assumed, a prior probability of 80% translates into a prevalence of 80. Therefore the disease-positive cells, *a* and *c*, must add to 80. The remaining patients, (1 – prevalence), are all in the disease-free cells, *b* and *d*. Therefore *b* and *d* add to 20. An ECG with a sensitivity of 70% will detect 70% of those with disease. Thus, cell *a* will be 56 (70% of the 80 patients with disease). Cell *c* is those patients with disease in whom test results are negative, or the false negatives. In this scenario there are 24 such cases.

Twenty patients are disease free in this example. Given a specificity of 60%, 12 of the 20 patients without disease will be correctly identified by

---

Box 2.6

The results of performing an ECG with a sensitivity of 70% and a specificity of 60% when the prior probability of angina is 80%. A population of 100 is assumed.

Disease

		+	−
	+	56	8
Test			
	−	24	12

$n = 100$

$(a + c) = 80$ $(b + d) = 20$

---

the cardiogram as being free of ischemia. Thus, cell d is 12. The remainder of the 20 disease-free subjects will be incorrectly identified as having disease. Cell b, the false-positives, is 8.

If the cardiogram is negative, the population we are now interested in is patients with a prior probability of ischemia of 80%, who subsequently have a nonischemic cardiogram. In Box 2.6, there is a total of 36 patients in whom the cardiogram is negative. Of these, 24 have disease. The probability of disease in this group, the posterior probability, is 24/36 (67%), and the NPV is 12/36 (33%). The PMN is 67%. In other words, the negative cardiogram has reduced the prior probability of 80% to a posterior probability of 67%. The FNI for Box 2.6 is 24/12, or 2. For every true-negative test result, there will be 2 false negatives. Thus, a negative cardiogram in this scenario does not allow us to exclude ischemia; ischemia is still quite probable despite the negative test.

What if the cardiogram is positive? In Box 2.6, test results are positive in cell a (true positives; 56) and in cell b (false positives; 8). Therefore, the denominator is $(a + b)$, or 64. The PPV, or the probability of ischemia in this group, is $a/(a + b)$, which in Box 2.6 is 56/64, or 87.5%. The remainder of those with a positive test result are false positives. In Box 2.6, the PMP is 8/64, or 12.5%. In other words, 12.5% of those from the population with an 80% prior probability of ischemia in whom the cardiogram is positive are disease free. In this scenario, the FPI, the ratio of false positives ($b = 8$) to true positives ($a = 56$), is approximately 0.14. For every 1 true-positive test, there will be 0.14 false positives. In this case, a positive cardiogram results in a high probability of ischemia, although a considerable degree of uncertainty persists.

Scenario 2.2c

Finally, consider another patient in whom, after history and physical exam, the probability of ischemia is estimated at 50% (highly uncertain). A cardiogram, with the same performance characteristics already noted (sensitivity of 70%, specificity of 60%) is obtained. The results are shown in Box 2.7.

If a population of 100 is assumed, a prior probability of 50% translates into a prevalence of 50; therefore the disease positive cells, a and c, must add to 50. The remaining patients, $(1 - \text{prevalence})$, are all in the disease-free cells, b and d. Therefore, b and d add to 50. An ECG with a sensitivity of 70% will detect 70% of those with disease. Thus, cell a will be 35 (70% of the 50 patients with disease). Cell c is those patients with disease in whom test results are negative, or the false negatives. In this case, there are 15 such cases.

Box 2.7

The results of performing an ECG with a sensitivity of 70% and a specificity of 60% when the prior probability of angina is 50%. A population of 100 is assumed.

		Disease	
		+	**−**
	+	35	20
Test			
	−	15	30

$$n = 100$$

$(a + c) = 50 \qquad (b + d) = 50$

In this example, 50 patients are disease free. Given a specificity of 60%, 30 of the 50 patients without disease will be correctly identified by the cardiogram as being free of ischemia. Thus, cell *d* is 30. The remainder of the 50 disease-free subjects will be incorrectly identified as having disease. Cell *b*, the false positives, is 20.

In this scenario, our patient is from a population in which the probability of ischemia is highly uncertain. If the cardiogram is negative, the population we are now interested in is those patients with a prior probability of ischemia of 50%, who subsequently have a nonischemic cardiogram. In Box 2.7, there is a total of 45 patients in whom the cardiogram is negative. Of these, 15 have disease. Thus, the probability of disease in this group, the posterior probability, is 15/45, or 33%. Conversely, the probability that ischemia is truly absent in the event of a negative cardiogram, or the NPV, is 30/45, or 67%. The remaining negative test results are false negatives (cell *c*) and reveal the probability of disease being present despite a negative test result. The PMN is 33%. Thus, the negative cardiogram has reduced the prior probability of 50% to a posterior probability of 33%. The FNI for Box 2.7 is 15/30, or 0.5. For every true-negative test result, there will be 0.5 false negatives. A negative cardiogram in this scenario does not allow us to exclude ischemia with confidence.

What if the cardiogram is positive? In Box 2.7, test results are positive in cell *a* (true positives; 35) and in cell *b* (false positives; 20). Therefore, the denominator is (*a* + *b*), or 55. The probability of ischemia in this group, *a* / (*a* + *b*), or the PPV, is 35/55, or 64%. The remainder of those with a positive test result are false positives. The PMP is 20/55, or 36%. In other words, 36% of those from the population with a 50% prior probability of ischemia in whom the cardiogram is positive are disease free. In this scenario, the FPI is approximately 0.57. For every 1 true-positive test, there will be 0.57 false positives. A positive cardiogram in this scenario leaves us with considerable uncertainty about the diagnosis of ischemia.

Summary: Altering Estimates of Disease Probability

While prevalence does not affect sensitivity or specificity, it directly affects both the positive and negative predictive values. Predictive values answer clinically relevant questions: if the test I order is positive, how probable is it that my patient has the disease in question? If the test I order is negative, how probable is it that my patient is disease free? The answers to these depend as much or more on *how probable disease was in the first place* (i.e., before the test was ordered) as they do on the accuracy of the test. No degree of test accuracy can compensate for extremes of prior probability. Predictive values are influenced by prevalence, or prior probability, because algebraically their denominators represent a mix of patients with and without disease. The denominator of a predictive value is a group of patients with a particular test result, not a particular disease status (see 2 × 2 table, Appendix C). As estimates of prior probability vary, so too will predictive values, even when test performance is held constant. The implications are that prior probability is as or more important in making a diagnosis, as the results of any testing done, and that the results of a test cannot be interpreted reliably if prior probability is not addressed.

※ TEST INTERPRETATION

So far, we have examined the effects of changing either the probability of disease based on the patient's characteristics (the prior probability), or the performance characteristics of the diagnostic test (the sensitivity and specificity), and found that either can substantively alter the posterior probability of disease. There is one additional factor that can similarly affect our clinical impression: the **cutoff point**. For any given diagnostic test that is not simply positive or negative, the cutoff point distinguishes values that will be taken to indicate disease, from values that will be taken to indicate the absence of disease. Often conventional cutoff points are established by the departments conducting the test: the laboratory or radiology or nuclear medicine. Nonetheless, cutoff points are subject to debate and should be interpreted in light of their statistical implications.

Consider that we are pursuing the diagnosis of myocardial infarction (MI) rather than ischemia in our patient with chest pain and that we are using the creatine kinase at 6 hours as the test of interest (troponin or the MB fraction of creatine kinase [CK] could be used instead).[4] Assume that the CKMB has been validated as a diagnostic test in populations with chest pain.[5] In such a population of 100 patients, 50 had MI and 50 did not. The distribution of CKMB values in mg/dl for the 100 study subjects are illustrated in Table 2.1 (note that these data are factitious and are used for illustrative purposes only).

TABLE 2.1   Example of Distribution of CKMB Values

CK Value	MI(+) (n = 50)	MI(−) (n = 50)
40–80	1	6
81–150	2	24
151–220	4	12
221–280	10	6
> 280	33	2

Scenario 2.3a

In Table 2.1, each range of CK values represents a potential cutoff point for the diagnosis of MI.[6] The performance characteristics of CK are determined in part by what criteria are used to define a positive test result.

Assume that, based on clinical assessment, the probability of myocardial infarction is 50%. The ECG is nondiagnostic due to either a permanent pacemaker or a left bundle branch block. The CK value at six hours is 68. What is the posterior probability of MI?

First, the sensitivity of the test needs to be determined. If a CK above 80 were considered positive, then 49 of 50 patients with MI would test positive, resulting in a sensitivity of 98%. But what about specificity? Of the 50 MI negative patients, 44 would test positive, and 6 would test negative. The resulting specificity is 12%. In a theoretical sample of 100 such patients, the scenario would appear as shown in Box 2.8. The posterior probability of MI is approximately 53%, minimally changed from our prior probability despite the positive test. What happened?

The very low cutoff point for the CK resulted in high sensitivity. When you set a cutoff point low, most patients with the condition will test positive. However, when the cutoff is set low, many of those who do not have the condition will also test positive. Therefore, many of those who do not have the condition will fail to test negative, and therefore the specificity will be low. Specificity is the measure of how reliably the test excludes disease by providing a negative result when disease is absent. In general, a low cutoff point improves sensitivity at the cost of specificity. As has been shown, the low specificity makes a positive test result unreliable. But what about a negative test result? The reliability with which MI can be excluded with a negative CK cutoff point at 80 (the negative predictive value) is 86%. A low cutoff point allows one to be confident of the accuracy of a negative test but not of a positive test.

Box 2.8

The results of applying a CK cutoff of > 80 to a patient with 50% prior probability of MI. The sensitivity of the test at this cutoff point is 98%, and the specificity is 12%. A population of 100 is assumed.

	MI +	MI –
CK +	49	44
CK –	1	6

$n = 100$

$(a + c) = 50$ $(b + d) = 50$

Box 2.9

The results of applying a CK cutoff of > 150 to a patient with 50% prior probability of MI. The sensitivity of the test at this cutoff point is 94%, and the specificity is 60%. A population of 100 is assumed.

	MI +	MI –
CK +	47	20
CK –	3	30

$n = 100$

$(a + c) = 50$ $(b + d) = 50$

Scenario 2.3b

What if the same patient had the same test, but we changed our interpretation simply by raising the cutoff point? If we required that the CK be greater than 150 to be considered positive, then the test would detect 47 of the MI's and miss 3, for a sensitivity of 94%. Of the MI negative patients, 30 would test negative, while 20 would test positive, for a specificity of 60%. This scenario is portrayed in Box 2.9. The posterior probability with a positive CK test is now 70%. By raising the cutoff point, we lowered sensitivity by making it more likely that someone with the disease would test negative. But we also made it much less likely that someone without the disease would test positive and thereby raised the specificity. Again, sensitivity and specificity are moved in opposite directions as the cutoff point is adjusted.

Scenario 2.3c

Finally, what would happen if we required that the CK be greater than 280 to be positive? As shown in Box 2.10, 17 patients with MI would now test negative, lowering the sensitivity to 66%. However, 48 of 50 MI negative patients would now also test negative, raising the specificity to 96%. The posterior probability of MI following a positive CK of greater than 280 is 97%. Thus, a cutoff point set high provides for high specificity; most of those who are truly disease negative will test negative. When a test with a high cutoff point is positive, it is unlikely to be a false positive

---

Box 2.10

The results of applying a CK cutoff of > 280 to a patient with 50% prior probability of MI. The sensitivity of the test at this cutoff point is 66%, and the specificity is 96%. A population of 100 is assumed.

		MI	
		+	−
CK	+	33	2
	−	17	48

$$n = 100$$

$(a + c) = 50 \qquad (b + d) = 50$

and therefore very likely to be a true positive. Therefore, a high cutoff point tends to result in a high PPV. But this comes at a cost. The high specificity of a high cutoff point results in low sensitivity. Many of the disease-positive cases will test negative. In this scenario, the probability of MI given a negative test is 41%. The NPV, the reliability with which a negative test indicates the absence of disease, is 59%. A high cutoff point allows one to be confident of the accuracy of a positive test but not of a negative test.

Determining the Optimal Cutoff Point: Likelihood Ratios (Boxes 2.11 and 2.12)

Having seen that varying the cutoff point can change the performance characteristics of a diagnostic test, we now need to consider how to compare such characteristics at different cutoff levels to determine the best one. One such approach is to create a ratio of sensitivity (true-positive test results) to false-positive error rate (FPER) and determine how likely it is at a given cutoff point that a positive result is true rather than false. This parameter is called the **likelihood ratio positive**. A related concept is the **likelihood ratio negative**, the ratio of false-negative error rate (FNER) to the specificity. A cutoff point is performing well when the likelihood ratio positive is high (i.e., it is much more likely that a positive test is true than false) and the likelihood ratio negative is low (i.e., it is much less likely that a negative test is false than true). Both likelihood ratios are constructed as they are so that the ratio of the likelihood ratio positive to the likelihood ratio negative can be used to provide the likelihood ratio as an overall measure of test performance at a given cutoff point. The higher the **likelihood ratio** (LR), the better the test is performing. A high LR implies that a positive test is very likely to be true and a negative test is unlikely to be false. Thus, a high LR simply indicates that the test is accurate or generally correct. Table 2.2 shows the use of likelihood ratios to compare test performance at different cutoffs for the CK values in Table 2.1.

The LR(+) should be greater than 1 and the LR(−) close to 0 for a test to be considered useful. Similarly, the LR should be large, generally near 50, to indicate that a test is performing well. In Table 2.2 a cutoff value of 280 produces the best likelihood ratio, although this cutoff is associated with a poor sensitivity (66%) and a high rate of false-negative error (34%). If missing actual MI's 34% of the time were clinically unaccept-

TABLE 2.2   Likelihood Ratios

CK Value	MI(+) (n = 50)	MI(−) (n = 50)	Cutoff Value	Sens	FPER	LR(+)	Spec	FNER	LR(−)	LR
< 80	1	6	80	98%	88%	1.11	12%	2%	0.17	6.53
80–150	2	24	150	94%	40%	2.35	60%	6%	0.10	23.5
151–220	4	12	220	86%	16%	5.38	84%	14%	0.17	31.65
221–280	10	6	280	66%	4%	16.50	96%	34%	0.35	47.14
281–800	33	2	800	0%	0%	—	100%	100%	1	—

FPER = false-positive error rate
FNER = false-negative error rate
LR(+) = ratio of sensitivity to FPER
LR(−) = ratio of FNER to specificity
LR   = ratio of LR(+) to LR(−).

able, using this cutoff value would be unacceptable. While the "numbers" can be used to demonstrate the cutoff value at which the test produces the greatest proportion of correct findings, the numbers cannot substitute for clinical priorities. In the case of a serious disorder such as myocardial infarction, false positives might be more tolerable than false negatives. Thus, likelihood ratios provide a reliable measure of the interaction between cutoff point and test performance but cannot be used to determine the appropriate cutoff point independently of clinical imperatives.

Receiver Operating Characteristic (ROC) Curves

Implicit in the above discussion of cutoff points is the inverse association between sensitivity and specificity. When the cutoff point is lowered, sensitivity rises and specificity falls. When the cutoff point is raised, the opposite occurs. The harder one tries to make sure that every last case of a disease will test positive, the more likely it is that noncases may also test positive. The harder one tries to be certain that all those who are free of disease test negative, the more probable it is that true cases will also test negative. Sensitivity is positively correlated with the false-positive error rate. The more one detects true positives, the more one detects false positives. Specificity is associated with the false-negative error rate. The more one detects true negatives, the more one detects false negatives.

The trade-off between sensitivity and the false-positive error rate is used to determine the optimal cutoff point for a particular test. The opti-

Box 2.11

Properties of the LR.

The LR expresses the likelihood that a positive test result is true rather than false, relative to the likelihood that a negative test result is false rather than true. The LR characterizes the accuracy of the test in terms of correct and incorrect test results among those with a particular test result (positive or negative). The likelihood that a test result indicates the presence or absence of disease can be assessed, using the LR, without knowing the disease prevalence in the underlying population. This can be shown using a 2×2 table:

		D	
		+	–
t	+	a	b
	–	c	d

sensitivity $= a / (a + c)$
specificity $= d / (b + d)$
false-positive error rate $= b / (b + d)$
false-negative error rate $= c / (a + c)$

- The LR(+) is $[a / (a + c)] / [b / (b + d)]$. Of note, both the numerator and denominator of the LR(+) are within columns of the table and therefore *independent of disease prevalence*.

- The LR(–) is $[c / (a + c)] / [d / (b + d)]$. Here, too, both numerator and denominator are contained within columns of the table and therefore *independent of prevalence*.

- The LR is $\{[a / (a + c)] / [b / (b + d)]\} / \{[c / (a + c)] / [d / (b + d)]\}$. This reduces algebraically to: $(a / b) / (c / d) = ad / bc$.

As will be discussed in Chapter 7, this parameter is also known as the **odds ratio**, i.e., the odds that a person with disease will have a positive test result (or exposure) relative to the odds of such a result (or exposure) in a person free of disease.

- **Odds ratio = LR**

$(\text{Tpos} / \text{Fpos}) / (\text{Fneg} / \text{Tneg}) = (\text{Tpos} / \text{Fneg}) / (\text{Fpos} / \text{Tneg})$
$(\text{Tpos} \times \text{Tneg}) / (\text{Fpos} \times \text{Fneg}) = (\text{Tpos} \times \text{Tneg}) / (\text{Fneg} \times \text{Fpos})$
$ad / bc = ad / cb$

Box 2.12

Likelihood ratios, probability and odds.

p is probability; LR is likelihood ratio; fner is the false-negative error rate; fper is the false-positive error rate; prev is prevalence; sens is sensitivity; and spec is specificity. Tpos is true positives, or cell a; tneg is true negatives, or cell d; fpos is false positives, or cell b; and fneg is false-negatives, or cell c.

$$odds = p/(1-p)$$

If probability=0.2; then odds= $0.2/(1-0.2) = 1 : 4 = 0.25$
probability = odds/(odds + 1)

$$p = 0.25/(0.25 + 1) = 1 : 5 = 0.2$$

pretest odds × LR(+) = posttest odds
Assume: $n = 100$; prev = 10%; sens = 90%; spec = 90%:

	D	
	+	−
T +	9 (a)	9 (b)
−	1 (c)	81 (d)

pretest odds = 1 : 9
LR(+) = sens/fper = 0.9/0.1
1/9(0.9/0.1) = posttest odds = 1
posterior probability = odds/(odds + 1) = 1/(1 + 1) = 50%

mal cutoff point is the one that minimizes the false-positive index. This value can be generated by use of a receiver operating characteristic (ROC) curve, as shown in Figure 2.1. ROC curves plot sensitivity on the y-axis against the false-positive error rate on the x-axis.[7] The upper left corner represents the ideal (100% sensitivity and 0% false-positive error). The lower left is 0% sensitivity and 0% false-positive error, while the lower right is 0% sensitivity and 100% false-positive error (the worst-case scenario). Finally, the upper right corner is 100% sensitivity and 100% false-

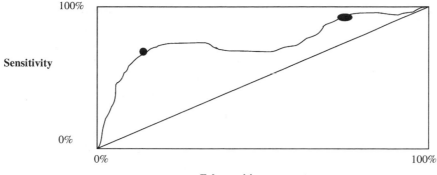

100%

Sensitivity

0%

0%   100%

False positive error rate

● The point closest to the upper left corner; minimizes the false positive index. This point represents 70% sensitivity and 10% false-positive error rate.
━ The point that results in nearly complete detection of positive cases with the least possible false-positive error. This point represents 96% sensitivity and 75% false-positive error rate.

Figure 2.1. Receiver Operating Characteristic (ROC) Curve.

positive error (everyone tests positive). The diagonal from lower left to upper right represents the **line of unity**, where one false positive is produced for every true positive (the false-positive index is 1). The false-positive index falls toward 0 (desirable) moving from the line of unity toward the upper left corner. In general the cutoff point that is closest to the upper left corner of the ROC is statistically the best, but it may not be clinically the best. For example, if one is testing for a very serious disease that is very treatable if caught early and if follow-up testing reliably excludes the disease among those who initially had false-positive tests, then one might prefer a lot of false positives to any false negatives. In this scenario, false negatives would go undiagnosed and suffer the consequences of untreated disease. But the high false-positive error rate associated with high sensitivity might require that a cutoff point be selected that is relatively near to the upper right corner in order to avoid missing any cases. While statistics can enhance clinical decision making when well applied, clinical priorities determine how statistical tools should be used.

Summary: Adjusting the Cutoff Point

With the exception of purely dichotomous tests (i.e., tests that provide a definitive negative or positive result), most diagnostic studies employing a cutoff point are subject to interpretation. Virtually any laboratory test result is more suggestive of disease when it is well outside the normal range than when it is just outside the normal range. This is an informal application of the cutoff point that almost every clinician uses without thinking. Does the abnormal test result warrant treatment or further workup? If the result is just outside the normal range, perhaps not. Why? Because at such a level, many disease-free individuals might also have a "positive" test. In other words, a cutoff point that makes it easy to detect disease when it is present makes it comparably easy to detect disease mistakenly when it is absent.

Conversely, what happens when the apparently healthy ("normal") patient has an extreme result on a routine laboratory test? Because a cutoff far outside the normal range makes it likely that some true cases of disease will be missed but unlikely that disease-negative individuals will test positive, a positive result almost certainly indicates disease (or laboratory error). Further investigation is clearly warranted. While such interpretations are second nature to any experienced clinician, knowing the statistical properties that underlie such decision making fortifies the process. When a test result is sufficiently outside the normal range to warrant careful evaluation but not so clearly abnormal as to provide definitive evidence of disease, an understanding of the relationship between variation in sensitivity and specificity and variation in the cutoff point can help determine when to test further, when to treat, and when to observe expectantly.

Generally when a disease is serious, when detection is important, and when false positives can be distinguished from true positives with follow-up testing that is readily available, a relatively low cutoff point is desirable. When a disease is less serious or indolent, when detection of disease is not urgent, and/or when distinguishing false from true positives is difficult without costly or invasive procedures, then a relatively high cutoff point is desirable.

The True Tests of a Test: Accuracy and Precision

Ultimately what one hopes for in a test is that it be correct, ideally all of the time. Of course, this expectation is unrealistic. However, a good test should be reliable, or precise. **Reliability** or **precision** refers to a test's reproducibility, its tendency to yield the same or very similar results when the same phenomenon is measured under the same conditions multiple times. It is worth noting that tests are apt to be repeated when they produce a result that deviates markedly from expectation. When a test producing an extreme value is repeated, it is likely to produce a less extreme result due to the **statistical regression effect**, commonly referred to as **regression to the mean**. This occurs because the extreme values are likely to represent (a) some deviation in the test itself that will tend to correct, on the basis of chance, when the test is repeated or (b) a deviation in the patient from their usual state. The more extreme the value, the less likely it is to be maintained at that level. Thus, when remeasured, it is likely to have shifted slightly toward less extreme values.

A test that is precise may fail to be accurate. **Accuracy** refers to the tendency of a test to approximate the truth with the average of its results. Accuracy does not require precision. Both accuracy and precision are desirable. A test that is precise but not accurate will yield consistent results that are wrong. A test that is accurate but not precise will yield results that are on average right but are inconsistent, at times deviating substantially from the truth. Accuracy and precision, as depicted by arrows or darts thrown at a bull's eye, are demonstrated in Figure 2.2 below.

Validity is a term used to characterize the overall correctness of a test, its tendency to reflect the truth. A valid test must be accurate and should be precise. To know the validity of a test requires that the true status be known. The determination of true status (e.g., true disease status) requires either a gold standard against which the test can be judged or the necessary time to disclose the condition as a result of its natural history. Often, gold standards are lacking in medicine, and thus assessments of test validity are themselves imperfect. Validity is often judged in several categories. **Content validity** refers to the degree to which a test assesses the pertinent outcome, all aspects of the pertinent outcome and nothing but the pertinent outcome. For example, a valid test of psychological stress should measure all of the manifestations of stress but not manifes-

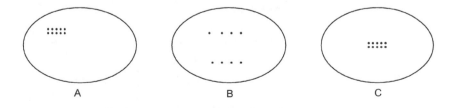

Figure 2.2. Accuracy and precision. A, Precision without accuracy; B, Accuracy without precision; C, Accuracy and precision.

tations of depression or anxiety unrelated to stress. **Face validity** refers to the apparent reasonableness of the measure, the extent to which its relation with the outcome of interest is plausible and believable (typically, among evaluators with relevant expertise). **Construct validity** is a measure of the correspondence of the results of the test in question with the results of other tests intended to assess the same condition or phenomenon. If, for example, tachycardia is characteristic of stress, then the results of evaluating stress should agree with the results of assessing heart rate. Finally, **criterion (or concurrent) validity** refers to the capacity of the test to predict the pertinent outcome.

The ultimate performance of medical tests depends on a complex interplay of assumptions and stipulations. The distinction between normal and abnormal test results will depend on the cutoff point chosen, the degree of variation in the measure of interest in the population under study, and perhaps the clinical circumstances as well. Test sensitivity and specificity will be assessable only once a decision is made regarding how to distinguish normal from abnormal, disease from the absence of disease. Test **responsiveness** is a measure of how reliably the test result changes in accordance with changes in clinical status. If, for example, Doppler ultrasound of the lower extremity remains abnormal after resolution of a deep venous thrombosis, the test is unresponsive to the change in the patient's status.[8]

The reliability and validity of test results will depend not only on intrinsic properties of the test but on the population (or patient) to which it is applied, the prior probability of the condition under investigation, and the correspondence between the patient or population under study and that in which the test was evaluated. Knowledge of true status based on some gold standard is often unavailable, and yet it is required to complete the definitive evaluation of a test.

SUMMARY/TAKE-AWAY MESSAGES

The scenarios above reveal important elements of the diagnostic process. While it is obvious that the reliability of a test result will vary according to inherent accuracy of the test, other factors are equally important. The cutoff point of a test can be set low or high, and the sensitivity and specificity will vary accordingly. The prevalence of the condition in question will influence how probable it is that a positive or negative test result is true rather than false.

In the diagnostic process, the disease state of the patient is *de facto* unknown. Therefore, the clinician decides whether studies are necessary, and which ones to order, on the basis of a semiquantitative estimate of disease probability. Is the estimate truly quantitative? It has to be; if disease is probable enough to warrant further testing, further testing is done. Not every patient with a headache needs on MRI, but those whose headaches suggest an intracranial mass do need one. How strongly must the headache suggest intracranial mass before the MRI is ordered? Strongly enough to reach the individual clinician's "threshold." None of us orders cranial imaging for every headache we see, and none of us is always unwilling to order such imaging. And each of us has a threshold for ordering such tests, based on our experience, on the literature, and in ways that are difficult to define, our unique application of the art of medicine. But for each of us there is a threshold, a point beyond which we are suspicious enough to warrant testing. "Threshold" and "enough" are quantifying terms.

Variation in the estimates of disease probability are reflected statistically as variations in the **prior probability** of disease. These estimates interact with the performance characteristics of the test we choose, including **sensitivity**, **specificity**, **false-positive error rate**, and **false-negative error rate**, to influence the **positive and negative predictive values** and therefore the **posterior probability** of disease associated with diagnostic testing. The tests must be interpreted based on *a priori* assumptions, such as the appropriate **cutoff point** between normal and abnormal values. The cutoff point conducive to optimal test performance can be assessed by use of the **likelihood ratio positive**, the **likelihood ratio negative**, and the overall **likelihood ratio** (measure of how probable a correct test result is relative to an incorrect test result). The trade-off between test sensitivity and false-positive error rate over a range of cutoff point values can be displayed by use of a **receiver operating characteristic (ROC) curve**. The overall performance of a test, its **validity** and **reliability**, depend on properties of the test, the population in which it is applied, and decisions and assumptions such as the appropriate cutoff point, the distinction between normal and abnormal, and the amount of variation incorporated into the range of normal or abnormal values.

The quantitative methods for modifying disease probability estimates based on test results are explored in Chapter 3.

🗱 🗱 🗱

〰 REFERENCEſ

1. Zalenski RJ, Shamsa FH. Diagnostic testing of the emergency department patient with chest pain. *Curr Opin Cardiol.* 1998;13:248–253.
2. Rathbun SW, Raskob GE, Whitsett TL. Sensitivity and specificity of helical computed tomography in the diagnosis of pulmonary embolism: A systematic review. *Ann Intern Med.* 2000;132:227–232.
3. Gorgels AP, Vos MA, Mulleneers R, de Zwaan C, Bar FW, Wellens HJ. Value of the electrocardiogram in diagnosing the number of severely narrowed coronary arteries in rest angina pectoris. *Am J Cardiol.* 1993;72:999–1003.
4. Mair J. Progress in myocardial damage detection: New biochemical markers for clinicians. *Crit Rev Clin Lab Sci.* 1997;34:1–66.
5. Morris SA, Helmer D, Pesce M, Giglio J. Clinical utility of CKMB isoform determinations in patients who present to the emergency department with continuous or resolved chest pain. *J Emerg Med.* 2000;19:21–26.
6. Mair J, Smidt J, Lechleitner P, Dienstl F, Puschendorf B. Rapid accurate diagnosis of acute myocardial infarction in patients with non-traumatic chest pain within 1 h of admission. *Corn Artery Dis.* 1995;6:539–545.
7. Jekel JF, Elmore JG, Katz DL. *Epidemiology, Biostatistics, and Preventive Medicine.* Philadelphia, PA: Saunders; 1996.
8. Markel A, Weich Y, Gaitini D. Doppler ultrasound in the diagnosis of venous thrombosis. *Angiology.* 1995;46:65–73.

Quantitative Aspects of Clinical Thinking

Predictive Values and Bayes' Theorem

INTRODUCTION

The diagnostic process begins with the interview of a patient whose condition is unknown. On the basis of history and physical examination diagnostic considerations are entertained, each of which is at least partially quantifiable. Those diagnoses deemed highly improbable will generally not be pursued unless the risk of failing to do so is extreme. Those diagnoses considered highly probable after the initial examination may be treated without recourse to further diagnostic evaluation. Often, however, substantial uncertainty remains following the history and physical examination. Diagnostic tests are applied to resolve, or at least attenuate, that uncertainty. The entire diagnostic process is directed toward a quantitative goal: establishing a diagnosis with sufficient confidence to justify treatment, or excluding a diagnosis with sufficient confidence to justify nontreatment. This chapter demonstrates how estimates of disease probability and test results interact during the pursuit of that goal.

Consider a patient presenting to you with abdominal distension. How likely a diagnosis is pregnancy? Of course, you have no idea. Or rather, not much of an idea; you are already beginning to consider. We can't help it. As clinicians, that's how we think. Give us a symptom or sign, and we naturally start composing our differential list. Abdominal distension: pregnancy is on the list. But how probable is it?

What we want before we can answer is additional information. What if we learn that the patient is 27 years old, is sexually active without contraception, and has been wanting to have a child. How probable is pregnancy now? Still hard to say, but certainly more probable. What if we also learn that the abdominal distension has been progressive over the past 6 months, associated with weight gain, and initially with nausea and vomiting in the morning that has now passed? What if we learn that nausea and vomiting were subsequently replaced by an increased appetite and a change in dietary preferences, some of which might be considered unconventional? Finally, what if we also learned that the syndrome were associated with breast tenderness, and an increase in breast size? I suspect we would all agree that pregnancy sounds quite probable, and certainly more probable than it did at first.

If we ordered a serum pregnancy test (beta human chorionic gonadotropin; β-HCG) now and it were positive, our suspicion would be confirmed and we would, of course, believe the test. We would, in other words, have *diagnosed* pregnancy. This is fairly typical of clinical practice; we choose a diagnostic study based on our clinical impression and then use the diagnostic study to make the diagnosis. Set up this way, the impression derived from the history and physical (H&P) and the results of subsequent diagnostic testing are distinct. Once we decide to test, we let the test results guide us. But should we?

Yes and no. What if the 27-year old with progressive abdominal distension and morning sickness is male? Now how likely is pregnancy? Barring tabloid miracles, pregnancy is impossible. And if we nonetheless order a pregnancy test and it is positive? Then it is wrong. No matter how reliable the pregnancy test, no matter its sensitivity and specificity, if it gives us an answer that we know can't be true, then it is wrong.

But the test has not changed, nor the patient's clinical characteristics. What has changed is simply our estimate of the probability of the condition in question. This extreme case, one in which the "disease" is impossible rather than merely improbable, makes a generic point: the probability of disease, the **prior probability**, remains important in the diagnostic process even after the decision has been reached to order diagnostic tests.

Intuitively, all clinicians understand that diagnosis is intimately related to probability. When we have sufficient confidence in a diagnosis derived from history and physical examination, treatment may be initiated without further diagnostic testing. Good examples might include asthma, bronchitis, or migraine headache. When the history and physical result in substantial uncertainty, or when there is hesitation to treat due to the toxicities of treatment, diagnostic testing is undertaken. But the results of testing cannot replace the prior probability estimate. They must be used together with that estimate, interpreted in light of it, and used to modify it.

When a condition occurs commonly in the population from which a patient comes, the patient is more likely to have the condition. The converse is also true: when a patient comes from a population in which a condition occurs very infrequently, the patient is relatively unlikely to have the condition. Obviously, the more closely the individual patient's characteristics can be matched to the characteristics of a population, the more helpful the comparison is. Clinical medicine is challenging because no two patients are alike, and an exact match between any patient and a population is impossible. Nonetheless, our ability to diagnose at all relics on approximating a match. How do we know someone with rhinorrhea has a viral upper respiratory infection rather than a cerebrospinal fluid leak? In fact, we do not actually *know*; we *infer*.

We infer because colds are common, CSF leaks are rare, and patients with colds share characteristics with all of the other patients with colds whom we've treated (the population of patients with colds), which makes the syndrome familiar and consequently diagnosable on the basis of probability. Diagnosis generally is made despite some residual uncertainty. We rarely can or do apply pathognomonic tests. We overcome the discomfort of residual uncertainty with our estimates of probability. And these estimates are population derived. If we do not know with absolute certainty what an individual patient has, how do we ever make a diagnosis?

There are only two ways. The first, unavailable to most of us, is fortune telling. If we could predict the future, we could know whether or not a patient would go on to have complications of a condition we think they may have. The only other way of knowing what will happen to a patient is by knowing what has happened to other, similar patients. The relative risks and benefits of treating versus not treating are unknowable in an individual patient until after they have or have not been treated. But the impact of such decisions on the patients who have come before is what our experience, and the medical literature, offer us. Therefore, all clinical decisions involve the application of what is known about populations to what is suspected about an individual.

▶ BAYES' THEOREM

This concept is rendered statistically useful by **Bayes' theorem**, developed centuries ago by a theologian.[1,2] In principle, the theorem asserts that the probability of any condition in an individual is related to the probability of that condition in the population of which the individual is a member (the underlying population prevalence of the condition). The theorem has been modified to indicate that the result of any diagnostic test alters the probability of disease in the individual patient because each successive test result reclassifies the population from which the individual comes (i.e., a patient with chest pain and a negative cardiogram versus a patient with chest pain and an ischemic cardiogram). In its basic, if intimidating, form the theorem is expressed as a series of conditional probabilities:

$$PD+ = \left[(pT+ \mid D+)pD+\right] / \left\{\left[(pT+ \mid D+)pD+\right] + \left[(pT+ \mid D-)pD-\right]\right\}$$

PD+: the **posterior probability** of disease (post-test probability)
|: given that; a symbol of conditional probability
pT+: the probability of a positive test
D+: disease is present
PD+: the **prior probability** of disease; (pretest probability or prevalence)
D−: disease is absent
pD−: the probability of nondisease; 1 − prevalence

Deconstructed, Bayes' theorem becomes less intimidating. Consider the numerator: [(pT+ | D+)PD+]. The probability of a test being positive *given that* (conditional probability) the disease is present is the test **sensitivity** (see Chapter 2). Expressed in a 2×2 contingency table (Box 3.1), the probability of a positive test in those who have disease is simply cell a, the true-positives. Bayes' theorem is now:

$$PD+ = true\text{-}positives / \left\{true\text{-}positives + \left[(pT+ \mid D-)pD-\right]\right\}$$

or

$$PD+ = a / \left\{a + \left[(pT+ \mid D-)pD-\right]\right\}$$

We've made good progress because the first term in the denominator of the theorem is the same as the numerator term. What of the second term in the denominator, $[(pT+ \mid D-)pD-)]$? As shown in Box 3.1, this is the probability of a positive test result among those without disease. This term reduces to cell b of the table shown in Box 3.1, the term representing the false-positives. The theorem can now be expressed as:

PD+ = true–positives / {true–positives + false–positives}

or

PD+ $= a / \{a + b\}$

Thus, intimidating though it first appeared, Bayes' theorem asserts the following: the probability that an individual with a positive test result truly has disease is the proportion of all positive test results (true and false) that are true-positives. As was shown in Chapter 2, this is the same formula as the **positive predictive value** (PPV), the probability that a positive test result truly indicates the presence of disease.

There is one other useful way of expressing the theorem. The probability of a positive test in those with the disease is the **sensitivity**, while the probability of disease is the **prevalence**. Thus, the formula can be expressed as:

PD+ = [sensitivity x prevalence] / {[sensitivity x prevalence]
+[(pT+ | D–)pD–)]}

The probability of a positive test result among those truly free of disease is the **false-positive error rate**, or 1 – **specificity**, and the probability of disease absence is 1 – **prevalence**. The formula can now be converted to:

PD+ = [sensitivity x prevalence] / {[sensitivity x prevalence]
+[(1 – specificity)(1 – prevalence)]}

In this form, Bayes' theorem permits calculation of the **posterior probability** of disease, the probability of disease after testing provided one knows the prior probability, and the sensitivity and specificity of the diagnostic test.

Working with Bayes' theorem rather than just the PPV offers both conceptual and logistical advantages. Conceptually, Bayes' theorem emphasizes the importance of prior probability to the probability of disease after testing. Logistically, Bayes' theorem allows us to determine the posterior probability of disease without resorting to a 2 × 2 table.

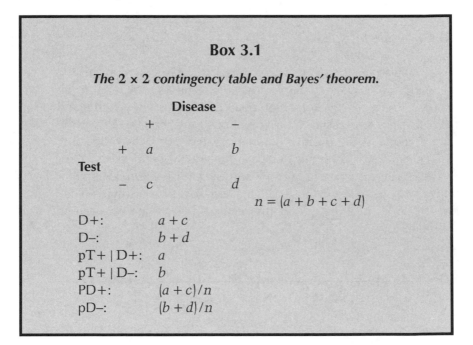

Box 3.1

The 2 x 2 contingency table and Bayes' theorem.

	Disease	
	+	−
Test +	a	b
−	c	d

$$n = (a + b + c + d)$$

D+:	$a + c$
D−:	$b + d$
pT+ | D+:	a
pT+ | D−:	b
PD+:	$(a + c)/n$
pD−:	$(b + d)/n$

⋙ APPLICATION

Consider a patient suspected of having deep venous thrombosis (DVT) on the basis of history and physical examination. In scenario 3.1a, the patient has overt risk for DVT, such as a long period of immobility or a known hypercoagulable state.[3,4] Consider that in scenario 3.1b, the patient is at intermediate risk for DVT. Finally, in scenario 3.1c, the patient is therapeutically anticoagulated on warfarin for a prosthetic heart valve, and therefore at low risk.

If each of these three patients presented with identical signs and symptoms of DVT in the left lower extremity,[5] our estimates of the probability of DVT would likely vary. The first patient seems very likely to have a DVT. Why? Not because of anything about the presentation; the patients are presenting identically. But rather because the patient *comes from a population of patients* in which the occurrence of DVT is known to be high. This is Bayes' theorem in action. The second patient has a moderate, or intermediate probability of DVT. The third patient, other things being equal, should be at low risk for DVT given that the INR (international normalized ratio) is therapeutic.[6]

Scenario 3.1a

Assume that the first patient is estimated to have an 80% probability of DVT. Although it may be uncomfortable to apply such a rigid estimate, the unavoidability of at least a semiquantitative estimate of disease probability has already been discussed. Would you order a Doppler ultrasound study of the lower extremity?[7] At some level of probability, you choose yes, below that level, you choose no. Not every patient who might have DVT gets tested, but some do. Whether intentional or unintentional, quantitative estimates of disease probability infiltrate the process of clinical decision-making. The 80% probability estimate implies that most patients with this risk factor profile and looking as if they have DVT do in fact have DVT. How does this estimate influence the results of diagnostic testing?

Assume that the venous Doppler is ordered, and that it has a sensitivity of 80% and a specificity of 75% for clot above the knee.[8,9] The test is positive. To what extent have we "clinched" the diagnosis?

Bayes' theorem provides an answer and forces us to consider that the test result must modify, rather than replace, our prior probability estimate. The posterior probability of disease is:

$$PD+ = \frac{[\text{sensitivity} \times \text{prevalence}]}{\{[\text{sensitivity} \times \text{prevalence}] + [(1 - \text{specificity})(1 - \text{prevalence})]\}}$$

In this scenario, the sensitivity is 80%, the prevalence is 80%, and the specificity is 75%. The formula becomes:

$$PD+ = (0.8 \times 0.8)/\{(0.8 \times 0.8) + (0.25 \times 0.20)\}$$

$$PD+ = 93\%$$

After a positive Doppler ultrasound test the probability of DVT is 93%. While this is certainly higher than 80%, is the difference clinically important? We started out with a 1 in 5 chance that the DVT we thought was present might actually not be. Even after a positive test, that possibility remains at just under 1 chance in 10. Diagnostic testing helped, but it did not provide certainty. Even so, the limitations of diagnostic testing interpreted out of context are more important than this one scenario can demonstrate.

Scenario 3.1b

What if the same test, with the same operating characteristics, were applied to a second patient who appears to be at intermediate risk for DVT? We can use a prior probability of 50% to convey our substantial uncertainty.

The approach to the posterior probability of disease is as before:

$$PD+ = \frac{[\text{sensitivity} \times \text{prevalence}]}{\{[\text{sensitivity} \times \text{prevalence}] + [(1 - \text{specificity})(1 - \text{prevalence})]\}}$$

$$PD+ = (0.8 \times 0.5)/\{(0.8 \times 0.5) + (0.25 \times 0.5)\}$$

$$PD+ = 76\%$$

Again, diagnostic testing has helped. But there is now a nearly 1 in 4 chance that a patient with a positive Doppler does not, in fact, have DVT. Of note, the posterior probability of DVT in this patient, the probability after a positive diagnostic study, is lower than the prior probability in the patient in scenario 3.1a. Also of note is the much greater change between prior and posterior probability estimates than in scenario 3.1a. When our prior probability estimate was 80%, a fairly reliable diagnostic test increased our posterior probability by 13%. Using the same test, but with a prior probability estimate of 50%, the posterior probability increased by 26%, or twice as much. In general, the greater the degree of diagnostic uncertainty (i.e., the closer the prior probability estimate is to 50%) the more helpful diagnostic testing becomes, and the more test results will modify the posterior relative to the prior probability.

Scenario 3.1c

The patient who is therapeutic on warfarin, but with a presentation suggestive of DVT has a low prior probability of the condition; we can estimate it at 10%. The same venous Doppler testing is applied, with the same operating characteristics. The formula becomes:

$$PD+ = \frac{[\text{sensitivity} \times \text{prevalence}]}{\{[\text{sensitivity} \times \text{prevalence}] + [(1 - \text{specificity})(1 - \text{prevalence})]\}}$$

$$PD+ = (0.8 \times 0.1) / \{(0.8 \times 0.1) + (0.25 \times 0.9)\}$$

$$PD+ = 26\%$$

Clearly demonstrated here is the hazard, to which we are all subject, of simply replacing our clinical estimates with the results of diagnostic testing. Despite a positive Doppler ultrasound (given the operating characteristics provided), the patient in question is far more likely *not* to have DVT than to have DVT. In fact, 3 out of 4 similar patients will be free of DVT.

Confronted with such a scenario, one is generally tempted to reconsider the prior probability estimate. *If the test is positive, then the patient seems to have the disease in question and therefore must have been more likely to have the disease in question than I originally thought.*

This kind of rethinking is both important and dangerous. It is important because the prior probability estimate is just that, an estimate, and one we tend not to like making in a strictly quantitative manner in the first place. Reconsideration of the prior probability estimate is appropriate. But if the prior probability estimate is reasonable, it should not be discarded or replaced based on the results of diagnostic testing. Discarding the prior probability estimate is an inappropriate use of test results, and gives them influence over the diagnostic process they should not have. Test results influence the probability of disease by converting the prior probability to a posterior probability. If the same test is used also to recalibrate the prior probability estimate, the same test is effectively being used twice. This distorts the information provided by the test and jeopardizes the diagnostic process. Test results should be interpreted in light of the prior probability of disease, not used to replace that estimate. That estimate may be revisited (such as is done in sensitivity analysis; see Chapter 10), but on the basis of clinical judgment, not a test result.

Naturally, the actual work-up of a patient is far more involved than the simple scenarios above would suggest. The first complication is that test results are not uniformly positive. What if the Doppler results were negative in each of the 3 scenarios just discussed? If we were inclined to believe a negative test result (we might be in scenario 3.1c where the prior probability of disease is thought to be low), we would be interested in knowing the probability of disease absence following a negative test result; this is the negative predictive value (NPV). As discussed in Chapter 2 and displayed in Box 2.1, the NPV is the true negatives (cell d in the 2×2 table) over all test negatives (the true- plus false-negatives; cells b and d), $d/(b + d)$.

This formula can also be cast in terms of Bayes' theorem. Cell d, the true-negatives, is the product of the probability of being disease free $(1 - \text{prevalence})$ and the probability of testing negative if disease free (specificity). Thus, the numerator for the negative predictive value is $(1 - \text{prevalence}) \times (\text{specificity})$; this is also the second term of the denominator. The first term of the denominator, the false-negatives, or cell b, is the probability of having disease (prevalence) and a negative test result $(1 - \text{sensitivity})$. Thus, the first denominator term is $(\text{prevalence}) \times (1 - \text{sensitivity})$. The Bayesian approach to NPV is displayed below:

$$\text{PD}- = \frac{[\text{specificity} \times (1 - \text{prevalence})]}{\{[\text{specificity} \times (1 - \text{prevalence})] + [\text{prevalence} \times (1 - \text{sensitivity})]\}}$$

$$\text{PD}- = d/(d + b)$$

This formula can be used to interpret a negative Doppler ultrasound result in each of the 3 scenarios just discussed.

Scenario 3.2a

Given a prior probability of DVT of 80%, a sensitivity of 80%, and a specificity of 75%, what is the probability that DVT has been ruled out if the Doppler study is negative?

To use the modified version of Bayes' theorem, we need the following:

specificity $= 75\%$

$1 - \text{prevalence} = (1 - 0.80) = 0.20$

$1 - \text{sensitivity} = (1 - 0.80) = 0.20$

The formula becomes:

$\text{PD--} = [0.75 \times 0.2] / \{[0.75 \times 0.20] + [0.80 \times 0.20]\}$

$\text{PD--} = 48\%$

Again, the hazards of simply substituting a test result for the clinical concern that led to the test are revealed. In a patient at high risk for DVT with pertinent signs and symptoms (i.e., a patient in whom the prior probability of DVT is 80%), a negative Doppler ultrasound with the operating characteristics described does not rule out DVT. In fact, the probability of DVT in this patient following a negative Doppler is still greater than 50%. Stated plainly, the patient is more likely to have the condition than to be free of it even after the negative test.

Scenario 3.2b

Given a prior probability of DVT of 50%, how confident can we be that the condition has been excluded by a negative Doppler study? The formula is:

$\text{PD--} = [0.75 \times 0.5] / \{[0.75 \times 0.50] + [0.50 \times 0.20]\}$

$\text{PD--} = 79\%$

We can now be 80% confident that DVT has been excluded. It is noteworthy how much more a diagnostic test contributes to our degree of certainty (i.e., how much more the posterior probability differs from the prior probability) when we have substantial uncertainty about the diagnosis. Also noteworthy is that 80% probability of disease exclusion still means 1 in 5 patients in this population has DVT.

Scenario 3.2c

Finally, what if the Doppler is negative in the low risk patient, in whom the prior probability of DVT is 10%?

$$PD- = [0.75 \times 0.9] / \{[0.75 \times 0.90] + [0.10 \times 0.20]\}$$

$$PD- = 97\%$$

In this case, we can be quite confident (although never absolutely certain) that DVT has been excluded. It is worth noting that we were more confident that DVT was excluded before ordering the Doppler for the patient in this scenario than we were after the negative Doppler for the patient in scenario 3.2b.

⚜ ALTERNATIVE APPLICATIONS

The scenarios above actually provide more information than discussed thus far. After a test result is positive, the posterior probability of disease tells us how probable disease is with such a result. But we may be interested in knowing how *improbable* disease is after a positive test. For example, if we have a low suspicion of a serious disease but feel obligated to order a study just to be sure, and the test comes back as a surprise positive, how do we react? As has been stated repeatedly, we cannot simply replace our low prior probability estimate with the test result. We may want to know, given the operating characteristics of the test in question, what the probability is that disease is absent despite a positive test. This may be particularly important if the test we ordered just to be sure is relatively noninvasive (e.g., a V/Q scan) but the confirmatory test we are now considering (e.g., a pulmonary angiogram) is invasive.[10] The probability that disease is absent following a positive test result is the proportion misleading positives (PMP) as discussed in Chapter 2, or (1 – positive predictive value) (see 2 × 2 table, Appendix C). In terms of the 2 × 2 table, the formula is $b/(a + b)$. In terms of Bayes' theorem, the formula is:

$$PD- \mid T+ \; = \; \big[(1- \text{ specificity}) \times (1-\text{prevalence})\big]/\big\{\big[(1-\text{specificity})$$
$$\times(1- \text{ prevalence})\big] + \big[\text{sensitivity} \times \text{prevalence}\big]\big\}$$

Alternatively, one may have a high suspicion of disease, yet feel similarly compelled to order a confirmatory test. How to interpret a surprise negative result in this situation? The probability of disease despite a negative test result is the proportion misleading negatives (PMN) or (1 – negative predictive value). In terms of the 2 × 2 table, the formula is $c/(c + d)$. In terms of Bayes' theorem, the formula is:

$$PD+ \mid T- \; = \; \big[(1- \text{ senstivity}) \times \text{prevalence}\big]/\big\{\big[(1-\text{sensitivity}) \times \text{prevalence}\big]$$
$$+ \big[\text{specificity} \times (1-\text{prevalence})\big]\big\}$$

〉〉 ODDS AND PROBABILITIES: BAYES' THEOREM AND LIKELIHOOD RATIOS

We have been discussing our clinical impression in terms of the probability of disease. The quantitative expression of this clinical judgment can be made alternatively with odds. The principal value in this is to be able to cast an estimate in whatever terms a patient (and/or clinician) most readily appreciates; a secondary benefit is the creation of linkages among various statistical applications.

The relationship between odds and probability is described by the following equations:

odds = probability/(1 – probability)

and

probability = odds/(odds + 1)

The validity of these equations is best demonstrated with an example. Consider that the prior (or pretest) probability of a particular condition is estimated at 50%. This can be expressed as 1 chance in 2. But how to express it in terms of odds? For every such patient who has the condition, there should be one such patient who does not. Thus, the odds are expressed as 1:1. When odds are even, there is an equal probability of the condition being present or absent, i.e., 1 chance in 2. The same result is derived from the equations:

probability $= 0.5$

odds $=$ probability$/(1-$probability$)$

odds $= 0.5/(1-0.5) = 0.5 : 0.5 = 1 : 1$

odds $= 1 : 1 = 1$

probability $=$ odds$/($odds $+ 1)$

probability $= 1/(1 + 1) = 1/2 = 0.5$

The likelihood ratio $(+)$ can be used along with pretest odds to produce post-test odds:

post-test odds $=$ pretest odds $\times$ LR$(+)$

Consider a situation in which the pretest odds of disease are estimated at 1 to 9 (1:9). A test is applied with 90% sensitivity and 90% specificity, and is positive. What are the odds of disease now (i.e., the post-test odds of disease)? The two approaches to this would be 1) to convert from odds to probability immediately and use Bayes' theorem, or 2) use the likelihood ratio to generate post-test odds, with the option of converting to probability thereafter. The likelihood ratio $(+)$, described in Chapter 2, is the sensitivity over the false-positive error rate, or the ratio of the rate of true- to false-positives. The false-positive error rate is $(1-$specificity$)$, therefore the LR$(+)$ is [sensitivity$/(1-$specificity$)$]. The post-test odds in the situation described would be:

(pretest odds) $\times$ [(sensitivity$/(1-$specificity$)$)] $=$

$(1 : 9)(0.90/0.10) =$

$(1 : 9) \times 9 = 1$

The post-test odds are 1, or 1:1. In terms of probability, this is:

probability = odds/(odds + 1)

probability = 1/(1 + 1) =

1/2 = 0.50

Thus the posterior or post-test probability is 50%. We can confirm the validity of this approach by setting up a 2×2 table with 100 patients of whom 10 have the disease and 90 do not. This provides for a pretest probability of disease of 10%, equivalent to the stipulated pretest odds of 1:9. A sensitivity of 90% requires that 9 of the 10 patients with disease have a positive test, while the 90% specificity requires that 81 of the 90 patients free of disease have a negative test. The table is shown in the box below.

		D		
		+	−	
	+	9	9	
T				
	−	1	81	
			$n = 100$	

prev = 10%

sens = 90%

spec = 90%

The posterior probability is the probability of disease given a positive test result, or the PPV. This is $a/(a + b)$, or 9/18. Again, we have 0.5, or 50%.

Finally, we can use Bayes' theorem directly. Pretest odds of 1:9 are the same as a pretest probability of 10%. With the prior probability, sensitivity, and specificity, we have all we need to apply the theorem:

PD+ | T+ = (0.90 × 0.10)/[(0.90 × 0.10) + (0.10 × 0.90)] =

0.09/(0.09 + 0.09) =

0.5 = 50%

Thus, the clinical impression of disease may be expressed in terms of either probability or odds to generate a revised impression following the use of diagnostic testing.

〽 IMPLICATIONſ OF BAYEſ' THEOREM FOR DIAGNOſTIC TEſTING

Does judicious application of Bayes' theorem to the process of workup and diagnosis require that we include a calculator in our proverbial black bags? The answer is a resounding *no* (although there are times it can come in handy), because there is generally substantial uncertainty about the prior probability estimate. Therefore, the use of the theorem to generate a very accurate posterior probability of disease is unreliable.

What is reliable is the theorem's capacity to demonstrate the interaction of prior probability estimate and a test result. If one is very confident disease is present, only a truly exceptional test can make one substantially more certain. Similarly if the test is negative, it can refute that impression reliably. If one thinks disease is very unlikely, only a remarkably good test can make one substantially more certain disease is absent. If the test is positive, it can provide firm evidence that disease is present. Bayes' theorem provides mathematical evidence to support the concept that the value of diagnostic testing depends both on the performance characteristics of the test and the clinical scenario in which the test is ordered.

Does application of Bayes' theorem result in more or less diagnostic testing? Ideally, both. That is, astute use of the theorem, or at least the concepts underlying it, should at times result in more diagnostic testing, and at times less. When one might be inclined to order a test despite considerable confidence that disease is present or absent, the theorem should highlight the extent to which test results will modify that level of confidence. When the test result is unlikely to change the clinical impression, the test may be unnecessary. Alternatively, when a needed test yields a surprise result, the theorem would argue against abandoning the prior probability and replacing it with the test result. In this situation confirmatory testing is likely to be required. The goal in applying the theorem to clinical practice is to do the right test at the right time for the right reason, not to increase or decrease testing generally.

How reliably can the theorem and its application be when the whole process begins with a prior probability estimate that is seldom more than an educated guess? Worse still, an educated guess that rarely receives unanimous agreement among a group of educated practitioners; a group of clinicians will invariably generate a range of estimates when asked to apply a numerical estimate to the probability of a disease.[2] And while the group members may feel comfortable with a range, no one is totally secure in their own estimate, let alone the estimates of the others. This seeming weakness is a strength in the application of Bayes' theorem. For while it is true that our estimates of disease probability are subject to considerable uncertainty, it is far better to confront the issue than ignore it. How do we decide when to order any test in any patient? When we feel sufficiently convinced that a test has value we order it, otherwise we do not. But what is "sufficiently"? The word connotes a quantity, albeit a vaguely defined quantity. If we accept that above a certain level of concern we pursue a diagnosis, below that level we do not (the only alternative would be to pursue every diagnosis in every patient, or no diagnosis in any patient), then we accept that we already do generate a semiquantitative estimate of disease probability. In a way it is reassuring that the estimates vary among a group of clinicians; no matter how statistics and evidence are applied, much of clinical practice will be shaped by judgment. The application of Bayes' theorem is not intended to eliminate uncertainty in the diagnostic process, but rather to disclose it, so we can wrestle with it more effectively.

One way to wrestle directly with the uncertainty in the prior probability estimate is to conduct a **sensitivity analysis**. This term is generic, referring to any situation in which the *a priori* assumptions are modified across some range of plausible values to determine whether conclusions are altered. In the case of Bayes' theorem, one can vary the prior probability estimate over a range of reasonable values. A reasonable value is the product of judgment, but it is also bounded by 0 and 1 (100%).

While one might be ill at ease in any given clinical situation to say, for example, that the prior probability of disease were 22%, one might be quite secure that it were between 5% and 50%. By interpreting the test result over the range of prior probability estimates, one can determine if the conclusion remains the same, or changes. When the implications of prior probability estimates vary over the "reasonable" range, one must apply judgment to determine how to proceed. Generally the course that minimizes risk to the patient and maximizes potential benefit is indicated, whether that means more testing or not.

Consider that a test with 95% sensitivity and specificity is applied to diagnose a condition for which treatment is absolutely necessary but invasive and painful (for example, osteomyelitis[11]). If the test, for example a MRI,[12] is positive, with what degree of confidence can one advise the patient to proceed with surgical resection or antibiotic implantation?

If the prior probability is set at 5%, the positive MRI (with sensitivity and specificity set at 95% each as noted above), results in a posterior probability of 0.5, or 50%. Although this is a substantial jump, it hardly is adequate to justify invasive therapy; there is still as much probability of the disease in question being absent as present. If the prior probability is set at 50%, the posterior probability under these conditions becomes 0.95, or 95%. This might reach the threshold of confidence required to begin treatment. If not, it certainly defines a reasonable boundary. If the prior probability estimate is greater than 50%, and the MRI is positive, the disease is almost certainly present, and treatment is indicated. If the prior probability is substantially lower than 50% a positive MRI will suggest a need for further confirmatory testing before invasive therapy is initiated.

⚜ CONCEPTUAL FACTORS INFLUENCING PROBABILITY ESTIMATES

Bayes' theorem is about probability. But probability is one of three concepts that should share equal prominence in the diagnostic process. The other two are **risk** and **alternatives**. (The subtleties of measuring and expressing risk are discussed further in Chapter 5.)

When a disease is very serious and can be modified with treatment (e.g., meningitis), the need to pursue a work-up cannot be discounted just because the condition is relatively improbable. A serious condition needs to be considered even if it is not probable. However, the seriousness and probability of a disease cancel one another at the extremes. If a condition is truly trivial, then no matter how probable it is diagnostic testing is unlikely to be valuable. And if a condition is extremely improbable, then no matter how serious, it should probably not be pursued. It is clear that we conduct our workups this way—not every patient with fever or headache has a lumbar puncture.

And this is where the third concept, alternatives, comes in. When an alternative diagnosis is very probable, then the diagnosis under consideration becomes less so. If the patient with fever and a headache appears to have a viral upper respiratory illness (i.e., a cold), then the probability that the symptoms are due to meningitis is that much less. Once a "cold" is diagnosed with confidence, the consideration of meningitis is resolved. But what of situations in which no good alternative suggests itself? For example, what of the patient with chest pain atypical for angina, but at least equally atypical for a gastrointestinal or musculoskeletal source? The lack of alternatives makes the principal diagnosis(es) in question more probable. When one has eliminated the impossible whatever is left, however improbable, is apt to be the truth. The building blocks of a solid diagnosis are considerations of probability, alternatives, and risk.

As noted throughout the text, statistical aspects of decision making and reasoning tend to insinuate themselves into the routine course of clinical practice. The history and physical is bounded by the type of prejudice upon which Bayes' theorem is based. Questions considered irrelevant are not asked, even though they might be relevant under highly unusual circumstances. Specific maneuvers in the physical exam that are unlikely to apply to a given patient are appropriately left out. Each question, and each component of the exam, is included or excluded based on the casual consideration of probability and risk. When used appropriately, each question and each examination maneuver follows those before it like diagnostic tests in sequence. The impression derived from a question leads to another question that "tests" the hypothesis generated by the previous question. The exam revisits and further tests the hypothesis(es) raised by the history. The process continues until a discrete range of possibilities amenable to diagnostic testing is produced. When the history and physical produce so characteristic a picture of a condition (i.e., when the patient is found to correspond almost perfectly with patients previously found to have a particular condition and therefore be a member of the population of patients with that condition), the list of possibilities is reduced to one item, and no further diagnostic evaluation is required. If one item seems much more likely than all others, but there are alternatives that are of sufficient probability and risk to warrant consideration, the dominant hypothesis (i.e., diagnostic consideration) requires further testing. Viewed this way, the process of hypothesis generation and testing begins even before the history and physical, by mere consideration of the practice setting, and then proceeds through the history and physical and any subsequent testing performed. The process continues until a single diagnosis is established with considerable certainty, or until a course of action is identified that will minimize the risk of adverse outcomes and maximize the probability of treatment benefit despite substantial residual diagnostic uncertainty. The particular value in viewing clinical inquiry as sequential hypothesis testing is that the interview and diagnostic technology lie on the same continuum. This perspective discourages undue reliance on "test results" without judicious interpretation of the appropriateness of test selection and performance.

⦻ BAYES' THEOREM AND THE SEQUENCE OF TESTING

When multiple diagnostic tests are ordered together, the approach is referred to as **parallel testing**. When one test follows another, the approach is referred to as **serial testing**. Bayes' theorem is better suited to serial than parallel testing, although it may be adapted to either.

Consider, for example, that a diagnosis of pneumonia is suspected in a 62-year-old male smoker with a productive cough. Among the tests one might consider are a complete blood count (CBC), a chest x-ray, and a sputum gram stain and/or culture. If the white blood count is elevated, it might be interpreted as evidence in support of the diagnosis, as might an x-ray that shows an infiltrate or sputum that reveals a dominant pathogen. But what if one of the tests is positive and others are negative? Will one positive test be sufficient to "clinch" the diagnosis and justify antibiotic therapy, or will two out of three or even all three be required? The basis for deciding should be the probability of benefit or harm to patients. If pneumonia is only "ruled in" when all pertinent tests are positive, one might expect the specificity of diagnostic testing to be high, but the sensitivity to be low, and the false-negative error rate correspondingly high. In other words, such an approach will prevent the over-diagnosis and treatment of pneumonia, but will likely cause cases of pneumonia to be missed. Conversely, if any positive test is used as adequate support for the diagnosis, few cases will be missed, sensitivity will be high, but specificity will be low and the false-positive error rate correspondingly high.

Instead of deciding in advance what the implication of multiple test results obtained concurrently would be, Bayes' theorem might be applied. With knowledge of the performance characteristics of each test (i.e., sensitivity and specificity), and an estimate of prior probability, the results of all tests can be used to produce a series of posterior probabilities. The ultimate posterior probability will be the same regardless of the sequence in which the test results are applied, as shown in Table 3.1.

TABLE 3.1   **Posterior Probability when 3 Diagnostic Tests Are Obtained Concurrently**

Test Sequence	Posterior Probability, 1	Posterior Probability, 2	Posterior Probability, 3
A–B–C	72%	83%	94%
C–B–A	75%	85%	94%

The prior probability of disease is 50%. Test A has a sensitivity of 65% and a specificity of 75%; test B has a sensitivity of 75% and a specificity of 60%; and test C has a sensitivity of 90% and a specificity of 70%. The final probability of disease is independent of the order in which the test results are considered. The results shown are based on positive results of all 3 tests.

When testing is performed serially rather than in parallel the use of Bayes' theorem, formal or informal, is almost unavoidable. The rationale for sequential testing is that testing will continue only as long as substantial uncertainty persists. Once "enough" evidence had been obtained that supports the diagnosis (i.e., positive test results produce a posterior probability high enough to warrant diagnosis and treatment), testing would presumably stop. Similarly, once enough evidence had been obtained (i.e., negative test results) to exclude the diagnosis with confidence, testing would stop.

In general, when testing is inexpensive, simple, and noninvasive, and/or when time is of the essence, parallel testing is preferred. This is often the case for hospitalized patients, because the cost of testing may be less than the cost of extra days in the hospital spent waiting for the results of sequentially ordered tests to come in. When tests are costly or invasive, when time is not the limiting commodity, and/or when the need for subsequent tests will depend on the results of initial testing, serial testing is preferred. Judicious application of Bayes' theorem, or at least a consideration of its relevance, is useful in the interpretation of tests under either circumstance.

S U M M A R Y / T A K E - A W A Y   M E S S A G E S

Application of Bayes' theorem provides for the quantification of disease probability based on the results of diagnostic tests. An estimate of disease **prior probability**, **test sensitivity**, and **test specificity** is sufficient to use a test result to determine the **post-test** or **posterior probability** of disease. The probability of disease given a positive test is the **positive predictive value**; the probability of disease absence given a negative test is the **negative predictive value**. Testing is of greatest utility when uncertainty is greatest. The performance of diagnostic tests depends in part on whether they are ordered **in parallel** (simultaneously) or **serially**. Testing may be interpreted as either **odds**, or **probability**, and translated to the other. The **pretest odds** of disease multiplied by the **likelihood ratio positive** (LR+) yields the **post-test odds** of disease. Because the probability of a given diagnosis following testing depends on the probability estimate prior to testing, the initial prior probability is of fundamental importance yet highly subject to uncertainty. This estimate may be varied over a range of reasonable considerations in a **sensitivity analysis** to determine at what values implications for clinical management are altered.

The probability of DVT in scenario 3.1a with no diagnostic testing at all is higher than the probability of DVT in scenario 3.1b following a positive diagnostic test. Provided that our prior probability estimates are reasonably accurate, this conclusion is correct and indisputable. But does any of us actually practice that way? Does any of us get the positive ultrasound result in scenario 3.2b and conclude that DVT is still less probable than it would have been in a high risk patient and that the diagnosis is yet to be made? By considering the importance of prior probability we would feel compelled to do so.

The counter argument, of course, is that the diagnostic studies are accurate and the estimate of prior probability is not. But is this really true? If it is, we should acknowledge that we simply have no basis to decide when a diagnostic test should be done because that decision is based on the clinical impression. In all of our work-ups, no matter how technological they may become, the clinical impression comes first and is therefore the foundation upon which all subsequent information must rest.

Perhaps that foundation is less solid than we might like, but even knowing that is important because it is our only foundation. Nor is it reasonable to refute the importance of prior probability by arguing that our clinical impression is not truly quantitative because it must be. Our clinical impression is like the philosophy question about the dollar bill with a piece missing, then another piece, then another. At what point is the dollar bill no longer worth a dollar? While we might have difficulty committing to the number of missing pieces acceptable to us, we know that somewhere between a whole and a wholly absent dollar bill is the threshold we would use. Perhaps we would only know it when we saw it, which is what happens in clinical practice. But the threshold itself is quantitative. If we are uncomfortable with the results of diagnostic testing based on an uncertain estimate of prior probability, how much more uncomfortable should we be when we base our diagnostic decision on probability estimates we are not willing or able to quantify at all? If the prior probability of disease is truly unknowable, then so, too, is the posterior probability. Acknowledging and confronting the quantitative challenges of medical reasoning and diagnosis is far more reasonable than ignoring or denying them.

〰 〰 〰

〰 REFERENCEƒ

1. Jekel JF, Elmore JG, Katz DL. *Epidemiology, Biostatistics, and Preventive Medicine*. Philadelphia, PA: Saunders, 1996.
2. Lurie JD, Sox HC. Principles of medical decision making. *Spine*. 1999;24:493–498.
3. Arfvidsson B, Eklof B, Kistner RL, Masuda EM, Sato DT. Risk factors for venous thromboembolism following prolonged air travel. Coach class thrombosis. *Hematol Oncol Clin North Am*. 2000;14:391–400, ix.
4. Ridker PM. Inherited risk factors for venous thromboembolism: Implications for clinical practice. *Clin Cornerstone*. 2000;2:1–14.
5. Gorman WP, Davis KR, Donnelly R. ABC of arterial and venous disease. Swollen lower limb-1: General assessment and deep vein thrombosis. *BMJ*. 2000;320:1453–1456.
6. Ageno W. Treatment of venous thromboembolism. *Thromb Res*. 2000;97:V63–72.
7. Bjorgell O, Nilsson PE, Jarenros H. Isolated nonfilling of contrast in deep leg vein segments seen on phlebography, and a comparison with color Doppler ultrasound, to assess the incidence of deep leg vein thrombosis. *Angiology*. 2000;51:451–461.
8. Richlie DG. Noninvasive imaging of the lower extremity for deep venous thrombosis. *J Gen Intern Med*. 1993;8:271–277.
9. Forbes K, Stevenson AJ. The use of power Doppler ultrasound in the diagnosis of isolated deep venous thrombosis of the calf. *Clin Radiol*. 1998;53:752–754.
10. Henschke CI, Whalen JP. Evaluation of competing diagnostic tests: Sequences for the diagnosis of pulmonary embolism, Part II. *Clin Imaging*. 1994;18:248–254.
11. Bamberger DM. Diagnosis and treatment of osteomyelitis. *Compr Ther*. 2000;26:89–95.
12. Sammak B, Abd El Bagi M, Al Shahed M, Hamilton D, Al Nabulsi J, Youssef B, Al Thagafi M. Osteomyelitis: A review of currently used imaging techniques. *Eur Radiol*. 1999;9:894–900.

Fundamentals of Screening

The Art and Science of Looking for Trouble

In many ways, screening represents the most explicit interface of individual patient care and population-based medicine. Clinical screening efforts are directed at the identification of disease or its precursors in an individual. Yet by definition screening is a practice conducted in populations, the characteristics of which determine the utility of such testing. Explicit criteria exist for determining the appropriateness of population screening. The performance characteristics of screening tests have implications for the reliability with which disease is ruled in or ruled out. Because the utility of screening is predicated on results in populations, cost is of particular importance. Even a test of clear benefit in a population may result in more harm than good for an individual; the potential human costs and benefits of screening for a given individual are considered.

⚡ SCREENING DEFINED

S creening is the effort to identify otherwise occult conditions (typically disease or disease precursors) in some appropriate segment of the general population. Such practices are distinct from **case finding**, which are efforts to identify occult, comorbid conditions in patients under active clinical investigation. As an example of the latter practice, consider the inclusion of so-called liver function tests (LFT's) among the admission labs of a patient with cellulitis. This is not a population-based screening program for occult liver disease, yet laboratory evidence of disease is being sought in an individual without relevant symptoms. Case finding is defined by its clinical context, and its inapplicability to the general population. Finally, the process of hypothesis-driven diagnostic studies may at times extend to conditions for which specific symptoms or signs are lacking. The applications of screening are maximally broad, pertaining to a defined segment of the general population. The applications of diagnosis are maximally narrow, pertaining only to populations with suggestive clinical presentations. The applications of case finding are intermediate, pertaining to clinical populations, but extending to conditions for which specific evidence is lacking.

⚡ SCREENING CRITERIA

The appropriateness of screening is contingent on three categories of criteria: disease-specific criteria; society, or system criteria; and test-specific criteria (see Table 4.1).[1,2] The disease-specific criteria stipulate that the disease must be serious enough to justify the screening effort; that the natural history of the disease must be known; that treatment must be effective and available; that the disease be neither too rare nor too common; and that early detection through screening must result in modification (for the better) of the natural history of the disease. Each of these criteria influences the capacity of the screening program to confer benefit, both to populations and individuals. If the disease is insignificant (e.g., seborrheic dermatitis), a population-based screening effort would be unjustified, even if early detection did improve outcomes. If the natural history of the disease is unknown, the impact of early detection through screening on the

TABLE 4.1

| | Screening Prerequisites | |
Disease Specific	Society / System Specific	Test Specific
• Disease is serious • Disease is detectable in asymptomatic state • Natural history of disease is known • Treatment is available • Natural history of disease is modifiable with treatment • The disease must be neither too rare, nor too common	• Confirmatory testing is available as needed • Follow-up is available for all screening positives • Treatment is available for all symptomatic cases, as well as all confirmed screening positives • The screening program is considered cost-effective relative to others	• The test should be sensitive so that disease is reliably detected when present • The test should be specific so that false positive results are minimized • The test should be safe, convenient, and not prohibitively expensive

course of the disease will be similarly unknown. In such situations, even apparent increases in survival become uninterpretable. The possibility exists that an individual lives longer after diagnosis because the timing of diagnosis has been shifted earlier, rather than because the timing of death has been shifted later. This phenomenon is known as **lead time bias**, and pertains equally well to nonlethal conditions. If treatment is unavailable or ineffective there is nothing to offer other than bad news if screening is positive. Screening is generally contraindicated under such conditions. If a disease is very rare, the expense of screening is apt to be unjustified, and false-positive tests are likely to outnumber true-positives. This criterion is waived when the benefits of treatment are extreme, such as in perinatal testing for phenylketonuria.[3,4] If a disease is extremely common, such as dental caries, preventive action, such as fluoridation, is more beneficial and cost effective than screening.[5,6] Finally, if treatment outcomes do not differ between those cases detected through screening and those detected because of symptoms, the expense and inconveniences of screening are unlikely to be justified.

Societal criteria for screening include the availability of confirmatory testing as needed; the availability of follow-up for all screening positives; the availability of treatment for all symptomatic cases, as well as all confirmed screening positives; and that the screening program be considered cost effective relative to others. As there are very few (if any) completely accurate tests in medicine, the results of the screening program must be subjected to additional testing whenever the clinical circumstances so require. For this to occur, such additional testing must be available. The provision of any screening test carries the responsibility of following up on the results obtained. If insufficient resources exist to provide needed follow up diagnosis and care to all patients who screen positive and appropriate interpretation for all patients who screen negatives, then screening is inappropriate. The availability of follow-up to screened patients presupposes that follow-up care and treatment is already available to all cases diagnosed due to the development of symptoms or overt clinical signs. Finally, a screening program will consume system resources that should be applied only if substantially greater health benefits are not procurable through alternative applications. Screening programs should be considered cost-effective by prevailing societal standards.

Most important for our purposes are the prerequisite test properties that determine the appropriateness of screening. The test to be applied should be accurate. **Accuracy**, the tendency to be correct, on average, even if results are actually quite variable, implies both sensitivity and specificity (see Chapter 2). **Precision** is the tendency to get the same or very similar result repeatedly, even if the results are actually quite far from being correct. As discussed in Chapter 1, **sensitivity** is the capacity to detect disease when it is present, while **specificity** is the capacity to exclude disease when it is absent. These performance characteristics of screening tests and their interaction with disease epidemiology are discussed in detail below. Finally, the test should be convenient, safe, and relatively inexpensive or its characteristics are likely to preclude application in a screening program. The test should also be complementary to other tests so that confirmation of disease status may be conveniently obtained. Note that the safety and convenience of screening tests are of greater importance than for tests used in diagnosis or even case finding. A test should carry minimal risks and inconvenience to justify its use in a large, asymptomatic population in which the majority of individuals are disease free. In clinical populations undergoing diagnostic workups, the relatively high probability of disease and the acute or even urgent "need to know" legitimize greater attendant inconveniences and risks.

※ STATISTICAL CONSIDERATIONS PERTINENT TO SCREENING

When clinicians are asked to explain the fundamental purpose of screening efforts, the most common answer (at least anecdotally) is to detect disease. Interestingly, and perhaps of general philosophical importance to modern medical practices, patients tend to offer a different response: to be reassured that disease is absent. In other words, clinicians are predisposed to rule in disease, patients to rule it out. Obviously, we as clinicians also prefer to rule out disease, and patients must be prepared to deal with the presence of disease even while hoping for evidence of its absence.

The pertinent test characteristics necessary to achieve the twin objectives of screening—to **rule in** disease, and to **rule out** disease—can be defined in terms of sensitivity and specificity. Recalling that sensitivity is measured in the population with disease, and that it defines the proportion of those with disease in whom the test is positive, one might be inclined to think it is useful to rule in disease. However, this is not so. A test with high sensitivity is needed to rule out disease. In other words, **a good rule-out test has a high sensitivity**. The rationale is quite simple once revealed. A test with high sensitivity will detect disease most of the time when it is present. Therefore, if the disease is present, the test will likely also be positive. The test is therefore unlikely to be negative when disease is present (i.e., a low false-negative error rate, as discussed in Chapter 1). If the test is negative it will likely be because disease is truly absent. Therefore, a negative result of a highly sensitive test reliably (more or less) rules out disease. The acronym *SnNout* may be of use (Sn = sensitive; N = negative result; out = disease ruled out).[7] A negative result from a highly sensitive test reliably rules out disease.

This is demonstrated in Box 4.1, in which the prevalence of disease is set at 5% in an arbitrary population of 100,000, and a test with a very high sensitivity (98%) and moderate specificity (60%) is applied. If the test is negative, there is only a 2% risk that it is a false-negative, because the false-negative error rate is (1 – sensitivity). The probability that a negative test result truly indicates disease absence (the negative predictive value)

Box 4.1

A 2 × 2 table depicting the results of screening a population of 100,000 in which the prevalence of disease is 5% with a test that has 98% sensitivity and 60% specificity.

$$
\begin{array}{c c c c}
 & & \mathbf{D} & \\
 & + & & - \\
 & + & 4900 & 38{,}000 \\
\mathbf{T} & & & \\
 & - & 100 & 57{,}000 \\
 & & & n = 100{,}000
\end{array}
$$

Positive predictive value (PPV) = $a/(a + b)$ = 11%
Negative predictive value (NPV) = $d/(c + d)$ = 99.8%
False-positive error rate = $1 - \text{specificity} = b/(b + d)$ = 40%
False-negative error rate = $1 - \text{sensitivity} = c/(a + c)$ = 2%

---

in this scenario is 99.8%, a product of both the high test sensitivity and low disease prevalence.

Intuition might suggest that a positive test with such high sensitivity reliably indicates that disease is present, but this is not so. Sensitivity indicates *the proportion of those who are disease positive* who will be test positive, but does not indicate *the proportion of test positives* who are truly disease positive. For this, the PPV is needed. In general, the false-positive error rate rises as the sensitivity rises (see ROC curves, Chapter 1). High sensitivity suggests that a high proportion of those who are disease positive are apt to have positive tests, but does not indicate anything about the rate of positive test results in those truly free of disease. In Box 4.1, the probability that disease is present after a positive test, the PPV, is only 11%. Clearly, a highly sensitive test is not adequate to rule in disease.

A good rule-in test has high specificity. The logic is comparable to that for the rule-out test. If a test is highly specific, it will be negative nearly always when disease is absent, meaning the test will almost never be positive when disease is absent. Therefore, if the test is positive it is highly probable that disease is present, or has been *ruled in*. The acronym

SpPin may be of use (Sp = specific; P = positive result; in = disease ruled in).[7] A positive result from a highly specific test reliably rules in disease.

This is demonstrated in Box 4.2, where the prevalence of disease is again set at 5% in a population of 100,000. This time, however, the screening test applied has a sensitivity of 60% and a specificity of 98%. As demonstrated in the table, a positive test now has a 61% probability (rather than 11% in the prior scenario) of truly indicating disease. The high specificity has significantly improved the capacity of our screen to rule in disease. Yet the PPV with a specificity of 98% is substantially lower than the NPV was when the sensitivity was 98%. Why? Because with a prevalence of 5%, the average individual screened is much more probable to be disease free than to have disease (by a factor of 20 to 1). As discussed in Chapter 3, predictive value varies not only with the test performance, but also with prevalence.

Therefore, the following can be asserted about screening tests to rule in and rule out disease. At any fixed prevalence, the higher the test sensitivity the lower the false-negative error rate, and the higher the NPV (although this depends in part on specificity as well), and the more reliably disease can be ruled out by a negative test. Similarly, given fixed preva-

---

Box 4.2

A 2 × 2 table depicting the results of screening a population of 100,000 in which the prevalence of disease is 5% with a test that has 60% sensitivity and 98% specificity.

		D	
		+	−
T	+	3000	1900
	−	2000	93,100

$$n = 100,000$$

Positive predictive value $= a/(a + b) = 61\%$
Negative predictive value $= d/(c + d) = 97.9\%$
False-positive error rate $= 1 - \text{specificity} = b/(b + d) = 2\%$
False-negative error rate $= 1 - \text{sensitivity} = c/(a + c) = 40\%$

lence, the higher the specificity the lower the false-positive error rate, and the higher the PPV (although this depends in part on sensitivity as well), and the more reliably disease can be ruled in by a positive test. Alternatively, given fixed values of sensitivity and specificity, positive test results will be more reliable (i.e., PPV will rise) as prevalence rises, while negative test results will be more reliable (i.e., NPV will rise) as prevalence falls.

This last point can be illustrated by extreme examples. Consider a pregnancy test with excellent sensitivity and specificity (99% each) conducted in a population of 1,000,000 males. The test is correct 99% of the time, yet every positive test result is wrong. Because 1% of those who are disease negative will have a positive test, 10,000 of the men will have a positive test. The PPV is 0. In contrast, the NPV is 100%; every negative test is true.

Applying an equally good test (99% sensitivity and specificity) to a population in which disease prevalence is 100% reveals the limitations at the other end of the spectrum. For example, if screening for the presence of a beating heart in a population of 1,000,000 conscious adults, 1% will test negative. Thus, there will be 10,000 negative test results, all of which will be wrong. Because there are no true-negatives, the negative predictive value is 0. Every positive test will be true, therefore the PPV is 100%. These properties are displayed in Box 4.3a and b.

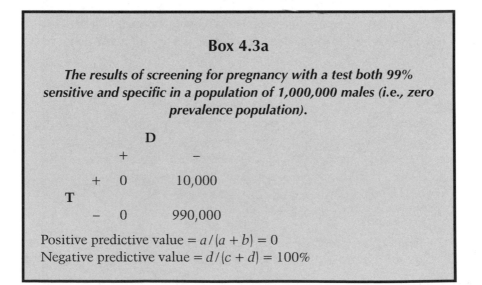

Box 4.3a

*The results of screening for pregnancy with a test both 99%
sensitive and specific in a population of 1,000,000 males (i.e., zero
prevalence population).*

	D	
	+	−
+	0	10,000
T		
−	0	990,000

Positive predictive value = $a/(a + b)$ = 0
Negative predictive value = $d/(c + d)$ = 100%

> ## Box 4.3b
>
> *The results of screening for a heart beat with a test both 99%
> sensitive and specific in a population of 1,000,000 conscious adults
> (i.e., 100% prevalence population).*
>
> | | D | |
> |---|---|---|
> | | + | − |
> | **T** + | 990,000 | 0 |
> | **T** − | 10,000 | 0 |
>
> Positive predictive value $= a/(a + b) = 100\%$
> Negative predictive value $= d/(c + d) = 0$

▓ SEQUENTIAL TESTING

While it may be enlightening to discover that sensitivity is required to rule
disease out and specificity to rule it in, this revelation (if it is one) creates
rather than resolves a clinical problem. The clinical problem, of course,
is that the patient's disease status, unknown before testing, should be
known after testing. The statistical considerations thus far discussed suggest that we need to choose between looking for disease and looking for
the absence of disease. As the patient may fall into either of these two
populations, and we cannot know which, the need to choose one undermines our efforts to learn the truth.

This dilemma is compounded by the relationship between sensitivity
and specificity, as discussed in Chapter 1. Because sensitivity pertains
only to those with disease, and specificity only to those without, they
are fundamentally independent. However, as sensitivity rises, the false-
positive error rate almost invariably rises. Specificity and the false-positive
error rate add to 1 (the sum of false-positives and true-negatives; all disease negatives), and therefore specificity will tend to decline as sensitivity
rises. As specificity rises, the false negative error rate almost invariably

rises. Sensitivity and the false negative error rate add to 1 (the sum of false-negatives and true-positives; all disease positives).

A good example of this phenomenon might be the reactions of contestants on a game show. One is generally penalized in such a contest for attempting to answer a question to which one doesn't know the answer. On the other hand, if one knows the answer but doesn't react first, the opportunity to respond is lost. One could respond very rapidly to be certain no opportunity to answer is lost but only at the risk of getting a question to which one didn't know the answer—*a false-positive reaction.* Alternatively, one could hold back to avoid getting stuck with an unanswerable question, but at the risk of missing a question one could have answered—*a false-negative reaction.* Efforts to maximize performance in either way will generally compromise performance in the other. There is the possibility that a contestant could have lightening fast reactions (no false-negatives) and always know the answer (no false-positives). Such contestants are rare, as are such diagnostic tests.

In screening, when the rare test with near perfect sensitivity and specificity is lacking, a sequence of testing is typically used. The strategy for HIV testing provides a good example, although there are many others. The initial step in screening requires that anyone who might have the disease be identified. For this, a test with high sensitivity is required. The ELISA, used as the initial HIV screening test, offers near perfect sensitivity.[8] With high sensitivity comes the capacity to rule out disease, as discussed above. Therefore, the initial round of screening is used to identify those who are reliably (more or less) free of HIV, those who can be reassured and undergo no further testing. The high sensitivity of the ELISA, however, comes at the "price" of some false-positive error. Therefore, a positive ELISA does not rule in disease. Rather, all positive reactions to the ELISA are further tested using Western blot (or alternative) assays with very high specificity.[8] The reliability of positive results is now enhanced in two ways. First, the second-stage test offers high specificity, resulting in a low rate of false-positive error. But equally important, the test is now being conducted on only those who had a positive ELISA. The prevalence of HIV in this group is much higher than in the general population. As prevalence rises and specificity remains fixed, the rate of false-positive error will decline. Thus, the second stage of testing is used to rule in disease.

Clinical rather than statistical considerations determine whether a premium is placed on sensitivity or specificity when there is a need to choose. If a disease is very serious, represents a public health threat, and/or has a very different outcome if detected early, the need to find disease whenever it is present takes precedence over the need to rule it out when absent. Needed in such a situation is a test with high sensitivity, so that few true-positives will be missed. In other words, when one cannot afford to miss a case of disease, a good *rule-out test* is required. Again, HIV is a good example. False-negative test results would represent a threat to both the individual and the public. However, in such situations the risk of false-positive results may be high. False-positive results not only require additional testing at additional cost but also if disclosed to the patient are likely to produce anxiety and "suffering" until the truth is disclosed. In the case of HIV screening, this is avoided by withholding information from the patient until two sequential tests have been completed. In other situations, such as breast cancer screening, such temporary nondisclosure is not possible, with ramifications discussed below.

When the disease being sought is relatively benign, when the disease is indolent, when later detection results in comparable outcomes as earlier detection, and/or when the consequences of false-positive results are more severe than the consequences of false-negative results, the need to exclude disease whenever it is absent takes precedence over the need to rule it in when present. Needed in such a situation is a test with high specificity, so that few true-negatives will test positive. In other words, when one cannot afford to identify disease in a disease-free individual, a good *rule-in test* is required.

A test with high specificity allows for few false-positives; those testing positive are very likely to have the disease. An example of such a test is the Pap smear used to detect early signs of cervical cancer.[9] Because the disease progresses very slowly, if missed on one occasion it can generally be detected at subsequent testing before harm comes to the patient. On the other hand, false-positive results might lead to unnecessary interventions, such as hysterectomy. Provided that a mechanism is in place to catch the false-negatives before preventable harm occurs, screening programs may reasonably prioritize specificity over sensitivity.

〰 STATISTICS, SCREENING AND MONETARY COSTS

Because screening is by definition a population-based practice, the cost of testing becomes an important consideration in developing strategies to optimize the public health. Societal resources are never unlimited, and choices must generally be made among potential services and interventions. Cost-effectiveness, discussed in Appendix B, is an appropriate arbiter of resource allocations with the potential to impact the public health.

In the case of screening, cost-effectiveness is used to identify the strategy that results in the greatest population benefit per dollar spent. Population benefit, fundamentally an aggregate measure of benefit experienced by individual patients, is the product of both early disease detection with resultant treatment and disease exclusion with resultant reassurance.

Scenario 4.1

Consider a hypothetical scenario in which a population of 100,000 is to be screened for "impending blindness syndrome." The disease is present in the population at a prevalence of 5%. If detected early, the course of the disease is modified so as to preserve vision, which is an outcome deemed important by society, and worthy of resource allocation. Screening test 1 offers a sensitivity of 80% and a specificity of 85% at a cost of $10 per test. Screening test 2 offers a sensitivity of 92% and a specificity of 95% at a cost of $12.50 per test. Either of these tests will be followed by screening test 3, which offers a sensitivity of 70% and a specificity of 99% at a cost of $100. These test characteristics are summarized in Table 4.2.

What is the most cost-effective way to screen the population? Statistical considerations are germane to the decision. Every individual with a positive result on initial screening, whether true or false, will require confirmatory testing. The costs of population screening will be the sum of the costs of the initial and confirmatory round of testing.

If test 1 is used as the initial screen, the costs of the initial screen will be $1million ($10 for each of the 100,000 tested). Of the 5000 disease positives, 80%, or 4000 cases will be detected. Of the 95,000 individuals who are disease free, 85% will test negative, and 15%, or 14,250 will test positive. These results are summarized in Box 4.4.

TABLE 4.2	Screening Test Characteristics for Scenario 4.1			
Test	Purpose	Sensitivity	Specificity	Unit Cost
1	initial screen	80%	85%	$10
2	initial screen	92%	95%	$12.50
3	confirmatory	70%	99%	$100

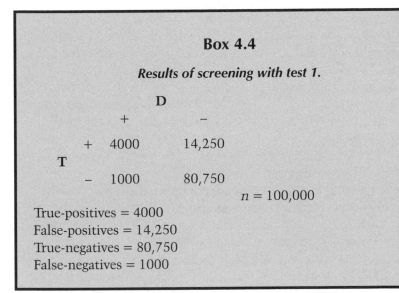

Box 4.4

Results of screening with test 1.

	D	
	+	−
T +	4000	14,250
T −	1000	80,750

$n = 100,000$

True-positives = 4000
False-positives = 14,250
True-negatives = 80,750
False-negatives = 1000

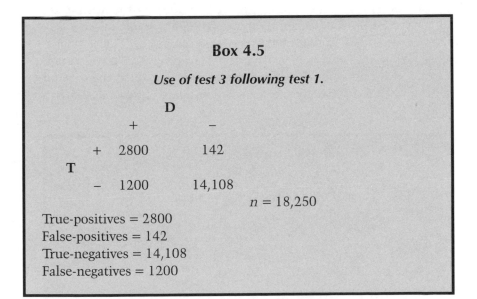

Box 4.5

Use of test 3 following test 1.

	D	
	+	−
T +	2800	142
T −	1200	14,108

$n = 18,250$

True-positives = 2800
False-positives = 142
True-negatives = 14,108
False-negatives = 1200

Confirmatory testing will now be required in those who tested positive. The total number of positive tests, false and true, is 18,250. Test 3 will now be applied to each of these, at a cost of $1,425,000 ($100 by 14,250). The results of applying test 3 after test 1 are shown in Box 4.5.

Thus, the sequence of test 1 followed by test 3 has identified 2800 cases out of 5000, while missing 2200 (1000 false negatives after test 1, and an additional 1200 false negatives after test 3), and has produced 142 false positives. The cost of screening was $2,425,000.

What if we begin with test 2? The higher cost of test 2 relative to test 1 might discourage us from doing so. However, test 2 has better performance characteristics than test 1—a higher sensitivity and equivalent specificity. Screening the population of 100,000 with test 2 will cost $1,250,000 ($12.50 for each person screened). The results of the initial screen with test 2 are summarized in Box 4.6.

Confirmatory testing will now be required in those who tested positive. The total number of positive tests, false and true, is 9350. Test 3 will now be applied to each of these, at a cost of $935,000 ($100 by 9350). The results of applying test 3 after test 2 are shown in Box 4.7.

Thus, the sequence of test 2 followed by test 3 has identified 3220 cases out of 5000, while missing 1780 (400 false-negatives after test 2, and an additional 1380 false-negatives after test 3), and has produced 47 false-positives. The cost of screening was $1,935,000. Starting with test 2 rather than test 1 produces a net savings of $490,000, while missing 420 fewer cases (i.e., 420 fewer false-negatives) and generating 95 fewer false-positives. While this analysis clearly favors screening with test 2 rather than test 1, two important considerations are missing. First, the societal costs of untreated disease are often high. In this hypothetical scenario

---

Box 4.6

Results of screening with test 2.

		D	
		+	–
T	+	4600	4750
	–	400	90,250

$n = 100,000$

True-positives = 4600
False-positives = 4750
True-negatives = 90,250
False-negatives = 400

Box 4.7

Use of test 3 following test 2.

<pre>
                        D
           +   −

       +   3220   47
   T
       −   1380   4703
                            n = 9350
</pre>

True-positives = 3220
False-positives = 47
True-negatives = 4703
False-negatives = 1380

---

the disease produces blindness in young adults if not detected early, while early detection preserves vision. The costs of screening should make allowances for the costs to society of lost productivity if disease goes undetected. The sequence of test 2 followed by test 3 results in 400 fewer cases of disease missed than the sequence of test 1 followed by test 3. Assuming a cost to society of $500,000 for every case of the syndrome not detected early, the test 2–test 3 sequence results in additional savings of $200 million.

Second, there will be intervention or treatment costs for those with positive results, whether true or false, on confirmatory testing. The total number of positive test results when test 1 is followed by test 3 is 2942. Of these, 2800 are true-positives and 142 are false-positives. Assuming treatment costs of $20,000 per patient, a total of $58,840,000 will be spent on treatment. The $2,840,000 spent on the false positives confers no benefit; $500,000 in societal costs are recouped for each of the 2800 true positives. The total number of test positives when test 2 is followed by test 3, is 3267. With treatment costs of $20,000 per patient, a total of $65,340,000 will be spent on treatment. The $940,000 spent on the false positives confers no benefit; $500,000 in societal costs are recouped for each of the 3220 true positives. A comparison of the total financial costs and benefits associated with using test 1 or test 2 prior to test 3 is provided in Table 4.3.

TABLE 4.3   Financial Costs and Benefits Associated with the Use of Either Test 1 or Test 2 Prior to Test 3

Screening Sequence	Costs of Screening[1]	Costs of Treatment[2]	Societal Costs without Screening Program[3]	Societal Costs Recouped due to Detected Cases[4]	Total Costs of Screening and Treatment	Net Financial (Cost) or Benefit to Society[5]
Test 1 – test 3	$2,425,000	$58,840,000	$2.5 billion	$1.4 billion	$61,265,000	$1.34 billion
Test 2 – test 3	$1,935,000	$65,340,000	$2.5 billion	$1.61 billion	$67,275,000	$1.54 billion
Savings (or losses) associated with use of test 2 rather than test 1	$490,000	($6,500,000)	—	$210 million	($6,010,000)	$198 million

[1]The costs of screening are the costs of the initial test for all 100,000 in the population, plus the cost of the confirmatory test in those initially testing positive.

[2]The costs of treatment apply to all of those testing positive on the confirmatory test, regardless of whether they are true- or false-positives.

[3]Society will incur a cost of $500,000 for each of 5000 cases of disease if screening is not performed.

[4]Every case of disease detected through screening will result in a savings of $500,000.

[5]The costs and savings associated with screening are compared to the societal costs associated with no screening program.

As demonstrated in the table, both screening sequences result in enormous savings to society relative to no screening program. The costs of screening are lower when test 2 is used as the initial screen, while the costs of treatment are higher due to a higher rate of disease detection. In the long term, use of test 2 rather than test 1 saves society nearly $200 million, given the conditions stipulated. While this scenario demonstrates the relationship between screening test characteristics and cost, it does not address all issues pertinent to the generation of screening policy. The costs of testing are immediate, the costs of treatment are slightly deferred, and the societal costs of not screening or the benefits of screening are substantially deferred. Additionally, those paying for and those reaping the benefits of screening may differ. The subtleties of policy generation and related aspects of medical economics are beyond the scope of this text.[10]

⧆ STATISTICS, SCREENING AND HUMAN COSTS

Screening is among the more important functions performed by primary care practitioners, and along with behavioral counseling and immunization, a leading priority in clinical preventive medicine.[1] While the disease and societal prerequisites to screening are more pertinent to public health than to clinical decisions, the statistical aspects of screening have important implications for individual patient care. First, the very act of screening implies that the individual patient is being handled less as an individual, more as a member of a population. Yet inattentiveness to the correspondence of the individual patient profile with the characteristics of the population for which screening is indicated is fraught with hazard. The results of screening are only interpretable if the prior probability of disease is known. As the patient is asymptomatic at the time of screening, the prior probability is based exclusively on population characteristics and the prevalence. If a test is indicated in a particular population with a particular prevalence of disease, it may or may not be indicated in any slightly different population with a different prevalence of disease. For every screening test recommended in certain populations, there are slightly different populations in which the performance of the test would be unacceptably poor. Screening, perhaps the primary activity of clinical prevention,[11] requires that we establish a population in which to place our patient before we can know if we are more likely to do good or harm.

TABLE 4.4	The Human Costs Associated with Use of Screening Tests 1 or 2 Followed by Test 3			
Testing Sequence	Number of Disease-free Individuals Referred on for Confirmatory Testing	Number of False Positives	Number of False Negatives	Total Number Misclassified at End of Screening Sequence
Test 1 – Test 3	14,250	142	2,200	2,342
Test 2 – Test 3	4,750	47	1,780	2,027

What harm? While the hypothetical scenario above was used to discuss monetary costs, it serves to demonstrate the human costs associated with screening practices. Despite using a sequence of 2 tests with reasonable performance characteristics, screening with tests 1 and 3 still missed 2200, while the sequence of tests 2 then 3 missed 1780. In the hypothetical construct, these misses are individuals who are destined to become blind.

Perhaps the harm resulting from false-negative screening can be discounted. After all, if no screening were done, all of the cases would be missed. At least those with disease who have tested positive have been helped by our screening efforts. But even if comfortable with this line of reasoning, what about the false-positives? In the hypothetical scenario, tests 1 and 3 produced 142 false-positives. The combination of tests 2 and 3 produced 42 false-positives. Each of these individuals went on to be "treated," at a cost of $20,000, for a disease they do not have.

Missing from the discussion is any consideration of the anxiety, discomfort, or risk involved in undergoing treatment. While the pain and risk of treatment may be very acceptable to an individual whose only alternative is blindness, what about to an individual who would be absolutely well if only that had not undergone screening? The human costs of the screening sequences discussed above are displayed in Table 4.4.

It has been well addressed in the medical literature that harm can come from even appropriate screening. One example should make the case. In a study of breast cancer screening by both clinical exam and mammography, Elmore et al. tracked the rate of cancer detection and false-positive error in 2400 women between the ages of 40 and 69 over a 10-year period.[12] A total of 88 breast cancers were diagnosed in the cohort, 58 by mammography, 7 by clinical breast examination, and an additional 23 that eluded the screen and came to attention when clinically apparent (false-negatives). Over the screening period, 31.7% of the women had at least one false-positive result on either clinical exam or mammography.

The benefits of the screening program are maximized if one assumes that all cancers found through screening are in an early stage; that all cancers found incidentally are in a later stage; and that a demonstrable clinical benefit results for each case of cancer detected through screening. Even if these unlikely assumptions were true, the human cost of breast cancer screening in the cohort was high: 870 follow-up appointments, 539 diagnostic mammograms, 186 ultrasound examinations, 188 breast biopsies, and 1 hospitalization.[12] All in women who would have been perfectly well if not screened.

〰 SCREENING PROS AND CONS

The purpose of this discussion is neither to encourage nor discourage screening. The benefits of screening for specific conditions are well established. Recommendations are summarized in the report of the US Preventive Services Task Force.[1] Rather, screening is placed where it should reside—at the interface of population-based and individual medicine. One does not know the disease status of the individual patient prior to screening; that is why screening is done. Yet however committed to the well being of the individual patient the test-ordering clinician might be, screening unavoidably subjects the patient to the statistical hazards of being part of a group. A certain proportion of those screened will test positive despite being disease free. A certain proportion of those being screened will test negative despite actually having the disease. While screening may offer a net benefit to the pertinent population, it will offer only benefit or only harm to the individual patient. All patients in whom screening reveals the truth will benefit (ostensibly). All those in whom screening errs will be harmed. The clinician cannot know in advance in which group any given patient will reside. The best one can do is to maximize the probability that the patient will benefit, and minimize the chances that they will be harmed. To do this requires familiarity with the performance characteristics of available tests; a reasonable estimate of the prior probability of disease; and an appreciation, shared between clinician and patient, of the nature and degree of benefit and harm associated with correct and incorrect results of screening.

SUMMARY/TAKE-AWAY MESSAGES

Screening is the effort to detect disease that is not readily apparent or risk factors for disease in an at-risk segment of the population. As is true of diagnostic testing, the results and implications of screening depend on both the prevalence of disease and test performance. If disease is rare, false-positives are apt to be relatively frequent compared to true-positives. If disease is common, false-negatives may be frequent compared to true-negatives. For these reasons, screening is generally inappropriate when disease is either exceedingly rare or extremely common.

A test with **high sensitivity** will rarely be negative when disease is present and thus negative results of such a test serve as a reliable means of **ruling out disease**. A test with **high specificity** will rarely be positive when disease is absent and thus positive results of such a test serve as a reliable means of **ruling in disease**. Often, **sequential testing** is indicated to first rule out, then rule in disease. The selection of tests and their order will depend on considerations of clinical imperative and cost. A serious disease for which early detection is considered highly valuable and essential to achieving good outcome will likely warrant greater emphasis on test sensitivity. Conversely, when later detection is as good as early detection, and when the adverse effects of false-positive results are considerable, high specificity may be the greater priority. Because the results of screening in an individual can only be positive or negative, correct or incorrect (excluding, for simplicity sake, inconclusive results), an individual may be harmed by even a reliable screening test. Consideration of the potential **human costs of screening** before testing is prudent for both clinician and patient. When sequential testing is indicated, **total program costs** may be reduced by choosing a better performing test initially, even if that test is more costly than the alternatives.

❧ ❧ ❧

❧ REFERENCES

1. U.S. Preventive Services Task Force (USPSTF). *Guide to Clinical Preventive Services*, 2nd ed. Alexandria, VA: International Medical Publishing; 1996.
2. Katz DL. *Epidemiology, Biostatistics, and Preventive Medicine Review*. Philadelphia, PA: Saunders; 1997.

3. Kwon C, Farrell PM. The magnitude and challenge of false-positive newborn screening test results. *Arch Pediatr Adolesc Med.* 2000;154:714–718.

4. Velazquez A, Vela-Amieva M, Ciceron-Arellano I, Ibarra-Gonzalez I, Perez-Andrade ME, Olivares-Sandoval Z, Jimenez-Sanchez G. Diagnosis of inborn errors of metabolism. *Arch Med Res.* 2000;31:145–150.

5. Edelstein BL. Public and clinical policy considerations in maximizing children's oral health. *Pediatr Clin North Am.* 2000;47:1177–1189.

6. Horowitz HS. Decision-making for national programs of community fluoride use. *Community Dent Oral Epidemiol.* 2000;28:321–329.

7. Sackett DL, Haynes RB, Guyatt GH, Tugwell P. *Clinical Epidemiology. A Basic Science for Clinical Medicine.* 2nd ed. Boston, Massachusetts: Little, Brown and Company; 1991.

8. Mylonakis E, Paliou M, Lally M, Flanigan TP, Rich JD. Laboratory testing for infection with the human immunodeficiency virus: established and novel approaches. *Am J Med.* 2000;109:568–576.

9. Frame PS, Frame JS. Determinants of cancer screening frequency: The example of screening for cervical cancer. *J Am Board Fam Pract.* 1998;11:87–95.

10. Jacobs P. *Economics of Health and Medical Care,* 4th ed. Greenwood Village, CO: Aspen Publishers; 1996.

11. Jekel JF, Elmore JG, Katz DL. *Epidemiology, Biostatistics, and Preventive Medicine.* Philadelphia, PA: Saunders; 1996.

12. Elmore JG, Barton MB, Moceri VM, Polk S, Arena PJ, Fletcher SW. Ten-year risk of false-positive screening mammograms and clinical breast examinations. *N Engl J Med.* 1998;338:1089–1096.

Measuring and Conveying Risk

INTRODUCTION

Risk is germane to every aspect of clinical practice. Every clinical intervention is predicated on the belief that the benefits of intervention outweigh the risks, and that the risks of nonintervention outweigh the risks of intervention. **Prognostication** is the projection (prediction) of personal risk based on some interpretation of prior experience reflected in population data. All preventive practices are justified only because those not injured or ill are at risk of becoming so without application of the appropriate precautions.

Given the fundamental relevance of risk to every aspect of clinical practice, a certain expertise in its measurement, its interpretation, and its communication might reasonably be expected of all clinicians. However, this expertise cannot be assumed. The communication of risk is subtle, and this subtlety is often exploited in the medical literature to cast outcomes in a light favorable to investigators and/or their sponsors. In addition, risk in the literature is pertinent to populations, while the clinical situation requires translation of population-based measures into terms of relevance to the individual patient.

⊰≋⊱ MEAƧURING RIƧK TO THE INDIVIDUAL PATIENT

Consider the clinical implications of the literature characterizing risks associated with thrombolytic therapy for myocardial infarction. While there are various ways of characterizing the treatment effects of thrombolysis,[1] data from the GUSTO trial[2] indicate a mortality risk reduction of 72% associated with thrombolytic therapy as compared to placebo. The figure is impressive; ¾ of the risk of dying of a myocardial infarction (MI) is eliminated by the use of thrombolytic therapy. But how would you convey this information to an individual patient? On hearing that they were 75% less likely to die with thrombolysis, the astute patient might ask, "75% less likely than what?" If the risk of death from MI were 100%, 72% risk reduction would yield a mortality risk of 28%. If the risk of death from MI were 1%, the death risk with thrombolysis would be 0.28%. The difference is large, important, and of clinical relevance.

What the difference highlights is the difference between relative risk and absolute risk, and the associated measures of risk change. **Relative risk** is the ratio of risk in one group to another. **Relative risk reduction** is the ratio of risk after the intervention that reduces risk to the risk without the intervention. The outcome measure can be death or any other adverse event of interest. In the case of myocardial infarction, the literature supports a mortality risk of approximately 25% without thrombolysis, and a risk of 7% with thrombolysis.[2,3,4,5] These are measures of **actual risk** to the population in question. The relative risk of death with thrombolysis is 7% as compared to 25%, or 0.07/0.25, or 28%. The relative reduction is the change in risk with therapy (25% − 7% = 18%) over the baseline risk (18%/25% = 72%). Depending on the point investigators are most interested in making, different versions of the same risk reduction are apt to be conveyed; often, the more impressive relative risk reduction figure, in this case 72%, is emphasized.

What is the problem with the relative risk reduction figure? As noted above, it is entirely *insensitive* to absolute risk. If the risk of death from MI were 0.0000025%, and thrombolysis reduced this to 0.0000007%, the relative risk reduction would still be 72%, even though the probability of benefit to any given patient would be extremely low.

Following any potentially dangerous intervention, an individual patient can only live or die. The relevance of a large relative risk reduction that changes the individual patient's actual chances of living or dying by a negligible degree is questionable. To provide patients with a measure of risk that is helpful, risk reduction must be cast in terms of individual experience. This can be done with use of a measure called the **number needed to treat (NNT)**. The NNT is the absolute risk reduction (ARR), divided into 1 (i.e., 1/ARR). It indicates the number of patients who need to be exposed to the absolute benefit of intervention before actual benefit is likely to occur in at least one patient. It is the number of patients that need to be treated before the actual benefit of intervention can be expected with confidence. The formula for the NNT is: 1/ARR, where ARR is the absolute risk reduction.

For example, in the case of thrombolytic therapy for MI, absolute risk of death is reduced from 25% to 7%. The absolute risk reduction is 18%. The number needed to treat is the number of patients who would need to experience this degree of risk reduction before an actual outcome benefit would probably occur in one. In this case, 1/0.18 is 5.56. Therefore, nearly 6 patients would need to be treated before one could expect to benefit. Stated alternatively, thrombolysis saves (or, on average, can be expected to save) one life for every 6 patients treated.

Of course, nothing in clinical practice is ever so simple. Any intervention with the potential to do good also has the potential to do harm. In the case of thrombolytic therapy, the principal harm is intracranial hemorrhage. An adverse outcome of varying but often devastating severity, this "harm" of treatment might be considered commensurate with the benefit of treatment, the prevention of MI-related mortality. There are, as well, other benefits of thrombolysis beyond the prevention of premature death. The prevention of left ventricular dysfunction and resultant heart failure is an obvious additional benefit. Bleeding elsewhere than in the head is an obvious alternative harm. The discussion could become bogged down in the innumerable variations on the theme of benefit and harm. However, limiting harm and benefit measures to the extremes facilitates discussion of the statistical implications for measuring risk.

Assume that thrombolysis raises the risk of intracranial bleeding from 0.5% to 1%.[6] The relative risk increase is 100% [(1 − 0.5/0.5) × 100]. The absolute risk increase is 0.5% (1 − 0.5). In this case, we need to consider the **number needed to harm (NNH)**, the number of patients subject to an increase in risk before one will probably experience the adverse outcome. The number needed to harm is 1 divided by the **absolute risk increase** (1/ARI), in this case 1/0.005, or 200. Thus, 200 patients would need to receive thrombolytic therapy before one intracranial bleed is likely to occur as the result of intervention.

But even these manipulations of risk measures fail to address the reality confronting the individual patient and their clinician. The same patient is subject to the absolute increases in both risk and benefit imposed by our interventions. We therefore need a measure of risk increase proportionate to benefit increase, or *vice versa*, to make informed decisions and recommendations about the merits of administering or withholding an intervention.

If by chance the NNT and the NNH are equivalent, the probability of treatment-related harm is the same as the probability of benefit. Such situations are best resolved by application of a patient value system: are the specific harms and benefits truly comparable, is one more acceptable than the other, is there a general preference for intervention or "letting Nature take its course?" This is to some extent still relevant when the NNH and NNT differ, as quantitative differences should not preclude qualitative considerations.

In the example provided, the NNH is much greater than the NNT. Whenever this is so, treatment is more likely to do good than harm, as the number of patients who need to be treated before one patient benefits is small, and the number that must be treated before one patient is harmed is relatively large. The NNH divided by the NNT (NNH/NNT) when the NNH is larger provides an **individualized benefit index**, a measure of the number of individual patients who stand to benefit from treatment for every one that is harmed. (The individualized benefit index, or IBI, is a newly coined term. Note that the same figure can be derived by dividing the larger ARR by the smaller ARI.) In this case, NNH/NNT is 200/5.56 is 35.97, or nearly 36 (equivalent to the ARR/ARI, 0.18/0.005). Thus, for every one patient who suffers an intracranial bleed as a result of thrombolysis, 36 lives will be saved. This provides the patient with a simple and fairly compelling basis for making an informed decision.

If the NNT exceeds the NNH (or the ARI exceeds the ARR), intervention would likely be contraindicated unless the pertinent harm were much less serious than the benefit. But situations in clinical medicine where harm is likely but trivial and benefit unlikely but extreme are fairly common. Consider a lumbar puncture (LP) in an adult with fever and a headache. The probability of a post-LP headache is high, perhaps 20%.[7] As this probability is zero without the procedure, the absolute risk increase is the same as the absolute risk: 20%. However, the LP may be life saving by diagnosing meningitis.[8] Consider that mortality risk with LP might be reduced from 1 in 200 to 1 in 10,000. The absolute risk reduction is 0.49%. Only 5 patients need to be subjected to the intervention for one to be "harmed", whereas 204 need to be "tapped" before one will benefit. In this scenario, the NNT divided by the NNH provides an **individualized harm index**, the number of patients likely to be harmed before one benefits. (The individualized harm index, or IHI, is a newly coined term. Note that the same figure can be derived by dividing the larger ARI by the smaller ARR.) The patient in the emergency department could be told that nearly 41 patients will get a post-procedure headache for every one whose life is saved by the diagnosis and appropriate management of meningitis.

Measures of risk reduction (or increase) are further complicated when time effects are considered. For example, the risk of stroke is reduced in patients with atrial fibrillation by anticoagulation with warfarin.[9] The same treatment increases the risk of hemorrhage. Neither risk effect is transient, however. The potential benefits of anticoagulation pertain throughout the period of treatment, as do the potential harms. Therefore, to calculate the NNT or NNH for a longitudinal intervention the measures must be adjusted to incorporate time. In this case, one could calculate the number of patients needed to treat for one year to reduce the risk of stroke by a fixed amount. If, for example, treatment with warfarin for a year reduced the stroke risk from 5% to 1%, the NNT would be 25 patients per year. Similarly, if such treatment increased the risk of a serious hemorrhage from 1% per year to 15% per year, the NNH would be approximately 7 patients per year. In this scenario, 3.6 patients treated for one year are "harmed" for every one that benefits. This approach to the incorporation of time into the estimation of NNT and/or NNH is still simplistic in that treatment effects may vary over time or as the age of the patient changes. Therefore the risks and benefits of treatment may not remain constant year to year, and the measures derived for the initial year of treatment may pertain less well thereafter. Nonetheless, these measures cast risk in terms clinicians and patients alike are able to understand and appreciate.

The NNT, NNH, and individualized benefit and harm indices will vary not only over time but with the individual patient's characteristics. For example, elderly and hypertensive patients are more subject than the young to the harmful effects of thrombolysis, as well as to life-threatening sequelae of MI.[10] Recent literature suggests that MI mortality may be especially high in young women.[11] All effort to cast risk into informative and relevant terms for the individual patient must be informed by an appreciation for the patient's characteristics and how they fit into the established body of evidence.

※ RISK FACTORS

Risk factors are exposures or traits associated with a particular adverse outcome. Intrinsic to the concept of risk factors is the anticipation of outcomes based on vulnerability rather than symptoms or signs. An individual with several risk factors for coronary artery disease is *more likely* than an otherwise comparable individual without those risk factors to have a MI. Because "more likely" begs the question, "more likely than what?" consideration of risk factors requires consideration of the quantitative aspects of prognosis.

While more accurate prognosis may be a desirable goal in and of itself, the greatest value in identifying risk factors resides in the potential to modify them. But the exploitation of that potential requires consideration of several quantitative factors. How much will modification of the risk factor in question modify overall risk? This can be measured as the **attributable risk**, the portion of total risk ascribed to the factor in question. But this is an insufficient basis to decide on intervention. Some estimate of the individual patient's actual, absolute risk of the adverse outcome (mediated by a variety of traits, such as family history, lifestyle, comorbidities, etc.), as well as any risks associated with the intervention itself, are also needed. For example, daily use of aspirin might reduce the risk of a MI, but at the cost of increased risk of bleeding.[12] For a clinician or patient to determine when intervention is warranted to treat vulnerability rather than disease the magnitude of vulnerability, the degree to which intervention modifies it, and the potential hazards of intervention all warrant attention.

※ MEASURING RISK IN CLINICAL INVESTIGATION

As noted above, expressing the effects of intervention or exposure on patient risk is an important aspect of clinical investigation. The specific measures of risk generated by studies are related to study design. The relative risk, or **risk ratio**, and an analogous measure, the **odds ratio**, are discussed in Chapters 7 and 8.

MEASURING RISK MODIFICATION

For clinical purposes, risk must often be translated from a population to an individual frame of reference. For purposes of public health planning, a population perspective is appropriate. But consistent with the theme of this book, there are ways in which the individual and population-based perspectives are closely linked. As was shown with the numbers needed to treat and harm, an individual patient's risks can be expressed in terms of small groups of similar patients. In efforts to modify risk by changing individual behavior, measures of population impact provide a gauge for the magnitude of benefit to be derived.

For example, consider that the risk of lung cancer in a nonsmoker is 5 per 10,000; the risk in the population is 30 per 10,000; and the risk in a smoker is 150 per 10,000.[13] How much can the individual patient reduce lung cancer risk if they quit smoking (assuming that the risk is lowered to that of a nonsmoker)? How much of the risk of lung cancer is attributable to smoking? How much of the lung cancer risk in the whole population is attributable to smoking? How much reduction in population risk could be expected if smoking were eliminated?

First, we need to generate a simple **risk difference**, the difference in risk between those with and without the risk factor. In this case, the risk difference is the risk of lung cancer in smokers (150) minus the risk in nonsmokers (5); the risk difference is 145/10,000. The risk difference between the exposed and the unexposed is the risk attributable to the exposure, or the **attributable risk** (AR). If the risk difference is made relative to the risk in the exposed it provides a measure of the degree to which risk in the exposed is attributable to the exposure. The **attributable risk percent** (AR%) formula is:

$$\frac{\text{risk}_{\text{exposed}} - \text{risk}_{\text{unexposed}}}{\text{risk}_{\text{exposed}}} \times 100$$

In this case, the attributable risk is $[(145/10,000)/(150/10,000)] \times 100$, or 97%. This indicates that 97% of the risk of lung cancer in a smoker is attributable to smoking. Stated alternatively for purposes of motivating behavior change, a smoker could be advised that they would reduce their risk of lung cancer by 97% were they to quit smoking (again, this assumes that the risk of lung cancer in a former smoker falls to the risk

TABLE 5.1   Clinically Relevant Measures of Risk

Measure	Formula	Application
Absolute risk	Outcome events/Population at risk	Identifies the actual event rate in the population in question
Absolute risk increase (ARI)	Pre-intervention absolute risk – Post-intervention absolute risk	Identifies the absolute increase in the rate of specific adverse events associated with an intervention
Absolute risk reduction (ARR)	Post-intervention absolute risk – Pre-intervention absolute risk	Identifies the absolute decrease in the rate of specific adverse events associated with an intervention
Attributable risk (AR)	Risk in the exposed – Risk in the unexposed	Provides a measure of the absolute risk associated with a specific exposure
Attributable risk percent (AR%)	(AR/Risk in the exposed) × 100	Expresses the degree to which risk for a specific outcome is due to a specific exposure
Individualized benefit index (IBI)	NNH/NNT (ARR/ARI)	When a procedure benefits more patients than it harms, this provides a measure of how many patients benefit for each patient harmed
Individualized harm index (IHI)	NNT/NNH (ARI/ARR)	When a procedure harms more patients than it benefits, this provides a measure of how many patients are harmed for each who benefits
Number needed to harm (NNH)	1/ARI	The number of patients who need to be exposed to the hazards of an intervention before one is likely to be harmed
Number needed to treat (NNT)	1/ARR	The number of patients who need to be exposed to the potential benefits of an intervention before one is likely to experience actual benefit
Population attributable risk (PAR)	Risk in the entire population – Risk in the unexposed	Provides a measure of the absolute risk for a particular adverse outcome in a population due to a particular exposure
Population attributable risk percent (PAR%)	(PAR/Risk in the entire population) × 100	Provides a measure of the degree to which risk of a specific adverse outcome in a population is due to a particular exposure, and the extent to which elimination of the exposure would reduce population risk
Relative risk	Risk exposed / Risk unexposed	Provides a measure useful in revealing the change in risk associated with an intervention
Risk difference	Risk in the exposed – Risk in the unexposed	The same as the attributable risk

in a nonsmoker). Of note, the risk difference is an expression of absolute risk, while the attributable risk percent translates risk into relative terms.

For purposes of encouraging an individual patient to change behavior and acquire the lower risk of the unexposed, the attributable risk percent is sufficient. But related measures, the **population attributable risk** (PAR) and **population attributable risk percent** (PAR%) are worth a mention due to their utility for populations. The PAR is the risk in the entire population minus the risk in the unexposed, while the PAR percent is the PAR divided by the risk in the population, and multiplied by 100. Measures of risk are summarized in Table 5.1.

SUMMARY/TAKE-AWAY MESSAGES

Risk is the number of events in the numerator divided by the susceptible population in the denominator. However, this simple formula is the basis for a variety of measures of varying utility in clinical practice. **Absolute risk** defines the actual impact of an event on a population. **Relative risk** is the ratio of one risk to another, or of risk in one group to risk in another group. Each measure may provide information concealed by the other. Characterizing clinical interventions in terms of the number of individuals who need to be treated before one can be expected to benefit, the **number needed to treat** is considered a risk measure of particular utility to clinicians and their patients. A corresponding measure for the adverse effects of treatment is the **number needed to harm**. These measures may be set as a ratio of one to the other to indicate the number of patients who derive benefit for each one harmed, or *vice versa*. The concept of **risk factors** presupposes semiquantitative estimate of the probability of future disease in a vulnerable individual, and the degree to which one or more traits or exposures alters that probability. The modification of risk factors derives from considerations of **attributable risk**, as well as the benefit/risk trade-off of intervening.

Alternative measures of risk may be of greater utility when making decisions about resource allocation for population benefit. The **population attributable risk percent** indicates how much of a hazard to the population is explained by a particular exposure and how much elimination of that exposure might be expected to reduce population risk. An understanding of the various measures of risk supports a more astute interpretation of the medical literature and more informative discussion with patients.

A nascent but evolving literature is beginning to explore and confront the challenges, statistical, ethical, psychological and otherwise, of quantifying and conveying risk to patients.[14,15,16,17,18,19]

⬛ ⬛ ⬛

⬛ REFERENCE∫

1. Simoons ML. Risk-benefit of thrombolysis. *Cardiol Clin.* 1995;13:339–345.
2. The GUSTO Investigators. An international randomized trial comparing four thrombolytic strategies for acute myocardial infarction. *N Engl J Med.* 1993;329:673–682.
3. Salomaa V, Rosamond W, Mahonen M. Decreasing mortality from acute myocardial infarction: Effect of incidence and prognosis. *J Cardiovasc Risk.* 1999 Apr;6(2):69–75.
4. Rosamond WD, Chambless LE, Folsom AR, et al. Trends in the incidence of myocardial infarction and in mortality due to coronary heart disease, 1987 to 1994. *N Engl J Med.* 1998;339:861–867.
5. Herlitz J, Hjalmarson A, Karlson BW, Bengtson A. 5-year mortality rate in patients with suspected acute myocardial infarction in relation to early diagnosis. *Cardiology.* 1988;75:250–259.
6. Brass LM, Lichtman JH, Wang Y, Gurwitz JH, Radford MJ, Krumholz HM. Intracranial hemorrhage associated with thrombolytic therapy for elderly patients with acute myocardial infarction: Results from the Cooperative Cardiovascular Project. *Stroke.* 2000;31:1802–1811.
7. Vilming ST, Kloster R. Pain location and associated symptoms in post-lumbar puncture headache. *Cephalalgia* 1998;18:697–703.
8. Aronin SI. Bacterial meningitis: Principles and practical aspects of therapy. *Curr Infect Dis Rep.* 2000;2:337–344.
9. Hart RG. Stroke prevention in atrial fibrillation. *Curr Cardiol Rep.* 2000;2:51–55.
10. Woods KL, Ketley D. Utilisation of thrombolytic therapy in older patients with myocardial infarction. *Drugs Aging.* 1998;13:435–441.
11. Vaccarino V, Horwitz RI, Meehan TP, Petrillo MK, Radford MJ, Krumholz HM. Sex differences in mortality after myocardial infarction: Evidence for a sex-age interaction. *Arch Intern Med.* 1998 Oct 12;158:2054–2062.
12. Awtry EH, Loscalzo J. Aspirin. *Circulation.* 2000;101:1206–1218.
13. Malarcher AM, Schulman J, Epstein LA, et al. Methodological issues in estimating smoking-attributable mortality in the United States. *Am J Epidemiol.* 2000;152:573–584.
14. Bogardus ST Jr, Holmboe E, Jekel JF. Perils, pitfalls, and possibilities in talking about medical risk. *JAMA.* 1999;281:1037–1041.
15. Elwyn G, Edwards A, Kinnersley P. Shared decision-making in primary care: The neglected second half of the consultation. *Br J Gen Pract.* 1999;49:477–482.
16. Lilly CM, De Meo DL, Sonna LA, et al. An intensive communication intervention for the critically ill. *Am J Med.* 2000;109:469–475.
17. Schneider AE, Davis RB, Phillips RS. Discussion of hormone replacement therapy between physicians and their patients. *Am J Med Qual.* 2000;15:143–147.
18. Penson RT, Seiden MV, Shannon KM, et al. Communicating genetic risk: Pros, cons, and counsel. *Oncologist.* 2000;5:152–161.

19. Matthews EJ, Edwards AG, Barker J, et al. Efficient literature searching in diffuse topics: Lessons from a systematic review of research on communicating risk to patients in primary care. *Health Libr Rev.* 1999;16:112–120.

Section II

PRINCIPLE∫ OF
CLINICAL RE∫EARCH

The artful interpretation of published studies is essential to the application of medical advances to individual patient care. Extensive advice on using the medical literature is available. The *Users' Guides* series in the *Journal of the American Medical Association* is a particularly noteworthy example (see Text Sources at the end of this book). Section II provides an overview of the considerations a clinician might have when reading and interpreting studies in the medical literature. Emphasis will be placed on the hypotheses tested in medical studies, the designs of the studies, and the statistics used to report results.

An important prerequisite to interpreting the specifics of a study and gauging its relevance to patient care is a simple, generalizable approach. For a busy clinician, the effectiveness of any aid in the interpretation of an article should be judged as much on the basis of efficiency as reliability. An approach that will help the clinician understand a study and use it efficiently is to answer four basic questions about it: what, why, how, and in whom?

The basic worth of a study is captured in its hypothesis. Knowing quickly what **hypothesis is being tested** allows a quick assessment of how much, if any, time should be invested in the article. The next question, why **was the particular hypothesis asserted and tested**, lends further support to the initial decision. Not all hypotheses are tested to change clinical practice. Knowing what question a study is designed to answer and why the question was posed is usually a sufficient basis for the clinician to determine if the study is worth the time it would take to read.

But these answers are not sufficient to determine if the study, once read, provides any basis for changing clinical practice. A first step toward that goal is reached by asking how **the study tested the hypothesis of interest**. The chapters in this section characterize the relative strengths and weaknesses of various study designs. These characteristics are the arbiters of evidence; hypotheses tested with varying methodologic rigor provide evidence of varying authority. A change in clinical practice on the basis of provocative but as yet inconclusive evidence might be misguided.

The ultimate clinical goal in reading the medical literature is to apply study results to the care of individual patients. This cannot be done before asking in whom **were the study results achieved**? To the extent that study subjects mimic the characteristics of a patient, results are more likely to apply. The opposite is also true; a patient not meeting eligibility criteria for a study cannot reliably be presumed to respond comparably to those subjects that did.

While the answers to *what*, *why*, *how*, and *in whom* go a long way toward providing a fundamental understanding of a study, the answers are potentially diverse and themselves raise additional and progressively subtler questions. It is hoped that the content of this section will help the clinician add sophistication to efficiency when he or she interprets and applies the medical literature to practice.

Hypothesis Testing 1

Principles

INTRODUCTION

Virtually all research is founded on the generation and testing of hypotheses. The interpretation of research requires an appreciation for the methods, performance, and pitfalls of hypothesis testing. While many aspects of hypothesis testing are quantitative and statistical, many salient principles are basic and conceptual. The characteristics of associative relationships, and the subtleties in establishing causality, are germane to the process of hypothesis testing. This material is relevant to the clinician not only because of its importance in interpreting the literature, but because the processes of clinical care are similarly dependent on the generation and testing of hypotheses. The generation of a differential diagnosis, and its ultimate reduction to a single diagnosis, or the estimation of prognosis, rely on hypotheses cast in terms of probability, alternative, and risk. These hypotheses are asserted and tested in the context of the history, physical examination, and subsequent testing and treatment. A refined appreciation for methods of hypothesis testing is therefore equally pertinent to the interpretation of the medical literature, and the clinical context in which that evidence is applied.

Medical investigation, and consequently the medical literature in which it is reported, is all about hypothesis testing. Beliefs or predictions about the actions of drugs or procedures, or the effects of exposures, are compared between groups to look for the differences that provide evidence of an association. The detection of a sufficiently robust association supports or even confirms the hypothesis.

The progress of medical science is dependent on the generation and testing of hypotheses. Only those hypotheses that are generated can be tested, which means that science is bounded and paced only by imagination and curiosity, and to some extent, bias. Beliefs about what is likely to be true in the absence of evidence represent biases, or prejudices. Yet such beliefs are the source of all hypotheses in medical science. If no one believed something to be true, it would not be a promising line of research. If corroborating evidence were already available, there would be little point in further study. Thus, scientific progress requires both curiosity and bias.

Of potential comfort to clinicians is the fact that clinical progress is achieved in much the same manner. Each new patient's story is judged in the context of all that has come before. Hypotheses generated about diagnosis, prognosis, and management are based in part on bias. Sometimes the bias is mediated by prior clinical experience. For example, a male patient with chest pain in the practice of a cardiologist in the US is presumed to be at risk for coronary disease because so many of his predecessors have had the condition. A male patient with chest pain in the practice of a pediatrician in a rural area in Tibet does not induce the same considerations. Yet it might be that the former patient does not have angina pectoris, while the latter patient, suffering an extreme familial dyslipidemia, does. Our biases can lead us astray but, because they are the product of what is usually true, they are more likely to guide us than misguide us.

It is because our biases (and by extension our hypotheses) about patients can misguide us that they generally need to be tested. The quantitative principles governing the process by which we test such hypotheses have been discussed in earlier chapters. But underlying the process of hypothesis testing in patient care is the evidence base informing clinical decisions. Evidence is the result when the bias leading to hypothesis generation is replaced with the results of hypothesis testing.

What one would hope to produce by testing hypotheses is ironclad evidence of causality, that exposure leads to disease or intervention to cure. However, **causality** is very difficult to establish. **Koch's postulates**, summarized in Table 6.1, are widely invoked as the acid tests of causality and are especially relevant to infectious disease. A more generalizable set of

TABLE 6.1	Koch's Postulates	
Association: it is always found with the disease	**Distribution**: is capable of explaining the manifestations of disease
Isolation: can be isolated and cultured and is distinct	**Susceptibility**: can produce the disease in susceptible individuals

conditions for causality is **Mill's canons**,[1] which state that causality is supported by associations that are[1]

- **strong**—the difference in effect mediated by the putative cause is large

- **consistent**—the effect is seen most/much of the time when the putative cause is present

- **specific**—the effect is generally not seen when the putative cause is absent

- **biologically plausible**—the effect relates to the putative cause in a manner consistent with current understanding of mechanism and natural history

- **dose-responsive**—the magnitude or risk of the effect appears to vary with the magnitude of the putative cause

There are several varieties of causality. A **necessary cause** must be present for the effect to occur. Exposure to mycobacterium tuberculosis is a necessary cause of tuberculosis. A **sufficient cause** will lead inevitably to the effect; decapitation is a sufficient cause of death. A necessary cause may or may not be sufficient to produce the effect. A sufficient cause may or may not be necessary.

Because causality is difficult to establish, there are preliminary standards of evidence that tend to come first. Because these standards of evidence are generated through the process of hypothesis testing, an appreciation for the mechanics of the process is fundamental to evidence-based practice. The key steps involved in hypothesis testing are summarized in Table 6.2.

TABLE 6.2   The Key Steps in Hypothesis Testing

Step in Hypothesis Testing	Description
Assert an association	Hypothesis generation generally requires some belief about a probable association in the absence of definitive evidence
Measure the magnitude (strength) of the outcome effect of interest by comparing outcome between groups with differing exposure	The degree to which differences in exposure or intervention correspond with changes in the outcome of interest provide the strength of the apparent association, or the "signal"
Measure variation among the observations of interest within exposure groups	Dispersion among the observations in the two or more study groups provide a measure of the variation, or the background "noise"
Measure the ratio of outcome effect to variation (signal to noise)	The critical ratio of the outcome effect to the variation (signal to noise) is the basis for statistical tests of association
Eliminate alternative explanations	To the extent possible, alternative explanations for the apparent association should be excluded, although this can never be done with complete confidence
Establish an association	If the ratio of signal to noise exceeds a conventional threshold, and alternative explanations are excluded or improbable, a "significant" association can be stipulated

❧ ASSOCIATION

The initial step in testing any hypothesis is to establish evidence that exposure or intervention appear to influence outcome. To do so requires detecting evidence of an **association** between the putative cause and the putative effect. Evidence supporting an association includes

  1) strength of the apparent relationship;
  2) consistency of the apparent relationship;
  3) an appropriate temporal sequence in the apparent relationship;

4) an apparent dose-response relationship;

5) biological plausibility; and

6) lack of an obvious alternative explanation.

The effort to exclude alternative explanations for an association under investigation underlies all clinical research. In order to eliminate alternate explanations, two or more groups need to be established that are alike in every way save the intervention, outcome, or exposure of interest. Chapter 8 discusses how this is incorporated into study design.

An association is more likely to be real and suggestive of causality if it is strong. If an antihypertensive drug is administered and blood pressure falls on average 1 mm Hg, doubt would persist for some time about whether the drug actually lowered blood pressure at all, about whether intervention influenced outcome. If the drug lowered blood pressure 30 mm Hg, its efficacy would be quickly apparent. The greater the change in the outcome after the intervention, the more clearly the evidence of an association emerges.

Similarly, an association is more apparent and is more likely to be real if it is consistent. A drug that appears to lower blood pressure a lot some of the time and not at all other times will be perceived to have an uncertain association with the outcome. A causal association with a small outcome effect is more convincing when it occurs all of the time.

In Western thinking, cause must precede effect; the apparent association must support a temporal sequence that is plausible. To increase the probability of a true association, other characteristics of the apparent association must be compatible with the prevailing understanding of biology. This notion of biological plausibility, though important, should not be imposed inflexibly, as the ideas of what is biologically plausible change as new knowledge is accumulated. The attribution of peptic ulcer disease to *Helicobacter pylori* was not considered plausible when the theory was first advanced.[2] Finally, if an increase in the magnitude of exposure ("dose") appears to change the magnitude of the outcome effect, association is more probable. Most exposures that produce effects do so more intensely at higher doses, although this is not invariably true.[3]

Once a potential relationship between causal and outcome variables satisfies these criteria, an association has been established. This association may be considered the "signal" that the putative cause is responsible for the putative effect. But for any signal to be perceived and interpreted correctly it must overcome the background noise. In hypothesis testing, the "noise" is variation in data.

※ VARIATION

Consider a simple clinical study in which a group of 10 patients is given an antihypertensive and another group of 10 is given placebo. To establish an association between the drug and a reduction in blood pressure, one looks for a lower blood pressure, on average, in the drug-treated group. But all members of the treatment group are unlikely to end with the same blood pressure, as are the members of the control group. Particularly if the groups are diverse, some members of the placebo group may have a greater fall in blood pressure than some members of the treatment group. Possibly the person (or people) responsible for measuring the blood pressure makes occasional errors or is somewhat inconsistent in their technique. This variability will naturally make it harder to detect a clear difference between the groups.

If every subject in the study had the same baseline blood pressure (160/90), and every member of the treatment group experienced a 20 mm Hg fall in systolic blood pressure, while blood pressure remained constant in every member of the placebo group, the post-treatment blood pressures would appear as shown in Figure 6.1.

At the other extreme, there might be a mean reduction of 20 mm Hg in the treatment group and no mean reduction in the placebo group, but such variable responses among the subjects that no treatment effect is clear. The results might look as shown in Figure 6.2.

In between these two extremes lie the results generally produced by clinical studies. There is almost always some overlap in the responses of treatment and control subjects. There is always variability in the re-

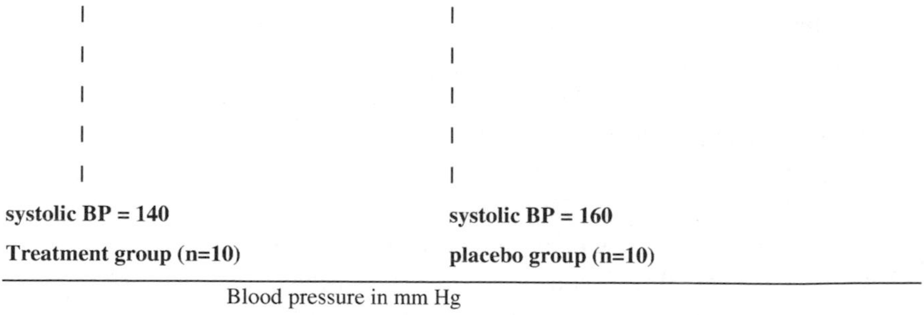

I	I
I	I
I	I
I	I
I	I
systolic BP = 140	**systolic BP = 160**
Treatment group (n=10)	**placebo group (n=10)**

Blood pressure in mm Hg

Figure 6.1. Outcome effects without variation.

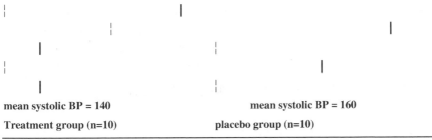

mean systolic BP = 140   mean systolic BP = 160

Treatment group (n=10)   placebo group (n=10)

Blood pressure in mm Hg

Figure 6.2. Outcome effects with extreme variation. The observations for the treatment group are shown in dashed lines, and those for the placebo group in solid lines.

sponses of individual subjects in each of the two or more groups. In the extreme example (Figure 6.2), the "signal" of the treatment effect is lost in the background noise of variability in individual responses; an association between intervention and outcome could not be discerned. In Figure 6.1, the artificial absence of variability in individual responses makes the association self-evident. Somewhere between these two extremes lies a dividing line or threshold that separates results supporting an association from results not doing so. To determine the existence of an association with confidence requires that some limit be set not only on the magnitude of the apparent outcome effect but also on the degree of variability in responses.

❧ MEAſURING CENTRAL TENDENCY: THE MEAN

Implicit in the concept of setting limits on variability is the need to measure variability.

Variability measures must be adapted to different types of data (see Types of Clinical Data below). Continuing with the example at hand, we need a method for measuring the degree of variability in blood pressure responses to treatment. The basis for comparison within a group of subjects is the typical response for a member of the group. Typical responses are expressed by **measures of central tendency**. Measures of central tendency include the **mean**, the **median**, and the **mode**. The mean is the average of all individual observations in the data set. The median is the middle observation(s) when the set is arranged in ascending order. The mode is the value(s) occurring the most times. The mean is the measure of central tendency with the best statistical properties and therefore the one most often used to characterize clinical data. Mathematically the mean is the sum of all observations divided by the sample size $\frac{1}{n}\sum_{1}^{n}x$.

☙ MEASURING DISPERSION: VARIANCE AND STANDARD DEVIATION

In almost every group of subjects undergoing almost any intervention outcome effects will vary. There are many sources of such variation. Individual subjects vary, in both apparent and inapparent ways, because of both genetic and environmental factors. This basic biological diversity is an important source of variation in clinical responses, both in the context of research and in clinical care. Variations in the intervention, variation in measurement, error, and chance all may introduce variation into clinical data.

To characterize **variability**, the degree to which individual observations are dispersed around the reference for the group must be measured. As noted, the mean is generally the reference for the group. A simple way of measuring dispersion around the mean would be to subtract the mean from each observation and add the differences. However, the sum of differences from the mean would always add to zero, as some observations are smaller and some greater than the mean. An alternative would be to use the absolute value of the differences, but because of advantages for statistical applications, the square of the differences is used instead. The sum of the squared differences from the mean for the group, or the **sum of squares**, is a useful measure of dispersion. The derivation of the sum of squares is shown in Figure 6.3.

Sum of squares $= \sum_{1}^{n}(\text{Distance from the mean})^2$

where 1 is the first observation in a sample, n is the last observation in the sample, and the distance from the mean for each observation from 1 to n is squared, and the squares then summed

$$= \sum(x_i - \bar{x})^2$$

where x_i is the value associated with the ith observation, and $\bar{x}$ is the value of the sample mean.

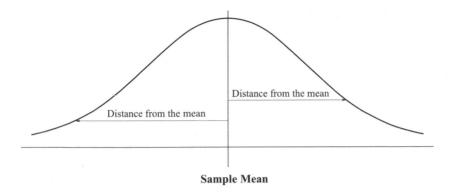

Sample Mean

Figure 6.3. The sum of squares. The sum of the squared distances of each observation in a sample from the sample mean is a useful measure of dispersion, or variation, in data.

The sum of squares can be manipulated to yield even more useful parameters. Instead of working with the total group variability, which will itself vary with the sample size, a measure of the average dispersion of each observation from the group mean is useful. The average, or standard, dispersion of each observation from the mean is called the **variance**. The variance would intuitively be the sum of squares divided by the number of observations, but it is not. It is the sum of squares divided by the sample size minus 1; this denominator is known as the **degrees of freedom**.[4] An extensive discussion of the degree of freedom concept is beyond the scope of this text but its use can be justified concisely. In measuring variation, only those values that actually can vary contribute. Once the mean value for a set of observations is known, and every value in the data set save the last has been established, the last observation is not free to vary; it is fixed by prior knowledge of the mean. Therefore, only the 1st through $(n-1)$st observations contribute to variation. The variance is the total group variation for all observations save the last. By convention, the sample variance is symbolized as s^2.

Because the dispersion of observations from the group mean was squared to produce the sum of squares, the variance does not provide a true measure of the average *distance* of each observation from the group mean. To obtain this measure, the square root of the variance must be taken. The square root of the variance, symbolized by s, is the **standard deviation**. The standard deviation is one of the more useful measures of dispersion for hypothesis testing and statistical analysis.

※ TEITINC HYPOTHEIEI: THE IICNAL TO NOIIE RATIO

In testing hypotheses, the strength of the apparent association under study may be considered the signal, a message of the treatment effect one is hoping to hear. The variation in the observations may be considered noise, the aggregate influences of true biological variation, random events, and measurement errors through which the signal must pierce to be heard. A very loud signal will be heard even amidst considerable background noise. A soft signal may still be heard clearly if the background noise is minimal. A loud (and clinically important) signal may go undetected if the background noise is deafening.

A ratio of signal to noise is required to find clear evidence of an association. When that ratio exceeds a certain, conventional threshold, the apparent signal may be considered sufficiently robust to overcome the background noise and provide meaningful evidence of a true association. When the ratio falls below that threshold, no matter how loud the signal, the data cannot be considered to provide evidence of the association under investigation.

The prototypical measure of the signal, or treatment effect, is the difference between the mean outcome for the treatment group and the mean outcome for the control group. The prototypical measure of the noise, or variation, is the sum of the variances for the two (or more) groups being compared. This ratio of outcome differences to aggregate variation is termed the **critical ratio**, as it provides the evidence needed to test a hypothesis. The conventions used to set the threshold for significance in hypothesis testing are discussed in Chapter 7.

※ TYPEI OF CLINICAL DATA

Continuous data

Not all clinical data can be analyzed in the same way. In the example above, the administration of a drug was used to induce a fall in blood pressure. Blood pressure is a **continuous variable**, with values falling along an uninterrupted continuum. Continuous data allow for the calculation of a mean. Continuous data may be further characterized as those that do and those that don't include a true zero. Blood pressure does, and therefore a value of 100 mm Hg may be considered twice as high as a value of 50 mm Hg. Such data are known as **ratio data**. In contrast, a variable such as IQ does not use a value of zero as a reference. While each point on the IQ scale is a fixed amount greater than the value below, a score of 120 cannot meaningfully be considered to reveal "twice" the intelligence of a score of 60. Such data are **interval**, not ratio data; both types are continuous.

An important characteristic of continuous data is their distribution. The distribution of data is how the multiple observations in a large sample tend to cluster. The distribution, or **frequency distribution** (it is based on the frequency with which specific values occur in the sample) most often applied to clinical data is the normal distribution. The **normal distribution**, also known as the Gaussian distribution, is displayed by the bell-shaped curve, in which most data cluster around the middle (the mean), with fewer and fewer observations at either extreme. The characteristics of the normal distribution are shown in Figure 6.4. Even if the data in a sample of observations are not distributed normally, they can often be analyzed as if they were because the means of multiple samples would be normally distributed if the "experiment" were repeated multiple times. This premise is known as the **central limit theorem**. The importance of

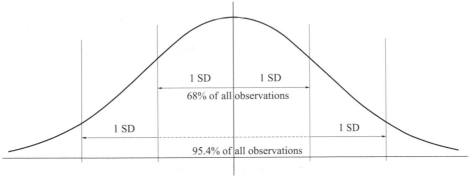

Sample Mean

Figure 6.4. Characteristics of the normal distribution. Distance from the mean is normalized, or rendered unit-free, by measuring in units of standard deviation (SD). The normal distribution contains 68% of all observations within 1 SD either side of the mean, 95.4% of all observations within 2 SD either side of the mean, and 95% of all observations within 1.96 SD either side of the mean.

the distribution to the interpretation of continuous data as well as the analytic approaches involved is discussed further in Chapter 7.

It is worth noting that the methods of hypothesis testing and statistical analysis are divided into two main groups, parametric and nonparametric. Continuous data may be characterized by both a mean and a standard deviation. These *parameters* permit the application of specific analytic methods, some of which are discussed in Chapter 7. Such methods make use of these parameters, and are therefore considered **parametric**. Data that cannot be characterized by a mean and standard deviation, or data that are clearly not distributed normally in either the sample or the underlying population, are **nonparametric**. Such data are analyzed using nonparametric methods, some of which are also discussed in Chapter 7.

Categorical data: ordinal

Many clinically useful data occur in levels that are discontinuous. Such data are categorical because the data are in discrete categories. When categorical data have an implied directionality, they are **ordinal**. One example is the intensity of a heart murmur, typically graded from 1 to 6. Another is the severity of edema, often graded from 1+ to 4+. Data that occur in a clearly ascending or descending order, but in a discontinuous manner, are ordinal. Ordinal data may or may not be interval data, depending on whether the increment between any two successive levels is consistent. Interval data may or may not be ratio data, depending on whether a true zero point is included. Continuous data such as age may be made ordinal by categorizing them. For example, subjects less than 30 years old might be made one "category", subjects 31–50 another, and subjects over age 50, a third.

Categorical data: nominal

Data that occur in discrete categories without implied directionality are **nominal**. Examples of nominal data are blood type and race.

Dichotomous data

Nominal data with only two levels are **dichotomous**, or **binary**. In a clinical trial with one treatment and one placebo group, treatment assignment is a dichotomous variable. Gender is another obvious example of a dichotomous variable.

The analytic approaches to these various types of data are briefly discussed in Chapter 7.

※ CHARACTERIZING AJJOCIATIONJ: UNIVARIATE, BIVARIATE, AND MULTIVARIATE METHODJ

This text is not intended to teach methods in statistical analysis. However, a basic understanding of how such methods are applied is helpful in interpreting the medical literature.

The initial step in analyzing data to assess the evidence supporting an association is to characterize the individual variables to be related. The characterization of individual variables includes such measures as mean, median, mode, range, standard deviation, etc., and is collectively referred to as **univariate analysis**. Statistical software packages will provide a full panel of variable characteristics in a univariate analysis.

Once the characteristics of the putative cause and putative effect have been assessed, the effort to characterize their association should proceed to **bivariate analysis**. As the name implies, bivariate analysis compares two variables to one another, providing statistical evidence of an association. The relationship between two variables can be assessed in a variety of ways, some of which are discussed in Chapter 7, and many of which are not discussed in this text (for further discussion of basic statistical methods, refer to *Text Sources*, p. 279).

Generally, the association between two variables is influenced by other factors. For example, even if a drug lowers blood pressure effectively, it may do so more or less reliably in older or younger patients, men or women, subjects with or without a variety of comorbid conditions. To factor all of these other influences into an association and assess the extent to which each contributes requires methods that allow for the analysis of multiple variables at once. Such **multivariable methods**, often incorrectly referred to as multivariate methods, construct models in which the outcome of interest is "explained" by all of the independent and/or interactive contributions of a variety of predictor variables. These methods generally perform a test to determine how well the model and its components account for the outcome, a so-called "goodness of fit" test.[5,6] For further discussion of multivariate methods, see Chapter 7.

☙ ELIMINATING ALTERNATIVE EXPLANATIONS: THE THREAT OF CONFOUNDING AND BIAS

The final step in establishing evidence to support an association is to exclude alternative explanations. If the apparent association between a causal and outcome variable can be readily explained by some other effect, no true evidence of the association under study has been garnered. There are three principal considerations in excluding alternative, or competing, explanations: alternative, biologically plausible hypotheses as yet untested; confounding; and bias.

Alternative hypotheses

One of the reasons why establishing evidence of causality is so difficult is because the exclusion of alternative hypotheses is often done with substantial uncertainty. Peptic ulcer disease is again a useful example. The hypersecretion of hydrochloric acid was associated with peptic ulcer formation long before *Helicobacter pylori* was identified.[7] The evidence in support of the acid hypersecretion hypothesis was strong, but it could not exclude an "alternative" explanation only made available through advances in science. To the extent that such advances are likely to modify our understanding of other causal pathways, no association is ever established with absolute certainty, and alternative explanations are never excluded with absolute confidence. Nonetheless, when all apparent or probable alternatives can be excluded, strength is lent to the association under study.

Confounding

When the apparent association, or apparent lack of association, between two variables is the result of the action of a third variable, the effect is known as **confounding**, and the variable as a **confounder**. When the confounder makes an association appear that does not exist, it is **positive**

confounding. When it masks a true association, it is **negative confounding**.

A basic requirement of any confounder is that it be associated with both the exposure (or intervention) and the outcome. For example, consider the hypothesis that coffee consumption leads to lung cancer. Evidence of a dose-response relationship might be found, with more coffee consumption associated with a higher risk of cancer. But cigarette smoking confounds this apparent association. Smoking is associated with both coffee consumption and with lung cancer. In this case, smoking is a positive confounder, creating the appearance of an association between coffee consumption and cancer where none actually exists.

If smoking were linked with coffee consumption but not with lung cancer it could not confound the association of interest. Subjects drinking a great deal of coffee might be more likely to smoke, but they would not, on the basis of their smoking, be at increased risk of lung cancer. Any apparent link between coffee consumption and lung cancer could not be attributed to smoking, and therefore the association of interest would not be confounded. Alternatively, if smoking were associated with lung cancer, but not with coffee consumption, it again could not confound the association of interest. Those subjects with high or low coffee consumption would be equally likely (or equally unlikely) to smoke. Thus, smoking would be comparably distributed across the levels of coffee consumption. If coffee consumption were linked with lung cancer it could not be ascribed to smoking, because the effects of smoking on lung cancer would be equally spread among the levels of coffee consumption. Thus, smoking could only confound the association between coffee consumption if it were associated with both, as in fact it is.[8] In this case, smoking is a positive confounder; coffee consumption is made to look like a risk factor for lung cancer when it is not.

Family history of a particular disease might act as a negative confounder. For example, data from the Nurses' Health Study suggest a lack of protective effect of dietary fiber on colon cancer risk.[9] However, an interaction among family history, dietary intake, and colon cancer risk is possible.[10] Consider the possibility that women with a family history of colon cancer made a concerted effort to increase their intake of dietary fiber, believing it to be protective. The association of interest is that between high fiber intake and reduced risk of colon cancer. However, if a family history of colon cancer were associated with both an increased risk of cancer and an increased tendency to consume a high fiber diet, family history might mask a true association between high fiber intake and reduced cancer risk.

If family history were associated with cancer risk but not fiber intake it could not mask the association of interest. Women with a family history of colon cancer would be at increased risk of colon cancer but would have variable fiber intake. If those with the highest fiber intake had reduced rates of colon cancer the association could be detected. Alternatively, if family history were associated with fiber intake, but not with colon cancer, it could not confound the association of interest. Women with a family history of colon cancer would tend to eat more fiber but would not be at increased cancer risk. Thus if fiber intake reduced cancer risk the effect would be detectable. If family history is associated with both fiber intake and cancer risk it acts as a negative confounder. Women at greater risk of cancer would reduce their risk by eating more fiber but would end with the same risk as women without a family history, eating less fiber. The true association would be masked.

There are various ways of preventing confounding. The most important of these is to make sure the groups to be compared are as similar as possible with the exception of the exposure, intervention, or outcome of interest. Specific approaches to avoiding confounding in study design are discussed in Chapters 8 and 9. Prevention of confounding is preferable to its management in the statistical analysis, although this, too, can be done.

A concept related to confounding yet different in important ways is **effect modification**. An **effect modifier** is a third variable, again associated with both the apparent cause and the apparent effect, which modifies, rather than obscures, the association of interest. For example, in the association between vigorous exercise and heart disease risk, the level of fitness can be considered an effect modifier. An individual who is basically fit will reduce his or her risk of heart disease by exercising vigorously. An individual who is unfit, however, may acutely increase his or her risk of MI by exercising vigorously; the clustering of MI's attributable to shoveling snow is a clear example.[11] The association between exercise and MI risk is real, but its direction varies with level of fitness.[12,13]

Bias

As noted above, hypotheses are the basis for all investigation, and hypotheses are the product of bias. Although bias in the hypothesis is acceptable, bias in the performance, analysis, or interpretation of a study is not. **Bias** is any approach to the study or the data generated by it that systematically distorts the "signals" being generated. Bias distorts the data in a particular direction, and is therefore known as **differential error**, or **systematic error**. It is distinguished from random, or nondifferential error. **Random error** increases variability, and therefore the background noise of a study, making the "signal" harder to detect. While random error does not produce a false signal, differential error can.

There are many ways bias can be introduced into a study. Often, subjects are recruited according to various inclusion and exclusion criteria. This recruitment strategy is essential to prevent confounding but it introduces **sampling bias**, systematic differences between the sample of study subjects and the general population (or other reference population). Sampling bias can be controlled, provided that sampling methods are described in detail. The criteria used to include and exclude subjects define the larger populations to which the study results are pertinent, or the **generalizability** of the results. Sampling methods influence the **external validity** of the study, which is another way of expressing generalizability. Sampling bias is introduced if the recruitment methods are not clearly described and the results are generalized to groups not eligible for the study, i.e., groups to whom the results cannot be known to pertain.

Once subjects are enrolled in a study, their assignment to the two or more treatment groups may introduce bias. If subjects are assigned in a way that will influence outcomes, e.g., if the most enthusiastic subjects in a study relying on behavior modification are assigned to active treatment and the disinterested subjects to the control group, it introduces a **selection bias** or **allocation bias**. While sampling bias refers to the distortions introduced by recruitment, selection bias refers to the distortions resulting from how subjects are placed into the groups once enrolled. Selection bias can be due to the selections made by the investigators (subject allocation) or by the subjects (self-selection) if they are at liberty to choose the group in which they would like to enroll. Selection bias distorts the comparison between or among the study groups and threatens the **internal validity**, often referred to simply as the validity, of the study. Once bias has compromised the internal validity of a study no adequate correction in the statistical analysis is possible.

If measurement methods differ between or among study groups, **measurement bias** is introduced. For example, if subjects in the group given the active antihypertensive agent have blood pressure measured with a large cuff, while those in the group given placebo have measurements

TABLE 6.3   Representative Varieties of Bias in Hypothesis Testing

Bias	Description
Assembly bias (Susceptibility bias)	The groups assembled for a cohort study differ systematically in some way other than the exposure of interest; group differences potentially lead to differences in susceptibility to the outcome
Detection bias	Subjects in one group are examined or tested more frequently or intensively than those in other groups, producing systematic differences in the probability of detecting disease; threatens the internal validity of the study
Lead time bias	Disease is detected early in its course by virtue of screening, distorting the apparent natural history of disease; may threaten either internal or external validity
Length bias	Subjects with disease of longer duration are more likely to be sampled, generally a threat to external validity
Measurement bias	Measures are obtained using different methods for subjects in one as opposed to other groups; threatens internal validity
Observer bias	Subjective measures are interpreted differently in treatment than in control subjects; threatens internal validity
Recall bias	When subjects with a disease recall exposures differently than those without disease in a retrospective study; threatens internal validity
Sampling bias	A nonrepresentative sample of the underlying population is recruited; a threat to external validity
Selection bias (Allocation bias)	Subjects with different characteristics are assigned or self-assigned to the two or more study groups; threatens internal validity
Spectrum bias	Subjects with disease of differing stage or severity are assigned differentially to the two or more study groups; a threat to internal validity
Treatment bias	Subjects in the different study groups are treated differently with regard to interventions other than the one of interest; a threat to internal validity

taken with a small cuff, a systematic difference in measurement methods distorts the study results. If subjects in one group are followed more meticulously than the other, undergo additional tests, or their findings are interpreted differently, **detection bias**, **treatment bias**, or **observer bias** are introduced, respectively. If subjects in one group have a more or less severe or advanced disease than those in other groups, **spectrum bias** is introduced. If early detection identifies some subjects earlier in the course of their illness than others, **lead time bias** can be introduced. If sampling and recruitment is influenced by the duration of illness, **length bias** may be introduced, with those individuals having their illness the longest most likely to be enrolled. These different types of biases are summarized in Table 6.3. Methods for avoiding several important varieties of bias are discussed in Chapter 8.

SUMMARY/TAKE-AWAY MESSAGES

The assertion and testing of hypotheses drives the process of medical investigation. Testing of hypotheses depends on such concepts as the strength of an apparent association and the degree of variation in the data. Strength of association is one signal of causality; others are expressed in **Mill's canons** and **Koch's postulates**. While a strong signal can lend support to a hypothesis, it may be drowned out by excessive variation, or noise. Thus, the concepts of hypothesis testing require some statistical discipline, the measure of signal in comparison to noise. In order to apply statistics to the testing of hypotheses, the various classes of clinical data—**dichotomous, nominal, ordinal, continuous**—must be handled distinctly. Measures of **central tendency** and **dispersion** are used to create the pertinent measures of signal and noise necessary in the construction of the **critical ratio** that tests the hypothesis. To interpret the apparent association between one variable and another, the influence of other variables must be controlled. A third variable associated with both putative cause and effect has the potential to be a **confounder**. A variable altering the relationship between dependent and independent variables can act as an **effect modifier**. Systematic distortions in the sampling and assignment of study subjects, or in the collection or interpretation of data introduce **bias** that may undermine or invalidate the hypothesis testing. Ultimately, hypothesis testing is subject to the same dominant influences as clinical practice—**probability, alternative**, and **risk**. A hypothesis is never proved true. When the null hypothesis is sufficiently improbable, it is rejected and the alternative hypothesis accepted. There is always some risk of asserting a false hypothesis, or rejecting a true one. And while associations require elimination of alternatives before considered supportive of a causal relationship, alternative explanations for an apparent association are never entirely excluded.

The basic mechanics of hypothesis testing are explored in Chapter 7.

〰 〰 〰

〰 REFERENCES

1. Mill JS. A system of logic (1856). In: Last JM. *A Dictionary of Epidemiology*, 2nd ed. New York: Oxford University Press; 1988.
2. Marshall BJ, Warren JR. Unidentified curved bacilli in the stomach of patients with gastritis and peptic ulceration. *Lancet*. 1984;1:1311–1315.
3. MacGregor JT, Casciano D, Muller L. Strategies and testing methods for identifying mutagenic risks. *Mutat Res*. 2000;455:3–20.
4. Jekel JF, Elmore JG, Katz DL. *Epidemiology, Biostatistics, and Preventive Medicine*. Philadelphia, PA: Saunders; 1996.
5. Dawson-Saunders B, Trapp RG. *Basic & Clinical Biostatistics*, 2nd ed. Norwalk, CT: Appleton & Lange; 1994.
6. Motulsky H. *Intuitive Biostatistics*. New York: Oxford University Press; 1995.
7. Cohen JC. Evolving therapies for peptic ulcer disease: *Helicobacter pylori* treatment. *Gastroenterologist*. 1995;3:289–300.
8. Nomura A, Heilbrun LK, Stemmermann GN. Prospective study of coffee consumption and the risk of cancer. *J Natl Cancer Inst*. 1986; 76: 587–590.
9. Fuchs CS, Giovannucci EL, Colditz GA, et al. Dietary fiber and the risk of colorectal cancer and adenoma in women. *N Engl J Med*. 1999;340:169–176.
10. Sellers TA, Bazyk AE, Bostick RM, et al. Diet and risk of colon cancer in a large prospective study of older women: An analysis stratified on family history (Iowa, United States). *Cancer Causes Control*. 1998;9:357–367.
11. Franklin BA, Bonzheim K, Gordon S, Timmis GC. Snow shoveling: A trigger for acute myocardial infarction and sudden coronary death. *Am J Cardiol*. 1996;77:855–858.
12. Mittleman MA, Maclure M, Tofler GH, Sherwood JB, Goldberg RJ, Muller JE. Triggering of acute myocardial infarction by heavy physical exertion. Protection against triggering by regular exertion. Determinants of Myocardial Infarction Onset Study Investigators. *N Engl J Med*. 1993;329:1677–1683.
13. Hallqvist J, Moller J, Ahlbom A, Diderichsen F, Reuterwall C, de Faire U. Does heavy physical exertion trigger myocardial infarction? A case-crossover analysis nested in a population-based case-referent study. *Am J Epidemiol*. 2000;151:459–467.

Hypothesis Testing 2
Mechanics

INTRODUCTION

The basic statistical approach to testing a hypothesis requires construction of a **critical ratio** of signal (apparent outcome effect) to noise (variation). This ratio is then interpreted on the basis of statistical conventions to assess its probability under differing assumptions. When the signal is strong relative to noise, the probability of a meaningful, or causal, association is high. When the signal is weak, and/or the noise loud, and the ratio therefore low, the probability of meaningful association, at least as indicated by the study in question, is also low. The means of comparing the results of a particular study, expressed as a particular type of data, to the conventional threshold for **statistical significance** constitute the mechanics of hypothesis testing, and are presented in this chapter.

Because all hypotheses are predicated on the absence of definitive evidence, and because in clinical practice the most cautious approach is to presume nothing untried is true until proved true, the convention is to assert a lack of association. This is done by formulating a **null hypothesis**, H_0, stipulating that two variables of interest are not related to one another, or that they vary independently. This convention calls for the establishment of an **alternative hypothesis**, H_a, that asserts what is sought, namely the association between the variables of interest. A threshold is then set for rejecting the null hypothesis. When the available evidence makes the lack of an association improbable (i.e., a rare occurrence), the null hypothesis is rejected, and the alternative hypothesis is presumed to be true.

While the conceptual approach to hypothesis testing is fairly constant, the methods applied vary with the nature of the variables and with the clinical question(s). A detailed discussion of statistical methods is beyond the scope of this text, but a basic understanding of the methods applied is useful in interpreting the literature.

\\\ PARAMETRIC METHODS

When the data to be analyzed are continuous, and can be described by a mean and standard deviation, and if the underlying data in the population are distributed normally (see Chapter 6), parametric methods of analysis can be used.

Student's t-test

The standard method of analysis when a continuous outcome variable is being compared between two groups is the **Student's t-test**. A discussion of this test is useful because it so clearly demonstrates the principles of hypothesis testing discussed in Chapter 6. The t-test is also helpful in revealing how intuitive hypothesis testing can be.

Consider that, as before, blood pressure reduction is to be compared between active treatment and placebo groups. The goal is to produce a critical ratio of signal to noise. The signal in this instance is the difference between the means for the two groups. The mean chosen is a matter of convenience; the actual blood pressure, or the magnitude of blood pressure reduction could be used as the basis for comparison.

By convention, a null hypothesis is asserted that stipulates no difference between groups. Therefore, if the mean blood pressure for the treatment group (A) and for the placebo group (B) are equivalent, the null hypothesis is confirmed. The more different the difference between the two means is from zero, the less consistent the results are with the null hypothesis. To reject the null hypothesis, we are initially looking for evidence that the difference between the means in not zero (that is, $\bar{x}_A - \bar{x}_B \neq 0$). Therefore, the numerator for the Student's t-test is $\bar{x}_A - \bar{x}_B - 0$.

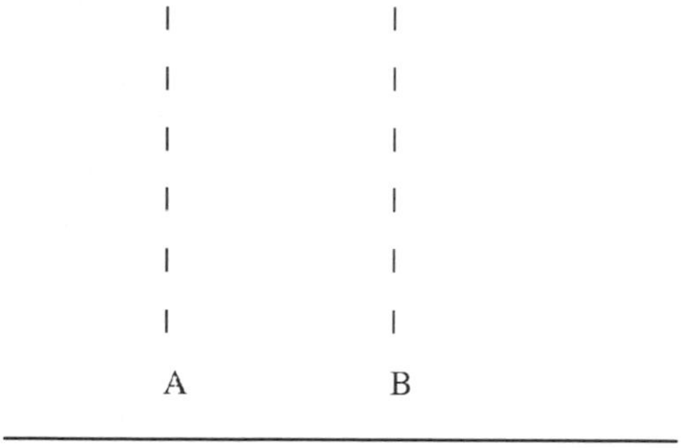

```
   |        |
   |        |
   |        |
   |        |
   |        |
   |        |
   A        B
```

Figure 7.1. A comparison of two group means when there is no within-groups variation.

Next, we need to compare the signal of treatment effect to the background noise. Background noise, statistically, is the combined variance in the two samples being compared. The methods for calculating the pooled variance for the two samples of interest (A and B) are not presented here, and are readily available elsewhere.[1] Suffice to say that the variances in the two samples are summed to produce a measure of the total interindividual variation among the subjects being compared. The **critical ratio** is a measure of the between-group variation to the total within-groups variation. When the variation between the groups is great relative to the within-groups variation, the null hypothesis can be rejected. Rejection of the null hypothesis, discussed further in Chapter 9, requires attaching a probability estimate to a given value of the critical ratio (called "t" for a t-test) by finding the value obtained in a table of possible values for that particular test.

The intuitive nature of t-tests is best revealed using frequency distribution plots. Consider that the blood pressures in group A and group B are identical before treatment, and their after-treatment distributions are shown in Figure 7.1.

No statistical methods are required to see that the treatment produced an outcome difference. But outcome data are virtually never this unambiguous. Far more typical would be one of the outcomes displayed in Figure 7.2.

In Figure 7.2**A**, the two curves, though differing slightly, cannot be said with confidence to differ significantly. While **significance** has particular statistical meaning (see Chapter 9), it also has intuitive meaning. These curves hardly seem to differ. What compells us to reach this conclusion

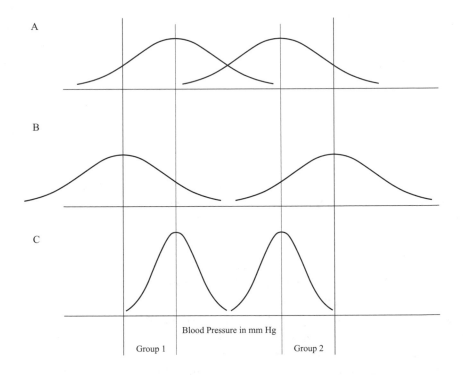

Figure 7.2. Frequency distributions for possible outcome data of a trial in which group 1 receives an antihypertensive medication and group 2 receives placebo. In **A**, there is substantial difference between group means, but also substantial variance, and therefore considerable overlap in values between the two groups. In **B**, there is identical variance as in **A**, but a larger difference between means. In **C**, there is the same difference between means as in **A**, but less variance.

is that the two curves have substantial overlap. The curves displayed in Figure 7.2**B** clearly differ "significantly," with significance again defined intuitively rather than statistically. Yet the degree of variation in these two curves is identical to those in **A**. What is different is the magnitude of difference between group means, the "between group" difference. Finally, in Figure 7.2**C**, the two curves are again seen to differ. Yet the difference between means for these curves is identical to those in **A**, where the difference was not apparently significant. What distinguishes the curves in **A** from those in **C** is the **degree of dispersion**; there is much less within-groups variation in **C** than in **A**.

In viewing this series of plots and deriving conclusions about the significance of the between groups differences, we are performing a t-test based on intuition. This recapitulates the intuitive handling of probability in the clinical assessment. Just as the features of a case are compatible enough with a diagnosis (i.e., with the features of previously assessed patients in whom a specific diagnosis was ultimately made) to rule it in, or sufficiently incompatible with a particular diagnosis to support it being ruled out, so, too, the results of trials are interpreted in terms of probability. We can tell that between-group difference alone does not determine significance, nor does the degree of within-groups variation. Only when the between-group variation is compared to the within-groups variation, allowing for assessment of the degree to which the two plots "overlap," can we reach conclusions about the significance of treatment effects. This is exactly what a t-test is set up to do.[1]

Probability in the process of diagnosis, or prognosis, relies on the correspondence observed between an individual patient and a population with particular characteristics and prior experience. Once a particular diagnosis emerges as the leading "contender" to explain a patient's syndrome, it is pursued with diagnostic testing that will confirm it, refute it, or provide misleading information in either direction. The putative benefits of a clinical intervention are assessed in much the same way. Treatment effect, much like disease, is presumed to be absent until there is evidence that it is present. The interpretation of a study (or test of hypothesis) relies similarly on the correspondence (or lack thereof) between the outcome observed and the outcome presumed (the null hypothesis). A patient at risk of MI with chest pain may be presumed to have angina until proved otherwise. With a sufficient body of evidence to prove otherwise, the diagnosis is at last discarded with some finite (defined or undefined) level of confidence. The results of a trial that diverge from the null hypothesis of no treatment effect similarly result in the null hypothesis being discarded. Whereas the profound influence of probability on this process in clinical medicine is handled informally, the requisite "thresholds" for reaching particular conclusions are formalized in the interpretation of trials.

Paired t-test

A technique often used in clinical research for a variety of reasons is to compare subjects to themselves, by sequentially treating them with the active agent and placebo. When this method is used, the analysis must correspond. A **paired t-test** relies on a before-after, or drug-placebo, comparison for each individual subject. The differences in outcomes under the two treatment conditions for each subject produce a set of differences with their own mean value. If the mean difference is quite different from zero, the null hypothesis of no treatment effect is more likely to be rejected. The mean difference is compared to zero to generate the signal, and this is compared to the within-groups variation (noise) to determine statistical significance. Because subjects (patients) are more like themselves than they are like anyone else, no matter how well matched, paired analyses reduce the variation ("noise") in the data set, and render the signal (treatment effect) easier to detect. Thus, such studies often require smaller samples, although they may require more time, as each subject must pass through the treatment assignments sequentially (see Chapter 8).

ANOVA

ANOVA,[2,3] an acronym for **analysis of variance**, is used when continuous data are being compared among more than two groups. For example, two active agents might be compared to one another and to placebo. The critical ratio for an ANOVA places the aggregate between-groups variation in the numerator, and the aggregate within-groups variation in the denominator. If the critical ratio is "significant" in a table of F-values (the name of the test statistic generated by an ANOVA), the null hypothesis can be rejected. In the case of ANOVA, rejection of the null hypothesis indicates that treatment had a significant effect, but not which treatment. For this, methods must be applied to conduct a pair-wise comparison among groups. The within-groups variation is generated by calculating the sum of squares (see Chapter 6) for each of the treatment groups. The between-groups variation is generated by calculating the sum of squares for all of the data as if they were in a single data set, and subtracting from this the sum of squares for the actual treatment groups. The difference is the variation eliminated by the assignment of subjects to their particular treatment groups. An example of the application of ANOVA is provided in Figure 7.3.

If the same test were administered to children at 3 grade levels (see Figure 7.3), intuition would suggest that the older children would perform better. In other words, some of the variation in test scores should be accounted for by grade level. Asserting a more detailed hypothesis, 2nd graders would be expected to perform better than 1st graders, and 3rd graders better than 2nd graders. The measure of performance would be the mean test score for the students in a given grade level. To test this hy-

A Test scores for 300 students, grades 1, 2, and 3.

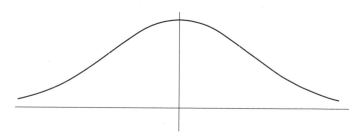

Sum of squares = 10,000

B Test scores of the same 300 students, plotted separately for grades 1, 2, and 3.

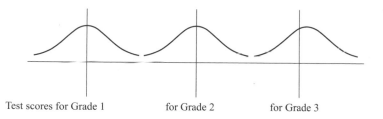

Test scores for Grade 1   for Grade 2   for Grade 3

Sum of squares per sample = 2000; Total sum of squares = 6000

Between groups variation explained by model equal 10,000 − 6,000 = 4000

Figure 7.3.   Application of ANOVA. A group of 300 students, 100 each in grades 1, 2, and 3, take the same exam. The test scores may be plotted on a single curve as shown in **A**, associated with a sum of squares (see Chapter 6), in this case stipulated to be 10,000. The test scores may be plotted instead with grade level serving as a "model" that could potentially explain some of the variation in test scores. The sum of squares for each of the three curves in **B** could be calculated and then summed. The difference between the residual variation in the three curves (the sum of squares for the three curves in figure **B**, or the within-groups variation) and the sum of squares for the curve in figure **A** is the between-groups variation. The between-groups variation is the amount of test score variation explained by grade level (or, more generically, the amount of variation in the outcome measure explained by the model). ANOVA generates an f statistic, the ratio of between-groups variation to residual within-groups variation. Tables of f statistics (or statistical software packages) indicate the statistical significance of this f ratio. As with the t-test, however, intuition is suggestive of the results of statistical significance testing. If the multiple curves produced by imposing the model are widely divergent, the model is likely to produce a significant f statistic.

pothesis, the degree of variation in the test scores accounted for by grade level needs to be assessed. If it is "large," or significant, then the "model" (grade level) is explaining variation in the outcome, and the hypothesis has been affirmed. If the variation in grades attributable to grade level is trivial, the hypothesis has not been supported. In Figure 7.3, the model is the division of test scores into categories of grade level. The difference between the sum of squares for all 300 test scores around the grand mean (10,000), and the sum of squares for the three curves accounting for grade level (6000), represents the amount of variation explained by the model (4000). If the variation between groups (grade levels) is large relative to the variation within groups (i.e., the variation left unaccounted for by the model), the model is useful in explaining variation in the measure of interest, in this case test scores. ANOVA, which creates a ratio of between-groups variation to within-groups variation using the sum of squares, will tend to generate evidence of statistical significance when the between-groups variation is large relative to the residual within-groups variation.

※ NONPARAMETRIC METHODS

When data are not continuous, or cannot be characterized by a mean and standard deviation, nonparametric methods are required. There are nonparametric analogues to virtually all of the parametric tests.

Chi-square

One of the most useful methods of nonparametric analysis, the **chi-square** is used to analyze dichotomous data in two or more groups. For example, if groups of subjects are given aspirin or placebo, and then followed to see whether or not they develop MI, the data would look as shown in Box 7.1.

With dichotomous outcome data, as with continuous outcome data, a null hypothesis must be asserted. The null hypothesis is **independence** of the treatment and outcome variables. To test this hypothesis, a ratio is created between what the data actually reveal, and what the data would reveal if the null hypothesis were true. If the data are very different from

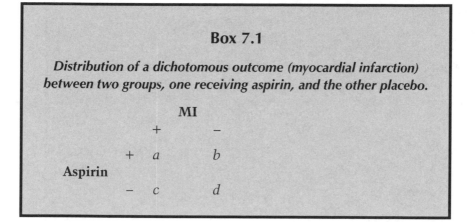

Box 7.1

*Distribution of a dichotomous outcome (myocardial infarction)
between two groups, one receiving aspirin, and the other placebo.*

		MI	
		+	−
Aspirin	+	a	b
	−	c	d

what would be expected under conditions of independence, the null hypothesis of independence is rejected. The implication of this is that the variables are dependent on one another, with treatment influencing outcome.

Assume that 100 subjects are given aspirin and another 100 subjects are given placebo ($n = 200$). If we know that a total of 100 subjects had a MI, how would the data be distributed if the null hypothesis were true, if treatment and outcome status were independent? Independence would require that the treated group have neither a higher nor lower risk of the outcome than the nontreated group. Therefore, the outcome events should be evenly distributed between the two treatment groups. If the 100 MI's were evenly distributed between aspirin and treatment groups, there would be 50 MI's in cell a and 50 MI's in cell c. If the 100 subjects who did not have MI were also evenly distributed between treatment groups, as would be expected under conditions of independence, 50 subjects would be expected in cell b and 50 in cell d (Box 7.2).

What if only 50 subjects had a MI, with 150 remaining MI free? If 100 subjects each again received aspirin or placebo and the null hypothesis of independence were true, we would expect the 50 MI's to be evenly distributed (more or less) between the treatment groups, with approximately 25 in cell a and 25 in cell c. Note that this expectation is predicated on chance, or randomness. Similarly, the 150 MI-free subjects would be (more or less) evenly distributed between cells b and d, with approximately 75 in each (Box 7.3).

Finally, what if only 50 subjects are given aspirin and 150 are given placebo, and a total of 60 subjects have a MI? We might expect that be-

---

Box 7.2

Even distribution of the outcome (myocardial infarction) between treatment groups as would be expected if treatment and outcome were independent.

	MI	
	+	–
Aspirin +	50	50
Aspirin –	50	50
		$n = 200$

Box 7.3

Even distribution of the outcome measure between exposure groups, when only 1 in 4 subjects experience the outcome.

	MI	
	+	–
Aspirin +	25	75
Aspirin –	25	75
		$n = 200$

---

cause 50 of 200 subjects, or ¼, are in the aspirin group, that approximately ¼ of the MI's would occur in this group (again, by chance). And as ¾ of the sample is in the placebo group, we might expect approximately ¾ of the MI's to occur in the placebo group; these conditions would fulfill the criteria of independence (i.e., outcome occurring independently of treatment assignment). The same would pertain to the 140 subjects free of MI, with ¼ in the aspirin group, and ¾ in the placebo group (Box 7.4).

What we have done in each of these permutations is calculate the **expected values** for each cell of the table (a 2 × 2 contingency table) un-

---

Box 7.4

Even distribution of the outcome event (myocardial infarction) relative to an uneven distribution of exposed and unexposed (treated and untreated) subjects.

		MI	
		+	−
	+	15	35
Aspirin			
	−	45	105
			$n = 200$

---

der the condition of independence required for the null hypothesis to be true. Our method for generating the expected value for each cell is easily replicated: in each instance, the expected value is the total for the row in the table, multiplied by the total for the column, and divided by the total number of subjects in the table. This is the algebraic expression of the concept that all of the outcome events and non-events should be distributed between the treatment and nontreatment groups based solely on the proportion of all subjects who are in each group. Stated mathematically, the expected value for any cell in a contingency table = [(row total × column total)/table total].

If treatment and outcome are actually not independent, treatment assignment will influence the distribution of outcome events. We would expect in this example that a disproportionate number of MIs would occur in the placebo group. To the extent that the actual distribution of MI's differs from the expected distribution of MIs under conditions of independence, we have evidence that the null hypothesis is unlikely to be true. This concept is the basis for the chi-square test. The chi-square value for each cell of the table is

$$(O - E)^2 / E$$

where O is the observed, or actual value of the cell, and
E is the expected value of the cell

The chi-square for the entire table is the sum of the chi-square values for each cell:

$$X^2 = \sum[(O-E)^2/E]$$

To interpret the value of chi-square, two additional steps are required. The first step is to establish the **degrees of freedom**. This is necessary for the same reason it is necessary in calculating the variance (see Chapter 6). Once row totals and column totals are known, as they must be to determine expected values, cells are free to vary until the outermost column and outermost row of the table are reached. In order for row and column totals to reach the required totals, the final entry in each row or column is fixed. Thus, the degrees of freedom for any contingency table is

$$(R-1) \times (C-1)$$

where R = number of rows

and C = number of columns

Once the chi-square value and degrees of freedom are known, the value is located in a table of chi-square values to identify the corresponding degree of statistical significance.[1]

Other nonparametric tests

A variety of other nonparametric tests allow for analysis of all varieties of clinical data. For the most part, these methods rely on **ranking** of ordinal or nominal data. For example, if two groups of students evaluate two lectures with scores ranging from "poor" to "excellent" across five levels, a method is needed that allows establishment of the "average" score achieved by each lecture to determine whether the rankings differ "significantly." A true average, or mean, is not applicable, as there is no way of averaging subjective measures. But a rank can be assigned to each score, with a "1" assigned to poor, and "5" assigned to excellent. The scores for both classes are then categorized by rank, and the rankings are compared between groups using methods roughly analogous to those of the t-test. Variations on this basic theme are applied in situations calling for nonparametric analogues to the paired t-test, ANOVA, and other methods.[2,3]

⚇ ODDS RATIOS AND RISK RATIOS

A common method of testing association in studies with a dichotomous outcome (such as presence or absence of disease or a risk factor for disease; survival or mortality) is to create a ratio of the occurrence of the outcome in those with exposure to those without the exposure, or a ratio of the exposure in those with to those without the outcome. When groups are assembled on the basis of exposure and followed for the outcome (cohort studies; see Chapter 8), the ratio of outcome in those with to those without the exposure is referred to as the **risk ratio** (RR). The risk ratio, also known as the **relative risk**, is the risk of the outcome in the exposed as compared to the risk in the unexposed. Calculation of the risk ratio is shown in Box 7.5.

When groups are assembled on the basis of outcome and assessed for exposure (case-control studies; see Chapter 8), risk of the outcome occurring cannot be assessed because the outcome has already occurred. Such groups can be assessed or compared on the basis of the "risk of having the risk factor" or exposure of interest. The method of comparing the risk of exposure between groups differing by outcome is the **odds ratio**, the calculation of which is shown in Box 7.6.

An odds ratio or risk ratio of 1 indicates no difference between groups. When the value of either differs markedly from 1, there is an obvious

---

Box 7.5

Calculation of the risk ratio. In a cohort study, with groups assembled on the basis of exposure, the risk of the outcome in the exposed $\{a/(a+b)\}$ over the risk of the outcome in the nonexposed $\{c/(c+d)\}$ is the risk ratio, or the relative risk.

		Outcome	
		Yes	No
	Yes	a	b
Exposure			
	No	c	d

Box 7.6

Calculation of the odds ratio. In case-control study, with groups assembled on the basis of outcome, the risk of "having the risk factor" (exposure) in those with the outcome expressed as odds is (a/c). The odds of the exposure in those without the outcome is (b/d). The odds ratio is the ratio of odds of exposure in those with to those without the outcome: $(a/c)/(b/d)$.

		Outcome	
		Yes	No
	Yes	a	b
Exposure			
	No	c	d

difference between groups. To determine the statistical significance (see Chapter 9) of either measure, statistical software packages surround it with a **95% confidence interval** (95% CI; see Chapter 9). When the 95% CI for either an odds ratio or risk ratio is entirely to one side of 1, the measure provides statistically significant evidence of a difference between groups.

Of note, case control studies (see Chapter 8) are often conducted when the outcome of interest is rare. Under such conditions, the odds ratio is a good approximation of the risk ratio. This is so because when disease (outcome) is rare, cells a and c (those with disease) are small relative to cells b and d (those without disease). The formula for the risk ratio $[\{a/(a + b)\}/\{c/(c + d)\}]$, can be converted as an approximation to $\{(a/b)/(c/d)\}$ when the values of a and c are small. This is algebraically equivalent to the odds ratio $\{(a/c)/(b/d)\}$, as both equal ad/bc, known as the **cross product** (because it is the product of diagonals in the 2×2 table). Thus, the odds ratio is legitimately used to approximate the risk ratio when disease/outcome is a rare event.

※ OTHER METHODʃ OF HYPOTHEʃIʃ TEʃTING

At times, both variables of interest in a comparison are continuous. For example, the relationship between physical activity and weight loss is of great interest to many patients. Our ability as clinicians to offer advice regarding this association requires, at first, that evidence of an association be generated. Ignoring the subtleties for the moment, what would be needed is a measure of the degree to which increases in physical activity produce decreases in weight. Such a measure is called **correlation**, and by convention, the Pearson correlation test is applied. The value generated is the **Pearson correlation coefficient,** r. The value of r corresponds with a measure of statistical significance, so that an assessment of change in physical activity and weight can be analyzed to determine whether or not increased activity is a significant predictor of weight loss. The square of r (r^2) is a measure of the proportion of variation in the dependent variable explained by the variation in the independent variable. There are non-parametric analogues of the Pearson correlation.[1,2,3]

Although knowing that activity and weight loss correlate is useful, it falls short of our clinical needs. A patient may want to know exactly how much of a particular type of exercise is required to produce a specific amount of weight loss. Correlation does not provide this information; **linear regression** does. In linear regression, a "regression line" is determined as the best linear approximation (i.e., producing the least mean square error) to the distribution of observations. The exact methods for generating the line are beyond the scope of this text,[2,3] but they essentially call for minimizing the sum of squares produced by the observations, using the line as the group mean. The slope of the regression line is a measure of exactly how much change in the dependent variable occurs per unit change in the independent variable.

One of the most important types of clinical data is **survival data**. While survival data are fundamentally dichotomous (live/die), the duration of survival is of interest to both our patients and us. Even if all patients with a particular disease in both the treatment and placebo groups have died at the end of 5 years, evidence that on average patients in the treatment group lived longer might support use of the treatment. Survival data are typically displayed in plots, with time on the x-axis, and the proportion surviving on the y-axis. **Survival analysis** is generally performed using one of two **life table methods**, the **actuarial method**, or the **Kaplan-Meier method**. The differences between these methods are beyond the scope of the current discussion.[2,3] The more popular Kaplan-Meier method generates plots with a step-wise, staircase-like descent.[4] The **log-rank test** is used to measure the significance of differences along the length of the curves so that even if mortality has equalized by the end of the observation period, interval differences can be appreciated. **Cox proportional hazards** modeling is a form of multivariable analysis for survival curves that allows the influences of multiple independent variables to be considered together.[2]

As noted at the start of the chapter, this brief overview of methods for testing hypotheses is intended only to cultivate an appreciation for the methods that are commonly applied in the literature. Considerably more information is required to prepare for independent data analysis (refer to Text Sources at the back of this book for further reading).

The rationale for including this material in a text on clinical epidemiology is based on practical considerations. Evidence-based practice is only as good as the evidence applied. The evidence applied in medical practice is predominantly that conveyed in the peer-reviewed literature. Hypothesis testing, and the resultant measures of statistical significance (see Chapter 9), are widely employed arbiters of "truth" in clinical evidence, and influence the pattern of publication in important ways.[5,6,7,8] Therefore, at a minimum one should recognize the type of analysis reported, and have some notion of whether or not it seems the appropriate method, before accepting the veracity of the reported evidence and applying it to patient care.

⚶ HYPOTHEƧIƧ TEƧTING AND THE ƧTIPULATION OF OUTCOME

The methods for testing hypotheses follow the assertion of the hypothesis(es) of interest. Intrinsic to the assertion of a hypothesis is the stipulation of measures, generally of both exposure and outcome. And these measures, in turn, depend upon the priorities in the setting in which the data will ultimately be applied. Increasingly, simple outcome measures, such as the presence or absence of disease, survival or death, are considered inadequate to convey the priorities in the practice setting. Both clinician and patient are concerned with symptoms, side effects, functionality, and more. These considerations are difficult to quantify, but quality of life measures attempt to do just that. The most popular of these measures is the **quality adjusted life year** (see Appendix B).[9] This measure assigns a value to a year of life, based on a scale from 0 (no quality, or death) to 1 (perfect health), and multiplies that by the years of life.

An example demonstrates how important the selection of outcome can be in the testing of hypotheses. In studies that have compared the rates of coronary revascularization between the US and Canada with survival as the outcome of interest, higher rates of CABG in the US have not been shown to produce a measurable benefit.[10] When morbidity is considered, however, as measured by the occurrence of angina, functional status, or overall quality of life, the higher rates of revascularization in the US may indeed be justified.[11] Rigorous methods of hypothesis testing cannot compensate for testing the wrong hypothesis, i.e., one predicated on the wrong measure of outcome. The "right" hypothesis is predicated on clinical priorities.

SUMMARY/TAKE-AWAY MESSAGES

While the detailed methods involved in hypothesis testing are not necessary for the clinician who is not involved in conducting research, an understanding of the basics is useful. The testing of hypotheses is the process by which outcome data of significance, and thus the "evidence base" for clinical practice (or at least one of its more important constituents), are derived.

The various methods of hypothesis testing share certain common characterstics. In general, a **null hypothesis** of no association is asserted. When the results of a trial are inconsistent with the null hypothesis, it is rejected, and the **alternative hypothesis** accepted. Thus, hypothesis testing does not and cannot prove causality. Rather, when the association observed seems too strong to be due to chance, the inference is drawn that it is not due to chance.

To assess the apparent strength of association, a critical ratio of "treatment" or group effect to variation is constructed. **Parametric methods** are used when the data are normally distributed, or when the underlying population data are normally distributed. A **t-test** is used to compare a continuous outcome between two groups, creating a ratio of the difference between means to the combined variation of the groups. When a group is compared to itself, a **paired t-test** is used. When more than two groups are being compared and the outcome variable is continuous,

ANOVA is used to create a ratio of between-groups variance to within-groups variance.

When data are not normally distributed in the underlying population, mean and standard deviation values needed for parametric analysis may not be meaningful, and **nonparametric methods** are used. For the most part, such methods assign rank values to data and compare groups on the basis of average rank. An exception is the **chi-square** test, used for dichotomous or nominal data, to test for independence. When the distribution of values in a contingency table is inconsistent with expectation under the assumption of independence, the chi-square test will provide statistical support for the dependence of one variable on the other. The **risk ratio** is a frequently applied outcome measure in cohort studies, and the **odds ratio** an analogue used for case-control studies. Both can demonstrate statistical significance by use of **95% confidence intervals**.

Data used in hypothesis testing are approached hierarchically, first using **univariate analysis** to characterize the individual variable, then **bivariate analysis** to establish simple associations, and finally with **multivariable methods**. Multivariable methods allow for the approximation of causality in the real world, with multiple influences acting at the same time. An example is **Cox proportional hazards** models, which are multivariable models often used to account for outcome differences in survival studies. While appropriate and sound methods of hypothesis testing are necessary in the generation of meaningful and interpretable outcomes, they are not sufficient. Methods cannot compensate for inappropriate selection of hypothesis or measure of outcome. Clinical priorities define the right measure of outcome, and the appropriate hypothesis(es) to test. The use of **quality of life measures** rather than survival as a measure of outcome in trials is a trend related to the evolution of clinical priorities. The various study designs that generate clinical data, and serve as the context in which hypotheses are put to the test, are explored in Chapter 8.

◊ ◊ ◊

◊ REFERENCES

1. Jekel, JF, Elmore JG, Katz DL. *Epidemiology, Biostatistics and Preventive Medicine.* Philadelphia, PA: Saunders; 1996.
2. Dawson-Saunders B, Trapp RG. *Basic & Clinical Biostatistics.* 2nd ed. Norwalk, CT: Appleton & Lange; 1994.

3. Motulsky H. *Intuitive Biostatistics*. New York: Oxford University Press; 1995.
4. Buccheri G, Ferrigno D. Prognostic value of stage grouping and TNM descriptors in lung cancer. *Chest.* 2000;117:1247–1255.
5. Ioannidis JP. Effect of the statistical significance of results on the time to completion and publication of randomized efficacy trials. *JAMA.* 1998;279:281–286.
6. Misakian AL, Bero LA. Publication bias and research on passive smoking: Comparison of published and unpublished studies. *JAMA.* 1998;280:250–253.
7. Callaham ML, Wears RL, Weber EJ, Barton C, Young G. Positive-outcome bias and other limitations in the outcome of research abstracts submitted to a scientific meeting. *JAMA.* 1998;280:254–257.
8. Sutton AJ, Duval SJ, Tweedie RL, Abrams KR, Jones DR. Empirical assessment of effect of publication bias on meta-analyses. *BMJ.* 2000;320:1574–1577.
9. Stone PW, Teutsch S, Chapman RH, Bell C, Goldie SJ, Neumann PJ. Cost-utility analyses of clinical preventive services: Published ratios, 1976–1997. *Am J Prev Med.* 2000;19:15–23.
10. Tu JV, Pashos CL, Naylor CD, et al. Use of cardiac procedures and outcomes in elderly patients with myocardial infarction in the United States and Canada. *N Engl J Med.* 1997;336:1500–1505.
11. Sollano JA, Rose EA, Williams DL, et al. Cost-effectiveness of coronary artery bypass surgery in octogenarians. *Ann Surg.* 1998;228:297–306.

Study Design

The capacity for evidence to support advances in medicine depends not just on the existence of such evidence but also on its quality. The designs of studies provide different strengths and weaknesses with implications for the quality of evidence produced and the appropriateness of application. An appreciation for the advantages and disadvantages, features and methodologic rigor of various study designs is useful in establishing optimal linkages between the sources of evidence and related modifications in clinical practice.

An understanding of **study design** is essential to the interpretation of the medical literature and, consequently, to the application of published evidence to individual patient care. The design of a study is the construct in which hypothesis testing is conducted, thereby linking study design to the nature of the hypothesis(es) the study is testing. Although the fundamental designs of medical studies are relatively simple, each carries with it implicit strengths and weaknesses worthy of note. There are subtle considerations in study methodology as well that are often only disclosed "between the lines" of the published literature. These considerations substantially impact the interpretability, reliability, and applicability of reported findings.

It is worth noting that there is a fundamental similarity between the construction and implementation of a research protocol and the process of diagnosis, prognosis, and treatment. Studies begin with hypothesis generation, just as the diagnostic process does. **Probability** is explicitly incorporated into study design, as it is in diagnosis and prognosis, in several ways.

The size and construct of a study are predicated on projections or expectations of treatment effects; similarly, the selection of diagnostic tests (or therapeutic interventions) is based on their projected performance. The projections in both research and clinical care are based on precedent—prior study for the former, prior patients (or patient populations) for the latter. And just as the diagnostic, prognostic, or therapeutic process is apt to go awry if probability estimates, such as the prior probability, are inaccurate, so the results of a trial are apt to be misleading if projections are erroneous.

In clinical care, the **risk** of intervening or failing to intervene is avoidable harm to a patient. In the generation of trial results, the risk is producing misleading information that will potentially contribute to harm to many patients. Diagnostic studies can fail in one of two directions, detecting disease that is not truly there or missing disease that is there. The results of trials also can suggest treatment effects that don't exist or miss treatment effects that do. Thus, studies must be undertaken with considerations for and safeguards against risk that are similar to those employed in clinical practice.

Lastly, the concept of **alternatives** is as relevant to research as it is to practice. One of Mill's canons (see Chapter 6) of causality is the exclusion of alternative explanations for an apparent association. Study methodology is founded on the controls required to exclude, or at least reduce, the likelihood that some alternative factor to the variable of interest is responsible for any outcome effect. A robust diagnostic process not only will exclude items from the differential with good confidence and lend strong support to a particular diagnosis but will also generate data that allow for the confident exclusion of alternative explanations for an association of interest. Important principles of good research are very much aligned with important principles of good clinical practice.

The literature is the end point of an often lengthy and labor-intensive process that began with curiosity, and to some extent preconception (or bias), on the part of one or more investigators. Curiosity and bias are both germane to generating a hypothesis. Curiosity underlies the clinical question, and bias underlies the belief in the probability of an association before conclusive evidence is available. Bias must be excluded from the conduct and interpretation of a study, but it plays a necessary role in study development.

Once a hypothesis is developed and supported by the prior literature, quantification of the exposures and outcomes of interest is necessary; the means of establishing an association depend on the measures of exposure and outcome. For example, if a putative association between psychological stress and immune function were to be studied, measures of stress and immunity would be prerequisite to considerations of study design.[1,2] If stress is to be measured as the loss of a spouse, the study cannot be interventional; if stress is defined alternatively, an interventional study might be feasible. Both the qualitative and quantitative aspects of the study hypothesis must be resolved before design can be considered.

Once a narrowly defined and quantitatively specific hypothesis has been developed, the advantages and disadvantages of different study designs can be considered. An understanding of this sequence—from hypothesis to measures to design—is as important to those interpreting a study as it is to those designing it. A study can only be interpreted in the context of what it was designed to measure. Therefore, recollection of the hypothesis and its quantitative components, is essential to interpretation of a study. This is especially true because associations are often reported, particularly from large observational studies, that are unrelated to the original hypotheses and aims. The process by which such associations are reported from large data sets is often referred to as "data dredging," a "fishing expedition," or "torturing the data until they confess."[3] The best defense against such potentially misleading disclosures is to recall the hypothesis(es) the study was intended to test. The same data set should not be used to both generate and test a hypothesis. Thus, any finding from a large study not addressed in its planning and design should be considered support for testing a new hypothesis, not its confirmation. Table 8.1 summarizes the steps in protocol development.

The purpose of any medical study is to conduct a controlled comparison that permits preliminary or secure inferences regarding causal associations. The need for comparison requires that all studies incorporate, minimally, two groups. This requirement can at times be met in studies with a single group, provided an external comparison group (separated by time, distance, or both from the study group) is clearly identified. Studies relying on a historical control group typify this approach.[4] Because a controlled comparison is central to the process of medical investigation, much about a study's merits and flaws may be inferred from an understanding of the composition of the groups being compared, the nature of the comparison, and the means employed to "control" the circumstances of the comparison. Figure 8.1 demonstrates the relationships among exposures, outcomes, and controls in the establishment of a particular study design.

TABLE 8.1   **Steps in the Development of a Research Protocol**

Step[1]	Comment
1. Generate a research question	The first step is the product of curiosity and should be followed immediately by a literature search (see Appendix A) to be certain that a definitive answer to the question is not already available. If the question has been answered, but not conclusively, the prior literature often is helpful in refining the question.
2. Assert a hypothesis	When curiosity generates a question, belief (or bias) suggests an answer. Assertion of that answer represents the hypothesis on which a study will be based. Bias is appropriate in the assertion of a hypothesis, but cannot be allowed to influence the conduct or interpretation of a study.
3. Establish discrete measures of exposure and outcome	The measures to be used for exposure/intervention and outcome are prerequisite to choosing a study design. Some measures require retrospective study, others require prospective interventions. Quantification of study measures often requires modification of the hypothesis(es), and is guided by the prior literature.
4. Revise the hypothesis	The hypothesis should be specific in addressing the measures of exposure and outcome, and it should suggest the methods necessary to measure each and thereby conduct the indicated "test."
5. Choose a study design	There is often more than one way to study an association of interest. The choice of study design is essentially an effort to select the construct that will facilitate the most definitive testing of the pertinent hypothesis(es) within the constraints imposed by ethical considerations, resource limitations, and feasibility.
6. Characterize the data to be generated	Beginning with the identification of measures in step 3, and ending with the selection/elaboration of study methods in step 6, the specific category(ies) of data to be generated by the study can be projected. The study "output" should be anticipated so preparations can be made for its management and analysis.
7. Select methods of analysis[2]	Once the data to be generated have been characterized, the appropriate analytical methods can be prepared in advance. Bivariate and multivariable methods can be chosen based on the characteristics of dependent and independent variables.

[1] Implicit between the steps is a review of the pertinent literature to determine whether or not the hypothesis(es) under development has (have) been adequately tested before, and to identify related studies that may be used for the adaptation of methods. Progression through the steps is an iterative process, with the product of one step modifying the step before. In particular, the identification/selection of measures will require revision of the hypothesis, which may then require revision of the measures, and both of these, as they change, will require changes in study methods, which may reciprocally require further changes in the measures and hypothesis.
[2] At the end of the process, sufficient information should be available to perform sample size or power calculations, which might then indicate/require revision of the measures or methods on the basis of feasibility or cost.

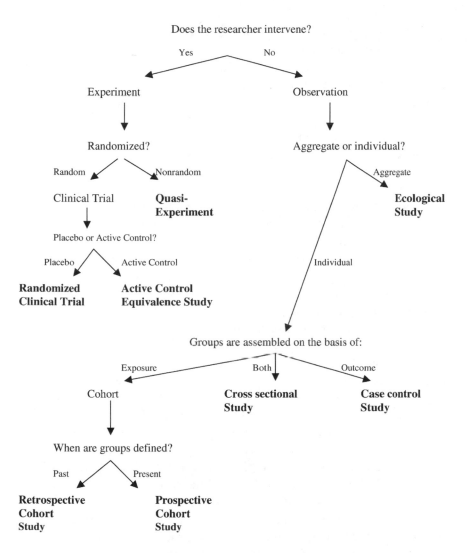

Figure 8.1. The defining characteristics of various study types.

▒ CAJE-CONTROL JTUDIEJ

Case-control studies involve comparison between a group of subjects with the outcome in question (cases) and a group without the outcome (controls). The *sine qua non* of case-control studies is assembling the groups to be compared on the basis of the outcome variable. In general, case-control studies are conducted retrospectively, that is, subjects with the outcome of interest are compared to those without, and questions are directed at exposures some time in the past. The exception is the **nested case-control study**. Nesting is the insertion of a case-control study within a cohort study (see below). While the cohort study may be prospective, the nested case-control study cannot be conducted until both the outcomes and exposures have occurred, therefore the nested study is again retrospective.

One of the great challenges in designing a case-control study is identifying the proper control group. If interested in studying risk factors for lung cancer, for example, the cases are clearly individuals with lung cancer. But what characteristics are appropriate for the controls? This question is best addressed by considering the goal in establishing a control group. The control group clearly cannot have the outcome, in this case lung cancer; that is what distinguishes them from cases. But ideally they should be just as susceptible to the outcome as the cases. If that is true, then the difference between groups with regard to outcome should be referable to some difference in exposure. Often, though, a case-control study is conducted when the relevant exposures are uncertain; that is the reason for conducting such a study. In the effort to assemble case and control groups as alike as possible, they might inadvertently be matched on the basis of an important exposure variable. For example, if the cases and controls in a study of lung cancer were required to have the same exposure to cigarettes, the association between smoking and lung cancer would be missed. This condition is referred to as "overmatching," and it is a threat to any case-control study.[5] If, however, the two groups differ too extensively, attribution of the outcome to any particular exposure becomes impossible. For example, if the cases are older than the controls, the development of lung cancer might simply be age-related, with the controls not yet experiencing the disease but destined to at some time in the future.

While all of the subtleties involved in the establishment of an appropriate control group are the problem of the investigators rather than the readers, the reader is ill prepared to interpret a case-control study if he or she is not appreciative of the implications of control group composition. If groups are too comparable, the causal role of important exposures may be missed. If not sufficiently comparable, differences in outcome between groups may be attributable to characteristics or exposures other than those reported. For better or for worse, there are no rules to apply that categorize a control as appropriate or inappropriate. Each reader needs to consider the issue and apply his or her own judgment. Reasonable guidelines would include comparability in age, gender, socioeconomic status, and population context. For example, if the cases are identified in the hospital, a hospital-based control group is generally indicated.[6,7] When cases are found in the "community" (i.e., not in a healthcare setting), controls should be community-based. Case-control studies in industrial settings generally require that both groups perform similar types of work.

The case-control study is limited with regard to outcome; only the outcome variable upon which group assignment is predicated can be studied. In contrast, multiple exposure variables can be evaluated. In the hypothetical example, subjects with and without lung cancer could disclose information, through direct questioning, the questioning of a surrogate, written survey, record review or some combination of these methods about diet, physical activity, alcohol, cigarettes, sunlight, illicit drugs, pharmaceuticals, or virtually anything else. The identification of a statistically significant association between the outcome and any exposure variable studied becomes the basis for reportable findings.

While the case-control study permits evaluation of a diverse group of exposure variables, certain caveats warrant mention. Support for a causal relationship is strongest if the apparent association both fulfills Mill's canons (see Chapter 6) and is consistent with prior hypotheses regarding the causal pathway. Statistically significant relationships that emerge from a case-control study that were not *a priori* hypotheses should be the basis for subsequent hypothesis testing. Again, no data set should be used both to generate and test a particular hypothesis. An additional and important limitation of the case-control study is that the temporal sequence of putative cause and putative effect can never be ascertained with certainty. As both outcome (effect) and exposure (cause) have already occurred, only inference can determine that exposure occurred first. Tobacco company executives exploited this weakness when case-control studies suggested that smoking caused lung cancer. They suggested, in congressional testimony, that nascent lung cancer came first, stimulating an urge to smoke.[8] While this incredible argument was eventually retracted, it nonetheless points out the inevitable limitations of a retrospective study.

In addition to the methodologic limitations of the case-control study, there are other threats to its reliability. As with other study designs, these come in the form of **confounding** and **bias**. The apparent associations between exposure and outcome in such a study may be masked or revealed by unstudied factors. Because all of an individual's exposures can never be inventoried, a case-control study never considers all possible explanations for the outcome. For this reason, and because the temporal sequence can never be asserted with complete assurance, a case-control study never provides definitive evidence of a causal association. That said, as noted below, sometimes the evidence from case-control studies is both quite convincing and the best evidence obtainable. Smoking and lung cancer again make for a good example. An intervention trial, in which one group were made to smoke, and another prohibited from doing so, is clearly not feasible for obvious reasons.

The creation of an apparent association where one does not exist is **positive confounding**. Any unstudied exposure in a case-control that is causally linked to the outcome and correlated with one or more of the exposures that are studied will positively confound the association between the studied exposure(s) and the outcome. Conversely, a third variable that correlates with a studied exposure and reduces the risk of the outcome may mask a true association; this **is negative confounding**. Only known confounders can be controlled in case-control studies.

While any systematic differences in the identification of exposures would introduce **bias**, such measures are under the control of the investigator. A threat unique to retrospective studies, **recall bias** may be nearly impossible to eliminate from case-control studies. Recall bias is differential recollection of past exposures by virtue of differences in the outcome. In general, cases are more likely to recall exposures that may have contributed to the development of disease; controls, not having developed the outcome, may lack the necessary stimulus to remember long-ago exposures.

Given these limitations, why are case-control studies conducted? First, case-control studies can assemble a group with a rare outcome so that its etiology can be explored. In an extreme example, the entire world's known cases of some very rare disease might be studied together. In most other types of study, the outcome would need to be awaited. In the case of a rare disease, the wait would be prohibitively long, or the sample size (see Chapter 9) required to achieve an adequate number of outcome events prohibitively large. This leads to another strength of the case-control study: it is inexpensive. No intervention is required, and no time needs to elapse. The study can be quickly completed, and the sample is often limited. As noted in Chapter 7, the odds ratio is often used to measure outcome in such studies, and serves as an approximation of the risk ratio.

∰ COHORT ﬆUDIEﬆ

Whereas case-control studies are defined by groups assembled on the basis of outcome, **cohort studies** are defined by the assembly of groups on the basis of exposure. The temporal sequence of events is not the defining characteristic of either study type. While case-control studies are inevitably retrospective, cohort studies may be retrospective or prospective.

The fundamental comparison in a cohort study is between (or among) groups with different exposures of interest. At the time that the groups are defined, the outcome has yet to occur. Because groups are assembled on the basis of exposure, **only those exposure variables defined at the start of the study can be evaluated**. However, cohort studies permit evaluation of multiple outcomes.

∰ RETROﬆPECTIVE COHORT ﬆUDIEﬆ

Cohort studies in which groups are identified on the basis of exposure at some point in the **past**, and then followed forward to the more recent past to establish the outcome(s) of interest are retrospective. Unlike case-control studies, **retrospective cohort studies** do permit reasonably secure inferences to be drawn about temporal association, although this association is somewhat dependent on the outcome measure. For example, if the outcome measure is death and the exposure is smoking, a cohort of smokers and a cohort of non-smokers is identified at some point in the past, then followed forward to determine the rate of mortality in each group. The outcome cannot have been present prior to the exposure. If, on the other hand, the outcome measure can go unnoticed for some time—such as hypertension or asthma—a retrospective cohort study cannot exclude the possibility that the outcome was already present at the time the cohorts were established.

Retrospective cohort studies offer the advantages of speed and low cost, as the entire subject experience of interest has already elapsed, and need only be elucidated. When the outcome measure is one that must have occurred after the exposure, such studies may offer fairly conclusive evidence of causality. One example is a study examining the mortality associated with exposure to coal dust among workers in Italy.[9] The study began by defining exposure, then followed the cohort forward through the past and collected mortality data. The death rate in the workers was then compared to the adjusted death rate for the general population.

This design has important weaknesses. As noted, relatively "soft" measures of outcome (those open to wide interpretation, and apt to vary by observer) or potentially latent measures of outcome cannot reliably be timed relative to exposure. Access to information obtained in the past may be difficult and at times impossible. Subjects in the study may have been treated, followed, and evaluated quite differently over the period of interest, introducing **measurement** or **detection bias**. By anticipating these potential weaknesses and compensating for them in the planning stage, retrospective cohort studies can be methodologically robust. They offer the advantage of time and cost efficiency. However, when the outcome of interest is rare, a case-control study is generally preferred.

∭ PROSPECTIVE COHORT STUDIES

In a **prospective cohort study** groups are assembled in the present on the basis of exposure or intervention and then followed into the **future** for the development of outcomes. When the outcome of interest occurs rarely, or takes a long time to occur, such studies are very expensive, lengthy, and large. For outcomes that occur commonly and/or rapidly, such studies provide the most convincing evidence of causality. When the exposure of interest occurs by chance or by subject choice, the study requires no intervention *per se* and is considered an **observational cohort study**. An example might be the evaluation, by comparable means and over a specified period, of workers in two industries for occupational injuries. When the exposure of interest is actively administered, the study is an intervention trial. An example is the assembly of a group to receive, and another group not to receive a particular vaccine, and then following both groups comparably for the detection of the infection of interest. Observational cohort studies, and non-randomized intervention trials, are subject to **selection bias** and **confounding**. Subjects choosing the "exposure" may differ systematically from those not choosing the exposure, and these differences might account wholly or partly for any differences in outcome.

In an **intervention trial**, selection bias may be overcome by randomly assigning subjects to receive the intervention or not. However, if subjects know that they either are or are not receiving the intervention, this knowledge might influence the outcome. The benefits of attention (or simply awareness of being the subject of investigation), regardless of the specific intervention, may influence outcomes; this influence is known as the **Hawthorne effect**. The Hawthorne effect is prevented by administering a placebo (either agent or intervention), and blinding subjects to their treatment status (i.e., active intervention or control condition). Under such circumstances, investigators might treat the subjects in each group differently to try and promote the outcome of interest unless they, too, are blinded to treatment status. Thus, the most rigorous prospective cohort studies are randomized, placebo-controlled, and double blind (i.e., neither subject nor investigator knows the subjects' treatment status). These so-called **randomized clinical trials** (**RCTs**) are considered state-of-the-art and provide the most conclusive evidence of causality in clinical studies of humans.

However, even when a prospective cohort study putatively carries all the requisite bells and whistles of methodologic rigor, such as randomization, placebo-control, and double blinding, bias can be introduced into the statistical analysis that could undermine, or even invalidate, the findings. Among the more flagrant, and common, liberties taken with RCTs is to analyze the experience of only those subjects completing all aspects of the intervention, rather than those randomized. Once subjects are deleted from the groups established by random assignment, the groups are no longer random, and **selection bias** is reintroduced. For example, consider a chemotherapeutic regimen effective in a small subset of patients, but leading to intolerable side effects in the majority. If such an intervention were analyzed in only those subjects able to tolerate it, it would look promising. If the entire group assigned to the treatment were analyzed, the outcomes of those unable to complete the treatment would be included, and would appropriately dilute the benefits of treatment so that the overall experience of those assigned to the regimen were revealed. The commitment to analyze the outcomes of an RCT on the basis of randomization, regardless of subject experience, is known as **intention-to-treat analysis**, as subjects are evaluated on the basis of what treatment was intended for them. This approach is also referred to as **the need to analyze as randomized**, and is considered an important aspect of investigative integrity. For example, a study of Ginkgo biloba reported in *JAMA*[10] reveals post-randomization adjustment of the cohorts that may compromise the validity of the outcomes claimed. In a compelling demonstration of the importance of intention-to-treat analysis, subject adherence, and the placebo effect, Horwitz and colleagues showed that while subjects in the Beta Blocker Heart Attack trial who complied with the intervention were less likely to have a fatal MI, so were those who were assigned to placebo and adhered to that.[11] While intention-to-treat analysis would reveal the effects of assignment to a particular treatment on outcome, analyzing only those who adhered to that assignment would automatically incorporate the characteristics of select subjects and potentially introduce bias.

The second common and potentially problematic liberty taken with otherwise rigorous RCT's is **data dredging** and **sub-group analysis**. As discussed in Chapter 9, only finite protection against false-positive and false-negative error can be accorded to any statistical test of association. By convention, the risk of a false-positive error is limited to 5%. However, this pertains to each hypothesis tested unless adjustments are made for multiple associations. If the risk of false-positive error is 1 in 20 and no adjustment is made for the testing of multiple associations, the probability of a false-positive outcome approximates 1 as the number of tests nears 20. The temptation to test multiple hypotheses and analyze patient subgroups is great when a large investment has been made in a randomized trial, some of which cost millions of dollars. This temptation can be legitimately indulged when statistical adjustments are made to keep the aggregate risk of false-positive error at the 5% level. While these methods are beyond the scope of this discussion,[12] an appreciation for their relevance is not. When multiple associations are reported from a single trial, either in one or a series of publications, and the papers do not specify an effort to adjust for multiple associations, the reported results should be approached with some degree of skepticism. However, the same large trials that are most likely to encourage multiple hypothesis testing are also most conducive to revealing true and important associations; the Nurses' Health Study is a good example.[13] This even scepticizm can be approached with a certain degree of scepticism!

≋ RANDOMIZED CLINICAL TRIALS

Randomized clinical trials, having become the gold standard for establishing evidence of causal associations in medical investigation, are a tempting consideration for any clinical researcher. However, that temptation is mitigated by the challenges of such trials. Depending on the outcome of interest, RCT's may require years to complete. Unless the outcome is very common, such studies will generally require very large samples. The combination of size, length, and rigorous controls leads to enormous expense. Multi-center RCT's may cost millions, or even tens of millions of dollars. As a consequence, funding for such trials from federal sources (such as the National Institutes of Health [NIH]) is extremely competitive. Most large RCT's are funded by the pharmaceutical industry.

Another factor that may preclude this approach is ethical considerations. These typically arise in two ways. First, once a practice has become the **standard of care**, subjecting it to a randomized trial is arduous at best, impossible at worst. The unfortunate aspect of this is that the RCT has only become the gold standard over recent years, and much of what was standard medical practice in the past was never subjected to what would now constitute rigorous investigation. A good example of such a practice is the insertion of right heart catheters (Swan-Ganz catheters) to obtain hemodynamic and volume status in critically unstable patients. Designed to provide needed information when none was previously available, such catheters were clinically embraced without ever being subjected to a randomized trial. In the non-randomized trials to date, including one by Connors et al. that generated quite a stir,[14] the insertion of these catheters has been associated with higher, not lower, mortality. Despite a call for either a RCT or a moratorium on the use of these catheters by editorialists in *JAMA*,[15] neither has occurred to date. This is not surprising in light of the clinical context: what patient or doctor would consent to randomization at a time of extreme clinical urgency? Whether correctly or not, clinicians have largely dismissed the results of non-randomized trials of right heart catheterization, attributing the results to selection bias or unknown confounders. This scenario re-emphasizes the comparability of the influential factors in research and clinical practice. The probability of benefit of a RCT is not deemed great enough to justify the anticipated risk, so to date the study has not been conducted. In more or less comparable ways, all established practices are difficult to investigate in RCTs.

The second situation in which an RCT is precluded is when the comparison of interest is unethical. Perhaps the best example of this problem is the research performed to establish the efficacy of AZT in interrupting the vertical transmission of HIV from mother to infant. An intensive zidovudine (AZT) regimen was studied in the US, and demonstrated that transmission rates were reduced by 70%.[16] The regimen involved protracted administration of AZT, which is often not feasible in developing countries with limited health care budgets. However, it was deemed unethical to study a shorter course of therapy in a RCT once the longer course was shown to be effective. Those subjects randomly assigned to the short course might not benefit, while those assigned to the longer course probably would. To overcome this concern, the decision was reached to study a shorter course of AZT in populations in Africa where only the shorter course could realistically be made available, and where *no treatment* was the standard of care. These trials resulted in intense and heated exchanges in the peer-reviewed literature in which the ethics of RCT's were debated.[17,18]

Finally, there is debate about the need for, and appropriateness of, placebo control in all clinical trials. This issue is addressed below (see ACES).

⚶ META-ANALYSIS

There are circumstances in which much-needed information cannot be obtained with a RCT. When results from less conclusive, often observational, studies are all that is available, a standard surrogate is meta-analysis. The approximation of RCT results with the aggregated results of observational studies has been described,[19,20] but also challenged.[21]

Meta-analyses, either qualitative or quantitative, aggregate the results of studies to establish a composite impression (qualitative) or measure (quantitative) of the strength of a particular association. A **qualitative meta-analysis** is essentially a systematic review of the literature on a particular topic. What distinguishes the qualitative meta-analysis from the review is the *standardized criteria* that are established to define the admissibility of a study. Only those studies with prestipulated methods and study populations are included.[22] All pertinent articles are reviewed, and the strengths and weaknesses of each described. Usually, the analysis indicates the number of controlled studies of the outcome in question and provides an impression, although not a statistical measure, of the weight of the evidence. Qualitative meta-analysis is the least methodologically demanding type.

Quantitative meta-analysis takes one of two forms. Either the data are analyzed as reported in the literature, or the raw data from multiple studies are obtained and aggregated.[22] The former is less demanding and time-consuming than the latter and does not require the same degree of cooperation from other investigators. A meta-analysis in which raw

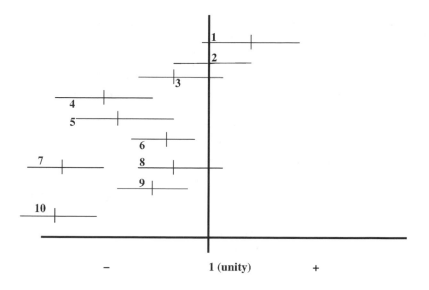

Figure 8.2. Display of results from a hypothetical qualitative meta-analysis of 10 trials of thrombolytic therapy. The vertical represents a relative risk of death of 1 (the line of unity).

data are aggregated requires that access to such data be accorded by the investigators responsible for each pertinent trial.

In either variety of quantitative meta-analysis, strict criteria are employed for the selection of pertinent studies. Despite these criteria, some variability in methods among studies is inevitable. This is generally measured in a **test of homogeneity**. The less variation in the trials included, the more meaningful the aggregate findings. Typically, when only the published data are used trials are displayed on plots that show whether or not they support an association, and if so with what degree of statistical significance. This is shown by setting a vertical line at a **relative risk** of 1 (no association), then plotting the 95% confidence intervals for the results of each study included. If, for example, one were trying to establish whether thrombolytic therapy reduces the risk of death from MI, the results of trials 1–10 might be displayed as shown in Figure 8.2. In this hypothetical scenario, 8 of 10 trials (trials 3–10) show a reduction in mortality as evidenced by a relative risk of death less than 1 with thrombolytic therapy. Of these 8 trials, the results are significant for 6 (trials 4, 5, 6, 7, 9, and 10) as evidenced by the displacement of the entire 95% confidence interval line to one side of the vertical line of unity (no effect). The other two trials (3 and 8) suggest a reduction in mortality, but failed to reach statistical significance. Two trials, 1 and 2, show no reduction in mortality. Trial 2 appears to show no effect on mortality of thrombolysis whatsoever, with the 95% confidence interval centered on the **line of unity**. Trial 1 suggests that thrombolysis actually increases mortality, but this trial did not reach statistical significance.

Would the aggregate information in Figure 8.2 be a sufficient basis to draw conclusions about the association between thrombolysis and MI survival? No. Information about the individual trials is still needed. While the weight of evidence strongly suggests a benefit, that is only true if all ten trials are comparable. If trials 3–10 are smaller or less rigorous than trials 1 and 2, the implications of these findings are quite uncertain. A quantitative meta-analysis is of use when it provides information on individual trial strengths and weaknesses, the comparability of the trials assessed, and the distribution of results.

The most rigorous form of meta-analysis is fully quantitative, aggregating raw data from multiple trials after assuring the comparability of subjects and methods among the trials included. Such meta-analyses are relatively rare, because they are very dependent on the availability of multiple, highly comparable trials. If such trials are convincing, a meta-analysis is generally unneeded. And if such trials are unconvincing, the probability of them having comparable subjects and methods is often low.

Despite these limitations, such analyses are occasionally done. As such analyses are typically limited to published data, they often assess the potential influence of **publication bias** by use of a **funnel plot**.[22] An example is an analysis of angioplasty in acute myocardial infarction,[23] in which the data from 23 separate trials were pooled together and reanalyzed.

Meta-analysis is predicated on either a **fixed effects** or a **random effects** model. In the former, the pooled data of the available studies are used to answer the question "is there evidence here of an outcome effect?" The data from the selected trials are considered to comprise the entire study sample. In random effects modeling, the data from the selected trials are presumed to constitute a representative sample of a larger population of studies. This approach is used to answer the question, "do the available data indicate that the larger population of data from which they were drawn provides evidence of an outcome effect?"[22]

Although it fills a niche among options for medical investigation, meta-analysis is itself subject to important limitations. Aggregated data invariably compound the errors intrinsic to the original sources. Heterogeneity of methods or of study subjects may result in the proverbial comparison between apples and oranges. The pitfalls of meta-analysis are revealed by the fact that their results may be different from the results of large RCT's.[24,25]

The **Cochrane Collaborative** is an organization devoted to the performance and dissemination of systematic reviews and meta-analyses based on consistent application of state-of-the-art methods. The organization supports a large number of study groups charged with the generation and updating of reviews in specific content areas. Cochrane reviews are accessible on-line at: www.Cochrane.org.

🍂 ACTIVE CONTROL EQUIVALENCE STUDIES (ACES)

There are times when the conventional approach to medical investigation, comparing an intervention to placebo, is simply inappropriate. Any time an established treatment exists for a condition that is known to be superior to placebo, the use of placebo should be weighed carefully.[26,27,28,29] While ethically laudable, this view poses a challenge to the study of new treatments in categories with established treatments. Against what standard should the new intervention be judged?

A logical answer is that the new therapy should be compared to the best old therapy. But to what end? Such a comparison might require that the new therapy be superior to the old, or simply that it be comparable, providing a new treatment option. The demonstration of *comparability* is particularly appropriate when the old treatment is effective but toxic. A new therapy comparably effective but less toxic would represent an advance.

An often overlooked method for such circumstances that is at times appropriate is the **active control equivalence study** (ACES).[30] As the name implies, in such studies the control is not a placebo but an active treatment. The goal of comparison is to demonstrate not difference but **equivalence**. A good example is a trial of a new chemotherapeutic regimen thought to be as effective as an old standard but also less likely to induce vomiting or neutropenia. For such trials, statistical methods are modified. Sample size is predicated on the need to detect a difference if one exists; false-negative error is minimized. Thus, the comparison will find a difference if there is one, and the failure to detect a difference becomes evidence for equivalence. The null hypothesis for such trials is the existence of a difference, while the alternative hypothesis is the absence of difference. Detailed discussions of ACES have been published.[30] Recent studies of gabapentin for painful neuropathies in which placebos were used are an example of opportunities for ACES that appear to have been overlooked.[31,32] The advantages, disadvantages, and optimal applications of ACES remain a subject of controversy.[26,27,28]

░ CROSSOVER TRIALS

When the effect of a treatment is transient, subjects may be assigned to sequential treatments and their responses to each compared. In such a study, subjects cross over from one treatment to the next, typically in random sequence. The advantage of such trials is that individual subjects may be compared to themselves rather than other controls with regard to the outcome effect(s) of interest, eliminating interindividual variation. The reduced variation (variance) in such trials allows for the use of statistical methods for paired comparisons, and smaller sample size. A smaller sample facilitates recruitment and generally reduces cost. A limitation of these studies is the need to account for any residual effects of one treatment before moving on to the next. This is addressed by interposing between active treatment cycles a **wash-out period**, the length of which should correspond to the time required for prior treatment effects to dissipate fully. A recent (2000) study of L-arginine in the treatment of interstitial cystitis provides an example.[33]

░ FACTORIAL TRIAL DESIGNS

Research tends to derive benefit from the "keep it simple" principle. A narrowly defined hypothesis is more readily tested than a complex one. That notwithstanding, the expense and effort involved in conducting a trial is such that there is a rationale for using the structure of a trial to derive as much useful information as possible. A factorial design represents a balance often struck between these opposing considerations. For example, in a 2×2 factorial design subjects are randomly assigned to

All Subjects			
Randomization			
Treatment A		Placebo A	
Randomization			
Treatment B	Placebo B	Treatment B	Placebo B

Treatment groups = Treatment A, Treatment B; Treatment A, Placebo B; Placebo A, Treatment B; Placebo A, Placebo B.

Figure 8.3. Treatment assignments in a 2 × 2 factorial design trial of treatments A and B.

treatment A or its placebo, and then the subjects in each of those two groups are randomly assigned to treatment B or its placebo. The result is four treatment groups, as shown in Figure 8.3.

The factorial design is appropriate when two treatments of interest are thought to interact in important ways, so that the comparison of each treatment alone to both together, as well as to placebo, is warranted. Alpha tocopherol and beta carotene effects on cancer prevention, for example, have been studied in this manner.[34,35]

※ OTHER STUDY DESIGNS

Often before the thoughts of association are entertained, information regarding general trends and prevalence of disease in a population is explored. The goal is primarily to elucidate the overall pattern of associations in a population (such as between exposures or risk factors and diseases) and to generate related hypotheses. **Cross-sectional studies** assess both exposure and outcome concurrently, often by use of survey or review of vital statistics or other aggregated data. The focus may be on individuals or on the population as a whole. Such studies are particularly suited for prevalence data but are of very limited utility in the elucidation of causality, because both exposure and outcome are measured simultaneously, and therefore temporal associations can be inferred but not shown. When cross-sectional studies are repeated sequentially, they are referred to as **longitudinal**, and can be used to demonstrate time trends in a population, again without definitive evidence of causality.

When a cross-sectional study assesses associations in a population, but not in the individual members of that population, it is referred to as an **ecological study**. Such studies might involve, for example, the proportion of a population using cell phones and the rate of brain tumors in the same population. A high rate of both cell phone use and brain cancer in a population would suggest an association, but would not (and could not) confirm one. The aggregate data for the population would not reveal whether the putative cause and the outcome were occurring in the same individuals. It might be that the brain tumors were occurring equally in those with and without cell phones, related to some unstudied variable also prevalent in the population. When causal inferences are generated based on an association in a population that is not applicable to the individuals in that population, it is known as the **ecological fallacy**, and is a particular weakness of ecological studies.[36]

Finally, the clinical literature often relies on other types of descriptive studies such as **case reports** and **case series**, which involve descriptions of individuals and small groups of individuals who share salient characteristics. In general, provocative descriptive studies should serve as the precursor to more formal studies of association.

The standard categories of medical investigation are not binding. The limits of study design are the limits of creativity and need. There are situations of need for which the appropriate study design has yet to be determined. The approaches described here are illustrative rather than comprehensive. An understanding of conventional trial designs, their applications, strengths, and weaknesses provides a basis for assessing the appropriateness and reliability of published studies of all varieties. Such informed assessment should be prerequisite to the application of published results to patient care.

∰ SAMPLING

There are various ways in which a clinical study or trial can be of value. It might generate novel and provocative hypotheses, or it might test hypotheses of clinical interest. For the clinician, the value of any trial resides in the applicability of its findings to practice. To transfer the results of a trial to the office or ward requires that the sample of study subjects share characteristics with the patient or population of patients. This correspondence is referred to as the **external validity** of the study, meaning its applicability to populations and individuals other than those actually studied. While the **internal validity** of a study is a gauge of its correctness and reliability, the external validity is a gauge of its relevance in the real world.

The external validity of a study depends in part on the sample of subjects and the methods used in the sample's assembly. To ensure that a study sample is representative of some larger population to which the findings will be considered relevant, **probability sampling** is the preferred method. In this approach, each member of the population has some defined probability of being selected to participate. The method can be adjusted so that subgroups in the population are sufficiently represented to allow for group-specific assessment of outcome and association. When there are no particular subgroups of interest, simple **random sampling** may be applied, in which each member of the population has an equal probability of selection.

When participation in a trial requires particular effort, exposure to a novel agent or intervention, or a willingness to accept placebo, many potential subjects are likely to decline participation. Therefore, random or probability sampling is unlikely to be feasible for most randomized controlled trials. The participants in such trials are likely to differ systematically from others unwilling to participate. A potential weakness of such trials, despite their rigorous methods and generally high degree of internal validity when well performed, is their questionable generalizability. The more burdensome the intervention in such trials, and the more it deviates from standard clinical practice, the less likely the participants are to represent the larger population of patients from which they were drawn. When sampling is based on the convenient accessibility of potential participants as well as their willingness to participate, it is referred to as **convenience sampling**. In interpreting clinical trials, consideration of sampling is helpful in making determinations of generalizability to a particular patient or patients.

﹌ AﬅﬅEﬅﬅING ﬅTUDY VALIDITY

The assessment of the validity of the medical literature is an essential step in its judicious application to patient care. To some extent, the busy clinician will be inclined to depend on the peer-review process and the editorial staff of journals to defend against the publication of invalid outcomes and conclusions. This is by no means unreasonable, as the peer-review and editorial processes, when working well, do indeed provide some protection.[37] Nonetheless, findings of dubious validity, and certainly of dubious applicability to one's patients, do find their way into the literature. A capacity to gauge the validity of any study oneself is a useful attribute and prudent precaution.

There are general criteria in the assessment of study validity that can be applied in virtually all cases. The clinical question should be clearly defined and the study type appropriate to answer that question. The outcome effect should be clearly stated, and the requisite measures of significance provided to know the probability that such an effect would be observed on the basis of randomness or chance. When multiple hypotheses or associations are tested in a single trial, the aggregate risk of a random, positive outcome must be explicitly addressed; statistical methods are available to compensate for the probabilistic hazards of multiple comparisons[38] and their use in such papers should be specifically cited. Such methods, in general, reduce the threshold of false-positive error for each individual association tested so that the aggregated risk of a false-positive is at an acceptable level, typically 0.05. When a data set is used to test multiple hypotheses without adjustment for doing so, the unflattering descriptions often applied include **data-dredging**, a fishing expedition, or torturing the data until they confess. The clinical significance of the outcome effect should be interpretable and considered separately from the statistical significance. The characteristics of the sample studied, the inclusion and exclusion criteria, should be considered to assess the external validity, or generalizability.

The specific characteristics of each type of study must be implemented appropriately to protect validity. For example, a cohort study requires that members of each cohort be comparably susceptible to the outcome, other than by virtue of the exposure under investigation. A case-control study is only valid if the cases and controls are sufficiently alike, and yet not too alike, other than with regard to the outcome of interest, to have comparable probability of prior exposures of interest. For the benefits of randomization to validity to be realized, the groups must be analyzed as randomized, regardless of their compliance or adherence to treatment, an approach referred to as intention-to-treat analysis. The assessment of validity based on specific study type or measure of outcome is addressed in many of the *Users' Guides to the Medical Literature* articles (see Text Sources, p. 279), as well as in other sources.[39]

Among the important steps in assessing and verifying study validity is consideration of bias and confounding (see Chapter 6). Confounding is introduced whenever a third variable is associated with both the exposure and outcome of interest, and either accounts for their apparent association (positive confounding) or masks their actual one (negative confounding). The definitive means of controlling for confounders (i.e., preventing them from distorting the measure of association and invalidating the study) is randomization, which protects against both known and unknown confounders. Other methods exist for protection against known confounders, including matching, restriction, stratification, and statistical adjustment. **Matching** requires that members of each study group share a particular trait. **Restriction** limits recruitment to those individuals with or without a particular trait, or particular traits. **Stratification** divides study subjects into groups based on one or more particular traits, and makes comparisons between comparable strata in each group. **Statistical adjustment** builds the potentially confounding variables into models that test for significance with the "third" variable(s) accounted for. However, adjustment cannot compensate for bias in the study design.

Valid results depend on the elimination of bias from the conduct of the study and the interpretation of its results. **Randomization** precludes bias in treatment assignment (allocation bias). **Blinding** of subjects (as opposed to an **open** or **open-label** approach), in which treatment assignment is concealed, along with use of a placebo, compensates for any possible **placebo effect**, and comparable contact for subjects in all groups prevents a **Hawthorne effect**. The placebo effect is a therapeutic response to an inert treatment,[40] and the Hawthorne effect is a change in outcome simply due to being under observation in a trial, or a therapeutic effect of increased contact time with investigators or care providers.[41] Blinding of the investigators protects against measurement and treatment bias. **Intention to treat analysis** preserves the protection afforded by randomization. **Random** or **probability sampling** protects against sampling bias with regard to the population of interest. A final consideration is how readily the results achieved in a trial might be translated to the less controlled circumstances of clinical practice, even when they are apparently generalizable. The **efficacy** of a treatment is a measure of its influence on outcome under near ideal circumstances, such as those produced in a controlled trial. **Effectiveness**, of greater clinical interest, is a measure of treatment influence on outcome under real-world conditions.

≫ THE STRENGTH OF EVIDENCE

Among the better examples of an evidence-based compendium of clinical guidelines is the work of the U.S. Preventive Services Task Force.[42] The Task Force has published reports providing guidance in the clinical application of preventive services based on the extent and quality of available evidence. In their report, the Task Force assigns a letter grade to indicate the overall strength of evidence, ranging from "A" for strong evidence of benefit, through "C" indicating substantial uncertainty, to "E" indicating evidence of probable harm. In the process, the Task Force established a semiquantitative approach to the evaluation of evidence of general utility. Large, randomized trials were considered to provide highest quality evidence. Well designed but nonrandomized controlled trials were considered one notch down. Rigorously controlled cohort or case-control studies were another notch down. Time series data were another notch down. Case reports and expert opinion were considered least definitive. Basic science research, including animal research, was not included in the Task Force algorithm, although such sources of evidence are of some use in generating hypotheses, and perhaps even in guiding clinical decisions when there is clear need for intervention and no other evidence available. The details of applying this scale are available in the report (see Appendix A). The general principles are sufficient, however, to facilitate a basic assessment of the strength of evidence conveyed by a single study or group of studies returned from a search of the literature (see Appendix A).

≫ CONSTRUCTIVELY DECONSTRUCTING THE MEDICAL LITERATURE

A building inspector may never have built a house, but he/she knows a good one (or bad one) when he/she sees one. Similarly, you may never design or conduct a clinical trial, but it will serve you well to know how a good one is constructed so you, too, know a good one, or bad one, when you see it.

As indicated in Chapter 6, study design should be a nearly final step in the development of means to test a particular hypothesis. Before a study is constructed, or a particular methodology adapted, specific measures of exposure (or intervention) and outcome should have been defined. The magnitude of the anticipated outcome effect, as well as the projected variance in the data, should be applied in sample size determination. The methods section of a paper should consistently indicate the level of alpha required for significance (conventionally, 0.05), and the level of beta or its complement, power. Often power is not reported, raising questions about the validity of negative findings.

When a study assembles subjects into groups on the basis of exposure, it is a cohort design. For such studies, a dichotomous outcome may be measured using the risk ratio, with 95% confidence intervals to indicate significance. Alternatively, if groups are assembled on the basis of outcome, the study is case-control, and cannot legitimately use the risk ratio for dichotomous outcome data; the odds ratio should be used as an approximation.

Methods of data analysis should be matched to the types of variables, both independent and dependent, of interest. When variables that are continuous and more or less normally distributed in the population are being analyzed, parametric methods are appropriate. When non-normal or non-continuous data are being used, nonparametric methods are more appropriate. When a dichotomous outcome measure occurs over time (e.g., death) survival analysis is appropriate. Sources are available with detailed information about matching analytical methods to various types of data.[12,38,43]

A basic understanding of any article (and the interest it holds) may be discerned by asking and answering *what* (is the hypothesis) *why* (does this hypothesis matter) *how* (was the hypothesis tested) and *in whom* (was the hypothesis tested). Additional questions are required to assess the study construction more fully. If cases and controls were matched, were they matched appropriately, neither too much nor too little? Were efforts made to reduce the influence of bias, especially recall bias? In a cohort study, were the groups at comparable risk of the outcome? Was sampling representative of the underlying population? Was randomization used to compensate for even unknown confounders? Were both subjects and investigators blinded in appropriate ways to prevent a Hawthorne effect, measurement bias and other related biases? If multiple hypotheses were tested, were statistical adjustments made? In a RCT, was there explicit acknowledgement of an intention-to-treat analysis?

By knowing the basic elements of sound construction for clinical trials, you may approach each article you read with specific expectations about methods. When these expectations are met, you may feel more secure that the results can be trusted. However, when these expectations are not met you should consider whether flaws in the design and construction of the study are such that the results cannot be trusted to stand.

SUMMARY/TAKE-AWAY MESSAGES

Variation in the design of clinical trials is necessary to allow for the testing and generation of diverse hypotheses. Although there is in general a hierarchy of methodologic rigor, culminating in the **randomized controlled trial** (**RCT**), not all hypotheses can, or necessarily should, be tested in a RCT. Among the considerations other than the quality of evidence is the ethics of the trial (i.e., use of a placebo or randomization might be unethical), time constraints, cost, and the frequency with which the outcome occurs.

Cross-sectional surveys, including **ecological studies**, are generally used to generate rather than formally test hypotheses. **Case-control studies** are particularly appropriate in the study of rare outcomes. In such studies, groups are assembled on the basis of outcome, and assessed for differences in exposure. Multiple exposures, but only one outcome, may be assessed. **Cohort studies** are defined by the assembly of groups on the basis of exposure (including exposure to an intervention) and their assessment for differences in outcome. Only one exposure, but multiple outcomes, may be assessed. Cohort studies may be **prospective** or **retrospective**. RCT's represent a particularly stringent variety of prospective cohort study.

Data from small trials may be more meaningful when aggregated. Various types of **meta-analysis** are used for this purpose.

Each trial design has intrinsic strengths and weaknesses. In addition, each is associated with constraints that help protect the validity of the data produced. For example, if a single study is used to generate and test multiple hypotheses, the risk of chance associations is high. Therefore, hypotheses generated in one study should be tested in another. When **multiple hypotheses** are tested in a single data set, protection against the statistical risk of a false positive result should be adjusted. In a randomized trial, groups should generally be **analyzed as randomized** (i.e., **intention-to-treat analysis**), or **bias** is likely to be introduced. The astute reader should approach the literature with particular expectations in mind; the trials that fulfill these expectations are more likely to be of clinical utility than those that fail to do so. Even methodologically rigorous trials, with a high degree of internal validity, may not provide data of true relevance to a particular patient or group of patients depending on the methods of **sampling** and the degree to which study participants represent the larger population from which they were drawn. The **validity** of a study should be assessed on the basis of explicit criteria, some of which are universally applicable, others of which pertain to specific study designs only. Among the principal goals in assessing study validity are the consideration of the adequacy of controls for bias and confounding, the generalizability, the statistical significance, and the clinical significance of the findings.

Understanding the principles of trial design allows one to approach articles with expectations in mind for appropriate methods. A comparison of the reported to the expected methods serves as a means of efficiently judging the likely quality of a trial. Trial results are almost invariably expressed in statistical terms that serve as the basis for discussion, implications, and recommendations. Thus an at least rudimentary understanding of the statistical results commonly presented in the literature is useful, if not essential, in the judicious interpretation and application of published evidence. Such interpretation is the subject of Chapter 9.

🖋 🖋 🖋

🖋 REFERENCES

1. Kiecolt-Glaser JK, Glaser R. Psychoneuroimmunology and cancer: Fact or fiction? *Eur J Cancer.* 1999;35:1603–1607.
2. Rozlog LA, Kiecolt-Glaser JK, Marucha PT, Sheridan JF, Glaser R. Stress and immunity: Implications for viral disease and wound healing. *J Periodontol.* 1999;70:786–792.
3. Feinleib M. Data bases, data banks and data dredging: The agony and the ecstasy. *J Chronic Dis.* 1984;37:783–790.
4. Stefanini GF, Foschi FG, Castelli E, et al. Alpha-1-thymosin and transcatheter arterial chemoembolization in hepatocellular carcinoma patients: A preliminary experience. *Hepatogastroenterology.* 1998;45:209–215.
5. Jorm AF, Easteal S. Assessing candidate genes as risk factors for mental disorders: The value of population-based epidemiological studies. *Soc Psychiatry Psychiatr Epidemiol.* 2000;35:1–4.
6. Cooper C, Eslinger D, Nash D, al-Zawahri J, Stolley P. Repeat victims of violence: Report of a large concurrent case-control study. *Arch Surg.* 2000;135:837–843.
7. Zodpey SP, Tiwari RR, Kulkarni HR. Risk factors for haemorrhagic stroke: A case-control study. *Public Health.* 2000;114:177–182.
8. Doll R. Uncovering the effects of smoking: Historical perspective. *Stat Methods Med Res.* 1998;7:87–117.

9. Petrelli G, Menniti-Ippolito F, Taroni F, Raschetti R, Magarotto G. A retrospective co-hort mortality study on workers of two thermoelectric power plants: Fourteen-year follow-up results. *Eur J Epidemiol.* 1989;5:87–89.

10. Le Bars PL, Katz MM, Berman N, Itil TM, Freedman AM, Schatzberg AF. A placebo-controlled, double-blind, randomized trial of an extract of Ginkgo biloba for dementia. North American Egb Study Group. *JAMA.* 1997;278:1327–1332.

11. Horwitz RI, Viscoli CM, Berkman L, et al. Treatment adherence and risk of death after a myocardial infarction. *Lancet.* 1990;336:542–545.

12. Motulsky H. *Intuitive Biostatistics.* New York: Oxford University Press; 1995.

13. Hu FB, Stampfer MJ, Manson JE, et al. Trends in the incidence of coronary heart disease and changes in diet and lifestyle in women. *N Engl J Med.* 2000;343:530–537.

14. Connors AF Jr, Speroff T, Dawson NV, et al. The effectiveness of right heart catheter-ization in the initial care of critically ill patients. SUPPORT Investigators. *JAMA.* 1996;276:889–897.

15. Dalen JE, Bone RC. Is it time to pull the pulmonary artery catheter? *JAMA.* 1996;276:916–918.

16. Connor EM, Mofenson LM. Zidovudine for the reduction of perinatal human immun-odeficiency virus transmission: Pediatric AIDS Clinical Trial Group Protocol 076— results and treatment recommendations. *Pediatr Infect Dis J.* 1995;14:536–541.

17. Perinatal HIV Intervention Research in Developing Countries Workshop participants. Science, ethics, and the future of research into maternal infant transmission of HIV-1. *Lancet.* 1999;353:832–835.

18. Lurie P, Wolfe SM. Unethical trials of interventions to reduce perinatal transmis-sion of the human immunodeficiency virus in developing countries. *N Engl J Med.* 1997;337:853–856.

19. Benson K, Hartz J. A comparison of observational studies and randomized, controlled trials. *N Engl J Med.* 2000;342:1878–1886.

20. Concato J, Shah N, Horwitz RI. Randomized, controlled trials, observational studies, and the hierarchy of research designs. *N Engl J Med.* 2000;342:1887–1892.

21. Pocock SJ, Elbourne DR. Randomized trials or observational tribulations? *N Engl J Med.* 2000;342:1907–1909.

22. Petitti DB. *Meta-Analysis, Decision Analysis, and Cost-Effectiveness Analysis. Methods for Quantitative Synthesis in Medicine.* 2nd ed. New York: Oxford University Press; 2000.

23. Michels KB, Yusuf S. Does PTCA in acute myocardial infarction affect mortality and reinfarction rates? A quantitative overview (meta-analysis) of the randomized clinical trials. *Circulation.* 1995;91:476–485.

24. Lelorier J, Gregoire G, Benhaddad A, Lapierre J, Derderian F. Discrepancies between meta-analyses and subsequent large randomized, controlled trials. *N Engl J Med.* 1997;337:536–542.

25. Bailar JC. The promise and problems of meta-analysis. *N Engl J Med.* 1997;337:559–560.

26. Temple R, Ellenberg SS. Placebo-controlled trials and active-control trials in the eval-uation of new treatments. Part 1: Ethical and scientific issues. *Annals Int Med.* 2000;133:455–463.

27. Ellenberg SS, Temple R. Placebo-controlled trials and active-control trials in the eval-uation of new treatments. Part 2: Practical issues and specific cases. *Annals Int Med.* 2000;133:464–470.

28. Simon R. Are placebo-controlled clincal trials ethical or needed when alternative treat-ments exist? *Annals Int Med.* 2000;133:474–475.

29. De Deyn PP, D'Hooge R. Placebos in clinical practice and research. *J Med Ethics.* 1996;22:140–146.

30. Makuch R, Johnson M. Issues in planning and interpreting active control equivalence studies. *J Clin Epidemiol.* 1989;42:503–511.
31. Backonja M, Beydoun A, Edwards KR, et al. Gabapentin for the symptomatic treatment of painful neuropathy in patients with diabetes mellitus: A randomized controlled trial. *JAMA.* 1998;280:1831–1836.
32. Rowbotham M, Harden N, Stacey B, Bernstein P, Magnus-Miller L. Gabapentin for the treatment of postherpetic neuralgia: A randomized controlled trial. *JAMA.* 1998;280:1837–1842.
33. Cartledge JJ, Davies AM, Eardley I. A randomized double-blind placebo-controlled crossover trial of the efficacy of L-arginine in the treatment of interstitial cystitis. *BJU Int.* 2000;85:421–426.
34. The Alpha-Tocopherol, Beta Carotene (ATBC) Cancer Prevention Study Group. The effect of vitamin E and beta carotene on the incidence of lung cancer and other cancers in male smokers. *N Engl J Med.* 1994;330:1029–1035.
35. Albanes D, Malila N, Taylor PR. Effects of supplemental alpha-tocopherol and beta-carotene on colorectal cancer: Results from a controlled trial. *Cancer Causes Control.* 2000;11:197–205.
36. Piantadosi S, Byar DP, Green SB. The ecological fallacy. *Am J Epidemiol.* 1988;127:893–904.
37. Earnshaw JJ, Farndon JR, Guillou PJ, Johnson CD, Murie JA, Murray GD. A comparison of reports from referees chosen by authors or journal editors in the peer review process. *Ann R Coll Surg Engl.* 2000;82(4 Suppl):133–135.
38. Dawson-Saunders B, Trapp RG. *Basic & Clinical Biostatistics.* 2nd ed. Norwalk, CT: Appleton & Lange; 1994.
39. Fletcher RH, Fletcher SW, Wagner EH. *Clinical Epidemiology. The Essentials.* 3rd ed. Baltimore, MD: Williams & Wilkins; 1996.
40. Thompson WG. Placebos: A review of the placebo response. *Am J Gastroenterol.* 2000;95:1637–1643.
41. De Amici D, Klersy C, Ramajoli F, Brustia L, Politi P. Impact of the Hawthorne effect in a longitudinal clinical study: The case of anesthesia. *Control Clin Trials.* 2000;21:103–114.
42. U.S. Preventive Services Task Force (USPSTF). Guide to Clinical Preventive Services, 2nd ed. Alexandria, VA: International Medical Publishing; 1996.
43. Jekel, JF, Elmore JG, Katz DL. *Epidemiology, Biostatistics and Preventive Medicine.* Philadelphia, PA: Saunders; 1996.

TABLE 8.2   Prominent Characteristics of Various Study Types

Study Type	Group Assembly	Outcomes	Exposures	Strengths	Weaknesses	Special Considerations
Case-control	Based on the outcome of interest	Only the outcome used in group assembly can be studied	Unlimited exposures can be studied	Rare outcomes can be studied; quick (retrospective), inexpensive	Temporal sequence is uncertain; subject to bias (especially recall bias) and confounding	The study relies heavily on the appropriateness of the control group, which is subjective
Prospective cohort	Based on exposure	Multiple outcomes can be evaluated	Only the exposure used in group assembly can be studied	Provides potentially conclusive evidence of causality; the temporal sequence of exposure and outcome is generally known with considerable certainty	Time-consuming and often expensive; if not randomized, subject to selection bias and confounding by unknown factors; if not blinded, subject to measurement and detection biases	The strength of the evidence provided should be judged based on the comparability of the two (or more groups) with regard to both baseline characteristics other than the exposure of interest, as well as the methods of assessment and follow-up
Retrospective cohort	Based on exposure	Multiple outcomes can be evaluated	Only the exposure used in group assembly can be studied	A quick, inexpensive alternative to a prospective cohort study, providing potentially conclusive evidence of causality when the timing of the outcome can be determined with confidence, and all pertinent data can be assessed	The timing of subjective or latent outcomes cannot be fixed relative to the exposure variable; pertinent data may be inaccessible; differences in the treatment of subjects over time may introduce measurement and/or detection bias	With careful attention to the timing of the outcome measure, and the potentially variable treatment of the subjects over the study period, retrospective cohort studies can approximate the rigor of prospective studies at considerably lower costs in money and time

TABLE 8.2   Prominent Characteristics of Various Study Types (cont.)

Study Type	Group Assembly	Outcomes	Exposures	Strengths	Weaknesses	Special Considerations
Randomized trial	Based on exposure	Multiple outcomes can be evaluated	Only the exposure used in group assembly can be studied	The "gold-standard" for obtaining evidence of causality; randomization protects against both known and unknown confounders, while double-blinding protects against bias	Time-consuming and expensive; because of the often exacting inclusion and exclusion criteria and the rigorous controls, pertinence to populations other than the precise one studied (external validity or generalizability) is often limited or uncertain	Post-randomization adjustments of the cohorts can compromise the benefits of randomization; intention-to-treat analysis should be indicated in the methods; unless methods are used to adjust for multiple associations, the probability of false-positive error increases with each hypothesis or subgroup tested; due to expense, studies may be underpowered, and therefore subject to false-negative error; finally, inclusion and exclusion criteria should be examined before pertinence to patient care can be determined

TABLE 8.2   Prominent Characteristics of Various Study Types (cont.)

Study Type	Group Assembly	Outcomes	Exposures	Strengths	Weaknesses	Special Considerations
Meta-analysis	Not applicable; group assembly should be consistent among the studies being analyzed	Those in the studies being analyzed	Those in the studies being analyzed	May permit a more definitive assessment of association than the individual trials it aggregates; useful when cost or ethical constraints preclude a RCT	The quality of the meta-analysis is ultimately bounded by the quality and comparability of the individual studies assessed; quantitative meta-analysis is time-consuming and labor-intensive; there is no evidence that meta-analysis provides information more likely to influence clinical practice than a review of the literature	Qualitative meta-analysis is essentially a systematic review of the literature, with explicit criteria for the inclusion and exclusion of studies from the analysis; quantitative meta-analyses may compare the results of multiple studies using a standard measure, such as relative risk or odds ratios, or may aggregate raw data to produce a true summary measure of association; the latter variety are most rigorous but relatively uncommon
ACES	Based on intervention	Outcomes of interest include a particular therapeutic effect of the intervention, as well as adverse effects of the intervention	The intervention of interest	Facilitates the evaluation of new therapies when existing therapies are effective but toxic, rendering placebo-controlled trials ethically questionable	Often requires large sample sizes for adequate power	Should be considered in any situation where the availability of therapy makes the use of placebo inappropriate

TABLE 8.2 **Prominent Characteristics of Various Study Types (cont.)**

Study Type	Group Assembly	Outcomes	Exposures	Strengths	Weaknesses	Special Considerations
Cross-sectional (ecological)	Not applicable; a single population is assessed	Associations between variables on a population basis	Those of interest; multiple exposures can be assessed	Ease, expediency; low cost; useful for hypothesis generation	Temporal associations are uncertain; not well suited to testing hypotheses; generally inadequate to establish causality; conclusions cannot be made about individuals; subject to the ecological fallacy	Potentially useful means of characterizing a population and generating hypotheses for future study
Cross-sectional (individual)	Not applicable; a single population is generally assessed	Associations between variables, either at one time or over time, in a given population, on an individual basis	Those of interest; multiple exposures can be assessed	Ease, expediency; low cost; useful for hypothesis generation	Temporal associations are uncertain; not well suited to testing hypotheses; generally inadequate to establish causality	Potentially useful means of characterizing a population and generating hypotheses for future study; if repeated over time, may provide useful information about temporal trends in the population

Interpreting Statistics in the Medical Literature

The statistical significance of trial data is thought to influence the probability of publication. Once published, the conclusions, implications, and recommendations derived from a study lean heavily on the statistical significance of associations reported. Consequently, significance testing has a profound influence on the base of evidence for clinical practice, at least that portion conveyed in peer-reviewed journals. A basic understanding of how statistical significance is determined and reported is therefore fundamental to evidence-based practice.

There is, in general, no particular need for the clinician to be expert in biostatistics. However, the ultimate arbiter of medical evidence is the reporting of **statistical significance**. The importance of statistical significance is even greater than it appears in the published literature; it is an important determinant of what does and does not get published, and at what pace.[1,2,3,4] In addition to influencing the opinions of editors and reviewers, statistical significance is often used by investigators as the acid test of data; failing to achieve it, results may never even be submitted. The evidence upon which clinical practice should be based is largely that reported in the peer-reviewed literature; the reporting of that evidence is largely governed by measures of statistical significance. Therefore, an appreciation for the methods by which such measures are produced and reported is germane to all clinicians.

Significance may be clinical or statistical, or both. Clinical significance does not necessarily require analytical methods to be perceivable. The splinting of fractures may never have been subjected to a randomized, placebo-controlled trial, but the procedure obviously, and significantly, alters outcomes for the better. A trial result may fail to reach statistical significance, yet appear to be clinically significant. As is addressed later in this chapter, such an outcome is generally due to a limited sample size and lack of statistical power. More often, a trial may report a statistically significant finding of questionable clinical relevance. The distinction between the two varieties of significance is noteworthy. While clinical significance is the product of judgment and prevailing clinical standards, statistical significance is the product of strict rules or conventions.

≋ ЈTATIЈTICAL ЈIGNIFICANCE

Fundamentally, statistical significance is a convention defining our tolerance of doubt in the reporting of associations. Causality is never entirely disproved, and rarely proved with absolute certainty. Even an apparently very strong association between putative cause and putative effect might be random. The case is brought home by looking at a mundane example. If you flip a coin 100 times and get 75 heads and only 25 tails, you will be suspicious that the coin may be rigged in some way. You will be even more suspicious if you get 85 heads, and perhaps quite convinced if you get 95. But even if you get 100 heads in a row, you do not have absolute proof that the coin is rigged. Consider all of the people in all of history who have flipped coins. If the total number of coin tosses is in the millions, or tens of millions, then a cluster of 100 heads in a row might just be random. But it would still be extremely unlikely that it would happen to you. Therefore, you could assert with reasonable confidence that the coin is rigged.

The notions of reasonable confidence and unlikely outcomes are the determinants of conventions for measuring statistical significance. By convention, and for no better reason than that, statistical significance is generally defined as the appearance of an association that would occur randomly less than 5 times in 100. In other words, statistical significance is a measure of the probability of the particular study outcome obtained. The study results are interpreted relative to the null hypothesis of no association (see Chapters 6 and 7). If the null hypothesis is true, the study should not provide evidence of an association. In our example, the null hypothesis would be that the coin is not rigged. No evidence of association in a trial would be, for example, the identical performance of active agent and placebo; in a coin toss, it would be half heads and half tails.

Experience tells us, however, that even when we know a coin is not rigged, we will not often get exactly 50 heads and 50 tails per 100 tosses. Similarly, even if a drug and placebo perform comparably, the results in two groups of subjects are unlikely to be identical. Because of chance, or randomness, we may get more tails than heads or heads than tails. Our trial may show a slight benefit of drug, or a slight benefit of placebo.

But what if we were to perform 100 tosses of 100 different but identical coins? We might not expect each coin to produce exactly 50 heads and 50 tails, but we would very much expect that result to be the average of the 100 coins tossed. Similarly, if the drug we were studying were truly no more effective than placebo, then while we might reasonably expect the placebo to look better sometimes, and the drug to look better sometimes, the average result of 100 trials would be no difference.

Were we to plot the results of our 100 experiments (clinical trial or coin toss), we could expect a **normal distribution**. Most of the 100 (or 1000 or 10,000) trials would show a result very close to the group mean: i.e., no association. Fewer trials would show small deviation from the mean in one direction or the other (more heads than tails or *vice versa*; drug better than placebo or *vice versa*); still fewer trials would show moderate deviation from the mean to either direction; and even fewer trials would show extreme deviation. The deviation would be the result of random factors. The distribution of our results would be as shown in Figure 9.1.

The normal distribution was discussed briefly in Chapter 6, and in the context of the t-test in Chapter 7. Its key properties are relevant here. The probability of deviation to varying degrees from the group mean on the curve can be quantified. To do this requires a measure of both distance from the mean and the frequency with which trials will produce a result that discrepant from the mean. Distance from the mean for a sample of individual observations is measured in units of **standard deviation**, discussed in Chapter 6.

A normal distribution always contains 68% of all observations within 1 standard deviation on either side of the mean, and 95.4% of all obser-

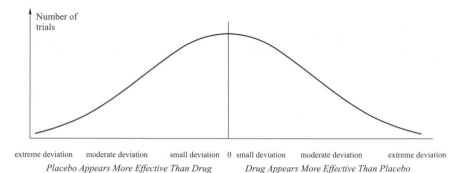

extreme deviation   moderate deviation   small deviation   0   small deviation   moderate deviation   extreme deviation

Placebo Appears More Effective Than Drug   *Drug Appears More Effective Than Placebo*

Figure 9.1. The distribution of the results of 100 trials comparing drug and placebo when the two have identical efficacy. The mean result of the 100 trials will be no difference between treatments. Studies will deviate to either side of the mean most commonly by a small amount, less commonly by a moderate amount, and least commonly by an extreme amount.

vations within 2 standard deviations on either side of the mean. Exactly 95% of all observations fall within 1.96 standard deviations on either side of the mean. When the sample of interest is not a group of individual data points, but rather a group of samples, such as when the results of multiple trials are being plotted, the appropriate measure of dispersion about the grand mean is the **standard error**. The standard error is the standard deviation divided by the square root of the sample size (*n*). The standard error is therefore smaller than the standard deviation, and the larger the sample size, the smaller the standard error becomes. This makes intuitive sense: the more observations on which a measure is based, the more reliable or stable it tends to be. A detailed discussion of the standard error is available elsewhere.[5,6,7]

Why is discussion of the dispersion of observations in a normal distribution pertinent and useful? If we know the probability that results of multiple trials will fall within a certain proximity to the mean, we also know the probability that they will not. The probability that a single trial will produce a result more than 1.96 standard errors in either direction from the mean of no effect is less than 5%. By convention, that result is improbable enough to cause us to think it is not due to chance. Thus, when a single trial gives a result more than 1.96 standard errors away from the null hypothesis of no treatment difference, we conclude that the result occurred not because of random factors, but because the null hypothesis is wrong. The null hypothesis (that there is no difference) is therefore rejected, and the conclusion drawn that the trial demonstrates a statistically significant treatment effect.

Statistical significance and rejection of the null hypothesis are essentially the same. For that reason, the portion of the normal distribution discussed above in which a result will cause us to reject the null hypothesis is known as the **rejection region**. The remainder of the curve constitutes values that are acceptable and is known as the **acceptance region.** Because the rejection region of the normal distribution is out at the periphery, it is also referred to as the *tails of the distribution*.

ONE-TAILED AND TWO-TAILED TESTS OF SIGNIFICANCE

Consider again that we are comparing an ineffective drug to placebo in a single trial. We would expect the average trial result of 100 such experiments to be no treatment difference. We therefore expect the result of our single trial to be close to that average result. If it is extremely different from that average, we reject that average (the null hypothesis) and conclude that drug and placebo are not comparable after all.

But extreme differences can occur in two directions; are both of comparable interest? The answer is that it depends. If we know relatively little about a drug, we may be interested in investigating whether its effects on a clinical measure differ from placebo. Such a difference could be in either direction. If the clinical outcome measure were serum cholesterol, such a drug might lower it or raise it relative to placebo. We would want to identify either effect. To conclude that the drug were significantly different from placebo, we would need a result in the tails of the normal frequency distribution. And because a result in either direction would be of interest, we would need tails at either end of the curve. Because the convention is to define a result as statistically significant if it is 5% or less likely to occur by chance, the probability of our result landing in either tail should sum to 5%. In other words, the total portion of the distribution that we consider the rejection region is the most extreme 5%, but equally divided into a rejection region above the mean, and a rejection region below the mean. In order that the portion of the entire area under the curve taken up by two identical rejection regions add to 5%, each of the two rejection regions must take up 2.5% of the entire area under the curve. These are the operative conditions whenever a paper reports a **two-tailed test**

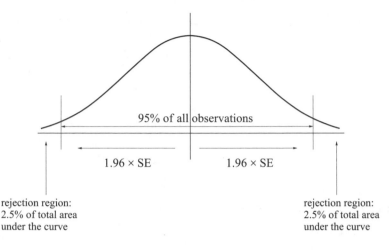

Figure 9.2. The rejection region of a normal distribution for a two-tailed test of statistical significance. The total rejection region constitutes 5% of the entire area under the curve, the conventional threshold for judging statistical significance. Each of two identical rejection regions takes up 2.5% of the entire area under the curve, and begins at 1.96 standard error units to one direction from the mean. SE = standard error.

of statistical significance. The two-tailed rejection region of a normal distribution is shown in Figure 9.2.

Alternatively, consider situations in which the effects of a treatment are known with some confidence. For example, an antihypertensive may be studied to see if it lowers blood pressure significantly more than a placebo, but there may be no concern that the drug will actually raise blood pressure. When the direction of treatment effect is known with considerable confidence, and only the magnitude of effect is under investigation, a **one-tailed test of significance** may be used. Under such conditions, 5% of the total area under the normal frequency distribution curve still represents the rejection region. But because any deviation from the mean (null) that is seen will predictably be in one direction only, the entire 5% rejection region can be placed to only one side of the mean. This places a large rejection region on one side of the curve, and none on the other side. These conditions are depicted in Figure 9.3.

When the direction of a treatment effect is known with some confidence, a one-tailed test of significance lessens the difficulty in producing a statistically significant result. Consider that the same experiment of an antihypertensive drug is conducted and subjected to either a one-tailed

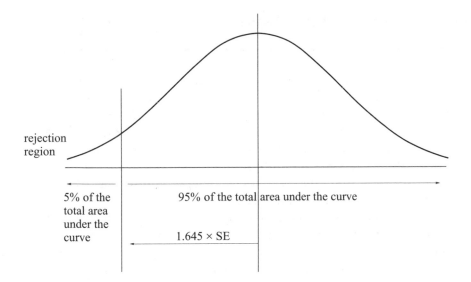

rejection
region

5% of the
total area
under the
curve

95% of the total area under the curve

1.645 × SE

Figure 9.3.   A normal distribution with one rejection region as used in a one-tailed test of significance. The total area under the curve allocated to the rejection region is still 5%, but it is now exclusively situated to one side of the mean. The rejection region begins 1.645 standard error units from the mean, rather than 1.96 standard error units as in a two-tailed test. Therefore, the rejection region occupies a larger portion of the half of the curve in which it is situated, even though it takes up no more of the total curve than the two rejection regions shown in Figure 9.2.

or a two-tailed test of significance. Assume that the drug lowered blood pressure an average of 10 mm Hg relative to placebo, and that this produced a result 1.7 standard error units from the mean of no difference. In a one-tailed test, this would reach statistical significance. In a two-tailed test, it would not.

The reason for this apparent paradox may well be self-evident by now. On the chance that it is not, an analogy may help. Consider that a football coach is screening potential quarterbacks by judging their throwing accuracy. They are asked to throw to a receiver within 5% of the sidelines (relative to the total width of the field). If they specify a preferred side in advance, they get to aim at the entire 5% on one side of the field. If they don't specify a side in advance, they have to divide the 5% in half, giving them a much narrower strip to aim for. This simple analogue demonstrates that the "target" is harder to hit for a two-tailed than a one-tailed test. For this reason, the more robust two-tailed test is considered the convention. A one-tailed test can be used, but generally must be justified.

☒ TYPE I AND TYPE II ERROR

Whenever a hypothesis is tested, two types of error are possible. The null hypothesis may be rejected when it is, in fact, true. This is the assertion of an association when none exists, and therefore a false-positive error. By convention, false-positive error is known as **type I error**, or **alpha (α) error**. Failure to detect an association when one does, in fact, exist, results in failure to reject the null hypothesis and a false-negative error. False-negative error is alternatively known as **type II error**, or **beta (β) error**. These error types are summarized in Table 9.1.

False-positive error and false-negative error are technically independent of one another, yet they interrelate in much the same way as sensitivity and specificity (see Chapter 2). As increasing effort is made to detect an association should one exist (increasing sensitivity), the risk of false-positive error rises. Conversely, should every effort be made to avoid detecting an association when one does not exist (specificity), the risk of false-negative error rises.

Prioritization of type I or type II error is a clinical matter, not a statistical matter. Generally, protection against type I error (or false-positive error) is the priority, and this may be attributed to the principle of *primum non nocere* (first, do no harm). If an association (e.g., a therapeutic drug effect) is reported but is not real, patients will be exposed to a drug

TABLE 9.1		A Summary of the Types of Conclusions and Errors that May Be Drawn from a Statistical Test of a Drug vs. Placebo	
		The truth	
		Drug Is Better Than Placebo	*Drug Is No Better Than Placebo*
The test result	Drug is better than placebo	*True-positive* Correct probability = $1 - \beta$ (power)	*False-positive* Type I error probability = α
	Drug is no better than placebo	*False-negative* Type II error probability = β	*True-negative* probability = $1 - \alpha$

with some potential to harm and no potential to help. Avoidance of such occurrences is essential to honor the ethical code of medicine and preserve public trust. The principal defense against false-positive error is to define the limits of uncertainty tolerable when an association is reported. By convention this threshold is referred to as **alpha** (α), and is generally set at 0.05, or 5%. As noted above, employing two-tailed tests of significance augments the stringency of this criterion. Thus, the actual limit of uncertainty (the risk of false-positive error) when a "statistically significant" association is reported in the expected direction (e.g., blood pressure *reduction* with a new antihypertensive agent), with α set at 0.05 and a two-tailed test, is 2.5% or less. As noted above, this rises to 5% when a one-tailed test is used.

There are clinical conditions, however, under which false-positive error is more acceptable than false-negative error. When a disease is serious and existing therapies are inadequate, the need for new therapies is particularly urgent. While approving ineffective therapies under such conditions would be undesirable, proffering false hope to seriously ill patients, it would nonetheless be preferable to withholding effective therapies because of an inability to recognize that effectiveness. This tension has been particularly overt with regard to FDA approval policies for desperately needed drugs, such as those to treat AIDS or cancer.[8] Protection against false-negative error is provided in the form of another conventional threshold, known as **beta** (β). Conventionally, beta is set at 0.2. As noted in Chapter 2, false-negative error and sensitivity sum to 1. Thus, the **sensitivity** of a study is $1 - \beta$. When β is 0.2, the sensitivity of the study is 0.8, or 80%. While referred to as sensitivity when describing the performance of a diagnostic test, the capacity of a study to detect an association when one exists is referred to as the **power** of the study. Thus, **power = 1 − β**. The comparability of the sensitivity of a diagnostic test to the power of a study highlights the comparable influence of probability and risk on the interpretation of results in both settings.

The risk of missing a case of disease generally rises as the specificity of a test increases, and the risk of false-positive diagnosis rises with sensitivity (see Chapter 2). These specificity and sensitivity correlations apply to type I and type II error as well. When false-positive error is a particular concern, as when a new therapy will be applied to a generally benign and/or self-limited condition (e.g., varicella vaccine), alpha may be set even lower than 0.05, with the understanding that a true treatment effect is more likely to be missed. When the need for a new therapy is extremely urgent (e.g., pancreatic carcinoma), beta may be set lower than 0.2 to increase study power.

There are several implications of the conventional use of alpha and beta in the literature of direct relevance to the clinician. First, the conventional level of protection against error may not be satisfactory for any particular patient for a variety of reasons. To the extent that a single patient differs from the subjects enrolled in a trial, the probability of benefit may also differ. If benefit is marginal relative to risk for those subjects in the trial, and if the benefit/risk ratio might be lower still for the patient in question, alpha of 0.05 may not be acceptably stringent. Similarly, if a patient is even more desperately ill than the subjects in a trial, beta of 0.2 may not be satisfactory. Reports in the literature should always be evaluated in the light of clinical imperatives.

Also of note, alpha and beta error both influence what appears in the literature. **Publication bias** (see Chapter 8 and Appendix A.3) is the tendency for journals to publish those papers that report a significant finding. This tendency is understandable; reports of association are generally more interesting than reports of non-association. Nonetheless, under conventional conditions with alpha set at 0.05, one outcome will *appear significant* for every 20 trials performed on the basis of chance alone. If, under such theoretical conditions, the one positive trial submitted is more likely to be published than the 19 negative trials, the literature will distort reality. This possibility has been debated both seriously[9] and whimsically,[10] but without obvious closure.

A related concern is that the primacy of alpha over beta has resulted in a relative inattentiveness to type II error. There is evidence that a certain number of published negative trials were **under-powered**.[11,12,13,14,15,16] A trial is under-powered when it lacks the means to detect a clinically important association with consistency. The best defense against false-negative error is an adequate sample size, as discussed below.

🕸 *p*-VALUEƒ

If grades are the currency of academia and money the currency of commerce, then ***p*-values** are the currency of clinical investigation. The symbol "*p*" designates probability. When a hypothesis is tested, a critical ratio is generated as discussed in Chapter 7. The particular ratio of apparent association (signal) to variance (noise) resulting from a single trial represents a fixed dispersion from the expectation of no association as stipulated by the null hypothesis. As discussed above, this dispersion from the null is measured on a normal distribution plot in units of standard error. The probability of landing a fixed number of standard error units from the null is precisely defined.* For example, the probability of a result $\leqslant 1.96$ standard error units from the null (given a two-tailed test) is 5%. A result even further out in the tail of the frequency distribution is associated with a lower probability still. Thus, the probability of any particular trial outcome is expressed as p. The outcome of a study is statistically significant whenever **$p \leqslant alpha$**. Conventionally, a result is significant when $p \leqslant 0.05$. Obviously, p may at times be substantially lower than alpha, indicating that the probability of a false-positive error is extremely remote.

〰 ſAMPLE ſIZE

The probability of type I and type II error are closely related to the size of a study. Consider a study in which an antihypertensive is given to one subject and a placebo to another subject. Even if the drug is highly effective most of the time, the single subject receiving it in this trial may not respond, resulting in a false-negative error. Conversely, if the one subject receiving the drug does experience a blood pressure reduction 10 mm Hg greater than the other subject, there is little assurance that this is not due to false-positive error. Any uncontrolled difference between the two subjects other than the intervention might be accounting for the apparent outcome difference. If, however, each group consisted of 1,000 well-matched subjects, and the outcome was the same (an average blood pressure reduction in the drug group 10 mm Hg greater than in the placebo group), we would feel confident that the drug was actually effective. Similarly, if blood pressure did not differ between the groups of 1,000 subjects each, we could feel confident that the drug does not work, at least in the population studied.

Thus, intuition suggests that a sample of some particular size is required to assure that an association (e.g., treatment effect) will be detected if it exists, and to assure that these associations are meaningful

---

* The probability value associated with a particular critical ratio is dependent on the method used for hypothesis testing and can be found in the appropriate table of probability for various statistical values (e.g., t-test, z, chi-squared, etc.).[5]

rather than random. What intuition cannot say is precisely what **sample size** is required to accomplish both goals. Statistics can provide this answer, however, serving as a tool with which the demands of intuition are addressed and refined.

A detailed discussion of sample size equations will not be provided here; such information is readily available elsewhere.[5,6,7] However, the basis for their construction is germane and will be discussed. Because studies are designed to test hypotheses by producing a critical ratio of effect (signal) to variance (noise) (see Chapter 7), sample size requirements are dependent in part on the anticipated effect and the anticipated variance. The larger the critical ratio, the more readily the null hypothesis is rejected. The critical ratio will be large when the outcome effect is large, and/or the variance is small. When the outcome effect is large it is detectable with a small sample, and when the effect is small a large sample is required to perceive it clearly. For example, a 2 mm Hg decline in blood pressure will look like random variation unless consistent among a large group of subjects, whereas a 50 mm Hg fall will be apparent in very few. Thus, sample size varies inversely with the magnitude of the outcome effect anticipated.

When variance is large, the **outcome effect**, even if robust, will be obscured by the underlying random variation. Only a consistent effect among a large number of subjects can overcome the interference of large variance and produce a clear signal. Conversely, when the background variation is modest, even a modest effect may be perceived clearly in a small number of subjects. Thus, sample size varies directly with variance.

Finally, given that the sample size offers protection against both type I and type II error, the acceptable limits of each must be factored into the pertinent equation. The capacity to detect a treatment effect when one exists (i.e., to increase study power and avoid a false-negative error) increases with sample size. The capacity to be certain that an apparent association is real (i.e., to avoid false-positive error) also increases with sample size. Thus, sample size equations incorporate measures of both alpha and beta, with sample size varying directly with the stringency of each. Representative sample size formulas are shown in Table 9.2.

TABLE 9.2   Representative Sample Size Formulas

Comparison	Formula	Explanation
Proportional outcome data compared between two groups, both type I and type II error considered	$N = \dfrac{(Z_\alpha + Z_\beta)^2 (2)(p)(1-p)}{d^2}$	• N is the sample size per group • Z_α is the Z-score* associated with the stipulated level of alpha, conventionally 0.05 • Z_β is the Z-score* associated with the stipulated level of beta error, conventionally 0.2 • p is the mean proportion of "successes" or outcome of interest in the two groups • d is the anticipated difference in the rate of "successes" between the two groups expressed in the same units as p
Continuous outcome data compared between two groups, with both type I and type II error considered	$N = \dfrac{(Z_\alpha + Z_\beta)^2 (2)(s)^2}{d^2}$	• N as above • Z_α as above • Z_β as above • s is the standard deviation associated with the outcome of interest, from prior study • d is the anticipated difference between the mean outcomes for the two groups expressed in the same units as s

To determine sample size, one must know or estimate the expected variation in the outcome data and the magnitude of the expected treatment (outcome) effect, as well as the acceptable thresholds for type I and type II error.

*A Z-score is the distance from the mean of a stipulated probability, in standard deviation units, of a hypothetical normal distribution with a mean of 0. For further discussion, see: Jekel JF, Elmore JG, Katz DL. *Epidemiology, Biostatistics, and Preventive Medicine*. W.B. Saunders Company. Philadelphia, PA. 1996.

▓ CONFIDENCE INTERVALS

Trial outcomes are often reported in the literature along with the associated p-value to indicate the degree of statistical significance. But how useful is the p-value clinically? Consider a trial in which 20 subjects with asthma each receives either inhaled corticosteroid or matched placebo for a month, and then has peak flow measures obtained. If the peak flows are greater with the inhaled steroid by an average of 10%, and $p = 0.02$, are we adequately informed to advise a patient how much they can expect to improve with the inhaled steroid?

Probably not. A single study produced a result consistent with a 10% improvement in peak flow. But we know that a single study falls somewhere on a normal distribution curve of hypothetical study results were we to repeat the same experiment multiple times.[5] Therefore, the results of a single study are not the truth *per se*, but one possible version of the truth, across a range of values.

But what if the above study were conducted in 200,000 or even 2 million subjects rather than 20? We might (and should) feel considerably more confident that the 10% improvement in peak flow is a stable estimate of what we can expect in a patient. Why? Because a large trial is more likely than a small trial to approximate the truth as it pertains to the whole population of interest. Statistically, the stability of estimates based on large trials is captured by the standard error, discussed above. The standard error is the standard deviation divided by the square root of the sample size. Thus, standard error falls as sample size rises, even if the standard deviation remains constant.

If a large trial and a small trial produce a comparable result with a comparable p-value, are they providing comparable information? Actually, no. The large trial is more informative, but only if the outcome is expressed in terms of a **95% confidence interval (95% CI)**. The 95% CI is the range within which 95% of results would be expected to fall, based on the one experiment conducted, were the experiment to be replicated multiple times. Essentially the 95% CI is established by assuming that the result of the one study conducted is the mean of a normal distribution, and then calculating the range of values within which 95% of that distribution would fall. As discussed earlier, 95% of the values along a normal distribution curve fall within 1.96 standard error units on either side of the mean. Thus, the 95% CI for the result of any study is the **result ± 1.96×SE**. When expressed this way, the results of large studies are distinguished from those of similar, but smaller studies. The large sample size of a trial reduces the associated standard error, producing a narrow 95% CI. A small sample size is typically associated with a wide 95% CI. Thus, following a small trial of corticosteroid, we might be able to tell a patient that the medication is effective and can be expected, with 95% confidence, to reduce peak flow by as much as 40%, or as little as 0.5%. Following a large trial, we might be equally confident that peak flow would fall between 8% and 12% (note that these are factitious data for illustrative purposes only).

Lastly, the 95% CI can be used not only to define the range of expected outcome effects but also to indicate statistical significance. In the example above, if the small trial were consistent with either as much as a 50% increase in peak flow, or as much as a 10% decline, the result would not be significant. Whenever the 95% CI encompasses values on both sides of the measure indicating no treatment effect, the result is not statistically significant. In the case of a risk ratio or odds ratio (see Chapter 7), the value of no effect is 1. In the case above, it is 0. When the entire 95% CI falls to one side (i.e., either entirely above or entirely below) of the "no effect value," the result is statistically significant.

⩩ OTHER CONSIDERATIONS

Although at times you may have been inclined to think otherwise, this is not a statistics text. Rather, the statistics included is only so much as is needed to enhance clinical decision making, or the interpretation and application of the evidence base on which clinical decision making rests. This chapter has as its objective the latter.

To interpret and thereby knowledgeably apply the statistical results reported in the literature demands neither a degree in statistics nor a calculator in hand whenever you pick up a journal. Rather, as is true of most disciplines, evidence-based medicine leans heavily on the simplest and most fundamental of its concepts. Statistics in the literature should be approached with this in mind.

Is the study hypothesis explicitly stated, and if not, is it at least implicitly clear? Is the study design explicitly defined in the abstract, and if not, is the design described adequately to support inferences about the relative methodologic rigor of the study? Is the study population characterized in sufficient detail to permit suppositions regarding the pertinence of results to individual patients?

Only after the answers to these questions are known does it make sense to pose similar questions regarding statistical methods. Does the study adhere to all pertinent stipulations (e.g., intention to treat analysis for a RCT)? Is alpha specified as being one- or two-tailed, and if one-tailed is it justified? Is beta (or power) specified? Do the methods used for hypothesis testing make sense in light of the type of data being analyzed? Is statistical significance expressed with a p-value or a confidence interval? Finally, is the clinical significance of the reported findings clear?

Some years ago, a study in the New England Journal of Medicine reported the statistical methods used in the trials the journal had published over a defined period of time.[17] Nearly 75% of the studies relied on fairly simple statistical methods. While the sophistication of statistical methods has increased over time, much of the clinical literature remains quite accessible to the reader who has only a basic understanding of statistical methods.

SUMMARY/TAKE-AWAY MESSAGES

Statistical significance is among the defining characteristics of evidence in medicine. Associations that appear robust may not achieve significance, those that appear weak may conversely be significant. While statistical significance cannot and should not replace **clinical significance** in decisions about the application of research findings, such testing asserts consistent criteria by which to judge the validity of apparent associations.

By convention, significance testing prioritizes protection against false-positive or **alpha error**. The value of alpha, typically **0.05**, represents the upper probability limit for an association to be considered causal rather than random. When the probability of a particular study outcome, represented by the p-**value**, is less than the value of alpha, the association observed is considered significant because it would occur randomly less than 5% of the time. Generally, alpha is **two-tailed**, meaning the 5% of the distribution of trial outcomes considered extreme enough to indicate causality is divided in two and located at either end, or tail, of the distribution. The distribution used to define the **rejection region** is a plot of the hypothetical outcomes of repetitions of the trial conducted, using the standard error as the unit of dispersion and the actual trial result as the mean. When an outcome is expected to deviate from the null in one direction only, a **one-tailed** test of significance may be appropriate, and makes the demonstration of statistical significance easier.

Significance testing does not directly address type II, false-negative, or **beta error**. This should generally be addressed in **sample size calculations**, to assure that an adequate sample is assembled to detect an association should one exist. **Power calculations** can be performed in the advent of negative study results to assess the probability of false-negative error.

While significance is indicated by a *p*-value less than alpha, the *p*-value provides no information about the range of results (e.g., treatment effects) likely for a given individual or group. This information is provided by a **95% confidence interval** (**CI**), which conveys significance when it does not contain the value of no effect (typically either 0 or 1), as well as the range within which 95% of results may be expected to fall. For any given treatment effect, the 95% CI, which is the mean plus or minus 1.96 standard error (SE) units, will be narrower the larger the sample size. This measure of significance is more informative than the *p*-value, and increasingly preferred.

〽 〽 〽

〽 REFERENCES

1. Ioannidis JP. Effect of the statistical significance of results on the time to completion and publication of randomized efficacy trials. *JAMA.* 1998;279:281–286.
2. Misakian AL, Bero LA. Publication bias and research on passive smoking: Comparison of published and unpublished studies. *JAMA.* 1998;280:250–253.
3. Callaham ML, Wears RL, Weber EJ, Barton C, Young G. Positive-outcome bias and other limitations in the outcome of research abstracts submitted to a scientific meeting. *JAMA.* 1998;280:254–257.
4. Sutton AJ, Duval SJ, Tweedie RL, Abrams KR, Jones DR. Empirical assessment of effect of publication bias on meta-analyses. *BMJ.* 2000;320:1574–1577.
5. Jekel, JF, Elmore JG, Katz DL. *Epidemiology, Biostatistics and Preventive Medicine.* Philadelphia, PA: Saunders; 1996.
6. Dawson-Saunders B, Trapp RG. *Basic & Clinical Biostatistics.* 2nd ed. Norwalk, CT: Appleton & Lange; 1994.
7. Motulsky H. *Intuitive Biostatistics.* New York: Oxford University Press; 1995.
8. Gould SJ. AIDS and FDA drug-approval policy: An evolving controversy. *J Health Soc Policy.* 1990;2:39–46.
9. Vickers A, Goyal N, Harland R, Rees R. Do certain countries produce only positive results? A systematic review of controlled trials. *Control Clin Trials.* 1998;19:159–166.

10. Vertesi L. Clinical Research Unmasked. *J Irreproducible Results*. 1997:12–13.
11. Ottenbacher KJ, Maas F. How to detect effects: Statistical power and evidence-based practice in occupational therapy research. *Am J Occup Ther.* 1999;53:181–188.
12. Mengel MB, Davis AB. The statistical power of family practice research. *Fam Pract Res J.* 1993;13:105–111.
13. Rossi JS. Statistical power of psychological research: What have we gained in 20 years? *J Consult Clin Psychol.* 1990;58:646–656.
14. Mittendorf R, Arun V, Sapugay AM. The problem of the type II statistical error. *Obstet Gynecol.* 1995;86:857–859.
15. Fox N, Mathers N. Empowering research: Statistical power in general practice research. *Fam Pract.* 1997;14:324–329.
16. Williams JL, Hathaway CA, Kloster KL, Layne BH. Low power, type II errors, and other statistical problems in recent cardiovascular research. *Am J Physiol.* 1997;273(1 Pt 2):H487–493.
17. Emerson JD, Colditz GA. Use of statistical analysis in the New England Journal of Medicine. *N Engl J Med.* 1983;309:709–713.

Section III

FROM REJEARCH TO REAJONING: THE APPLICATION OF EVIDENCE IN CLINICAL PRACTICE

Probability, alternative, and risk assessment all quide the decisions made by clinicians and patients. An understanding of the role of quantitative estimation in medical reasoning and research has the potential to enhance decisions as well as the clinical processes and outcomes that ensue. Yet the constraints and assumptions imposed in illustrating principles of clinical epidemiology create scenarios very unlike those encountered in clinical practice.

In clinical practice, multiple hypotheses are entertained at once. Alternatives are never excluded with complete confidence. Patient preference and clinical judgement may correspond or diverge. Prior probability is an educated guess at best, a genuine guess at worst, and necessary evidence is often either unavailable, difficult to find, or of questionable quality or relevance. Yet decisions must be made, advice must be offered, and treatment must be provided.

The true test of clinical epidemiology is at the proverbial bedside. To demonstrate the utility of the concepts presented throughout the text, decision analysis will be discussed as the formal application of probability, risk, and alternative to medical decision making. Then a hypothetical case will be tracked from presentation to treatment, with the applications of quantitative reasoning and evidence highlighted.

10

Decision Analysis

The statistical principles underlying medical reasoning are fundamental to sound decision making, yet they generally are (and generally should be) subtle in application. Few if any of us are inclined to approach the bedside or exam room with a calculator in hand. Fortunately, our natural capacity to generate and compare semiquantitative estimates of probability and risk based on judgment, evidence, and personal experience generally guides us and our patients through the labyrinth of therapeutic options. Unfortunately, profound uncertainty at times leads to an impasse. The identification of such impasses, clinical dilemmas in which the probability of discrete risks and benefits associated with alternatives in diagnosis or management are nearly comparable, is both important and valuable. Such situations are important because they define a need for more robust estimation of potential benefit and risk than is typically required. They are valuable because methods for such estimation are available.

The formal application of quantitative decision making—incorporating probability, risk, and alternatives as well as patient preferences and values—finds expression in decision analysis. A science of medical decision making in its own right, decision analysis has been characterized in the medical literature, both succinctly[1,2,3] and at greater length.[4,5] Succinct treatment will be sufficient in this text; the reader interested in greater detail is encouraged to pursue other sources.

undamentally, **decision analysis** is an effort to make the quantitative principles upon which a given clinical or health policy decision is based explicit. By formalizing quantitative estimates associated with alternatives in clinical management, their comparison may be approached more formally, with assumptions and uncertainty made explicit and exposed. In this way, both the clinician and the patient may identify and challenge the considerations upon which decisions rest. Just as a debate may expose and clarify controversy that might have been overlooked otherwise so decision analysis may expose the robust or dubious presuppositions that influence clinical decisions and choices.

In decision analysis, a **decision tree**[6] is developed to facilitate comparison of discrete options in management. In such trees, a square represents a juncture at which a decision must be made, a circle represents a juncture at which chance operates, triangles represent outcomes, and lines track strategies. An example is provided in Figure 10.1.

Along each of the strategy lines, numbers are inserted to indicate the **probability** of particular outcomes.[7] These numbers should be obtained from a systematic search of the pertinent literature in published decision analyses. When relying on a published decision tree, you must evaluate its adequacy in several ways. The first is the quality of the evidence on which the quantitative estimates in the tree are based; these should be explicit in a published source. The second is correspondence of the tree to the range of options and outcomes under consideration. If important management alternatives or outcomes are missing from the available trees, perhaps due to treatment advances since their publication, they are unlikely to offer meaningful utility. In the absence of a published decision tree, you might construct one that more effectively exposes and explores the influence of uncertainty and your various "educated guesses" on your preferences and those of your patient. Of course, the success of this exercise will depend substantially on the quality of the estimates applied.

Once a decision is made (represented by the lines of strategy emanating from a square, or decision node), the tree must provide all possible **alternative outcomes** of the decision. These outcomes occur on the basis of probability, or chance. If the outcomes are undesirable, the probability of occurrence may be considered a measure of **risk**. The probabilities emanating from a chance node range from 0 to 1, and must sum to 1.

When a single outcome is of exceptional importance, such as death, the probability of occurrence is an adequate measure of utility. Those strategies that minimize the risk of death are preferred to those associated with greater risk. When multiple outcomes are being considered, however, a

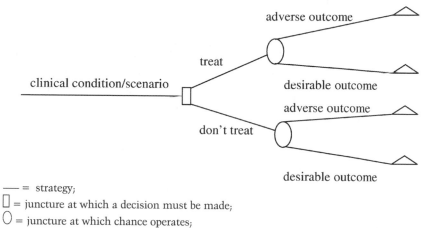

— = strategy;

▯ = juncture at which a decision must be made;

〇 = juncture at which chance operates;

△ = outcome.

Figure 10.1. The basic anatomy of a decision tree.

consistent measure of **utility** must be applied so that outcomes can be compared on a single scale.[7,8] Because the utility of various clinical outcomes is subjective, the patient is the appropriate source of these measures, which are often chosen across the range from 0 (worst outcome, such as death) to 1 (best outcome, such as perfect health).

Once a decision tree is identified or constructed that incorporates all pertinent alternatives of treatment and outcome, and acceptable estimates of probability and utility, it can be used to disclose the preferability of one choice over another. The first step is to quantify the aggregate results of making a particular decision. This is done in a process called "averaging out." The probability estimate for each outcome following a chance node is multiplied by the corresponding utility measure. At times, the tree may display chance outcomes that precede a single outcome of interest, such as death. For example, anticoagulation might or might not lead to hemorrhage, which then might or might not lead to death. When the tree presents outcomes as intervening variables between a decision and the ultimate outcome, the probability of the intervening outcome is multiplied by the subsequent probability of the ultimate outcome, the latter substituting for the utility measure.[9] In either case, the products obtained by multiplying probability and utility for each outcome that emanates from a chance node are summed to produce the overall measure

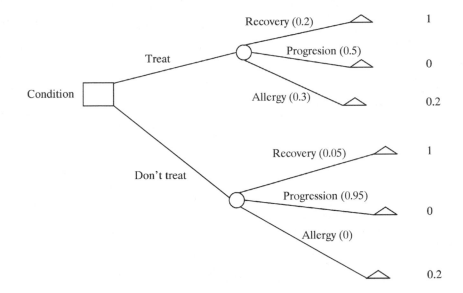

Figure 10.2. The process of "averaging out" the results associated with a particular decision. In this simplified construct, the decision to "treat" or not to treat is associated with three possible outcomes: cure, failure, and allergic reaction. Recovery denotes full recovery, progression in this case denotes death, and allergy denotes a severe (anaphylactic) reaction to treatment. Each outcome occurs at a defined probability, and is associated with a defined utility. The product of probability and utility for each outcome, summed, represents the "averaged out" utility of the decision. The utility of complete recovery is 1, and the utility of death is 0. The utility of an allergic reaction is set at 0.2 for illustrative purposes (arbitrary value). In this case, the decision to treat is associated with a net utility of $[(0.2 \times 1) + (0.5 \times 0) + (0.3 \times 0.2)]$, or 0.26, and the decision not to treat with a utility of $[(0.05 \times 1) + (0.95 \times 0) + (0 \times 0.2)]$, or 0.05. Thus, there is a greater net utility associated with the decision to treat than with the decision not to treat. All else being equal, this tree would support a decision to treat.

of utility associated with the decision preceding the node. An example is provided in Figure 10.2.

Once the utility associated with particular decisions is determined, the range of decision options must be compared. The explicitly quantitative approach used in decision analysis makes such comparison easy, if not altogether reliable. Those decisions associated with low utilities are undesirable. A complex (realistic) decision tree will often portray many options and outcomes.[10,11] To reach an ultimate decision, the alternatives depicted in such a tree must be systematically eliminated until a clear preference emerges. By establishing the average utility at each chance node, the utility of making a particular decision is defined. If low, that branch of the decision tree can be eliminated, or "pruned." The process of pruning back continues until only decisions of comparable and/or acceptable utility remain. At times a single option will be revealed as the clear choice. At times, two or more options may be so close in utility as to represent a "toss up." These are the options worthy of consideration by the patient and clinician, assuming the quantitative input of the tree was reliable.

However, that final stipulation is the proverbial "big if." The evidence base for comprehensive, reliable decision analysis is often unavailable. Estimates of probability and utility may be subject to substantial uncertainty. That uncertainty might be enough to change the interpretation of the tree, and the choice of intervention or strategy. The method for determining whether or not the decision reached is susceptible to reasonable changes in the estimates of probability and utility is **sensitivity analysis**.[4]

In sensitivity analysis, the important assumptions upon which a decision rests are varied across the range of reasonable or plausible values (another potential source of error in quantitative estimation) to determine whether or not this variation of values changes the preferences that emerge from the table. When decisions are stable across the range of estimates considered reasonable (based on published data, or clinician and patient opinion), the tree provides a robust basis to support a particular decision. (Naturally, the more obvious a given choice or decision is, the less likely that decision analysis will be required in the first place.) When varying quantitative estimates across the range of reasonable values changes the decisions supported by the tree, decision making becomes very dependent on identifying which estimates correspond most closely to the patient in question.

Finally, a variant of decision analysis allows for the projection of changes in utility and probability over time. Called **Markov Analysis** or Modeling, such methods require the use of dedicated software.[12] While their use by anyone not devoted to research in decision making is unlikely, such models occasionally are reported in the literature.[13,14,15,16,17] Therefore, clinicians should recognize the method as decision analysis adjusted for the dynamic character of the pertinent variables over time.[4]

As an example of a clinical dilemma for which formal quantification of probability and risk across the range of alternatives would be helpful, consider a patient with a prosthetic heart valve on warfarin, who suffers an intracranial bleed induced by a minor trauma. The valve is an "absolute" indication for anticoagulation, the bleed an "absolute" contraindication. A recent case series and review addresses this very issue.[18] Many challenging scenarios in clinical decision making could potentially benefit from the application of decision analysis.[17,19,20,21,22,23]

SUMMARY/TAKE-AWAY MESSAGES

Decision analysis is a formal application of many of the quantitative principles discussed throughout the text, and in particular probability, risk, and alternatives. **Decision trees** are constructed to represent the alternative interventions and outcomes pertinent to a particular clinical scenario. The construction of such trees requires sufficient literature to allow for the identification and quantification of such alternatives. **Clinical dilemmas** for which there is a lack of evidence are generally not conducive to decision analysis, although a rudimentary tree might be constructed simply to help the clinician and patient struggling through such a scenario better confront the options.

For dilemmas in areas of adequate evidence, decision trees may be available. When they are, they identify the **alternatives** and quantify **probability** and **risk**. **Sensitivity analysis** allows for adjustment of the quantitative estimates over a range of plausible values to determine which estimates can vary without altering the implications of the tree, and upon which estimates the ultimate decisions are most dependent. **Markov Analysis** allows for the incorporation of changes in utilities and/or probabilities over time into the analysis. The implications of a particular decision may be discerned in a process called **averaging out**, and those branches of the tree associated with undesirable outcomes or unacceptable risk eliminated in a process called **pruning back**. The remaining branches of the tree represent the alternatives among which the "right" choice is likely to be found. Once quantitative principles have trimmed the tree, the selection of a strategy is subjective, depending, as all clinical decisions ultimately do, on patient and clinician values, beliefs, and preferences.

〰 REFERENCEſ

1. Birkmeyer JD, Welch HG. A reader's guide to surgical decision analysis. *J Am Coll Surg.* 1997;184:589–595.
2. Richardson WS, Detsky AS, et al. Users' guides to the medical literature. VII. How to use a clinical decision analysis. A. Are the results of the study valid? *JAMA.* 1995A;273:1292–1295.
3. Richardson WS, Detsky AS, et al. Users' guides to the medical literature. VII. How to use a clinical decision analysis. B. What are the results and will they help me in caring for my patients? *JAMA.* 1995B;273:1610–1613.
4. Petitti DB. *Meta-Analysis, Decision Analysis, and Cost-Effectiveness Analysis. Methods for Quantitative Synthesis in Medicine.* 2nd ed. New York: Oxford University Press; 2000:152–158,229–243.
5. Skinner D. Introduction to Decision Analysis: A Practitioners Guide to Improving Decision Quality. Gainesville, FL: Probabilistic Publisher; 1999.
6. Detsky AS, Naglie G, Krahn MD, Redelmeier DA, Naimark D. Primer on medical decision analysis: Part 2—Building a tree. *Med Decis Making.* 1997;17:126–135.
7. Naglie G, Krahn MD, Naimark D, Redelmeier DA, Detsky AS. Primer on medical decision analysis: Part 3—Estimating probabilities and utilities. *Med Decis Making.* 1997;17:136–141.
8. Djulbegovic B, Hozo I, Lyman GH. Linking evidence-based medicine therapeutic summary measures to clinical decision analysis. *MedGenMed.* 2000;(6):E6.
9. Jekel JF, Elmore JG, Katz DL. *Epidemiology, Biostatistics, and Preventive Medicine.* Philadelphia, PA: Saunders; 1996:103.
10. Romano PS, Waitzman NJ. Can decision analysis help us decide whether ultrasound screening for fetal anomalies is worth it? *Ann N Y Acad Sci.* 1998;847:154–172.
11. Greenberg ML, Malenka DJ, Disch DL. Therapeutic strategies for atrial fibrillation. The value of decision analysis. *Cardiol Clin.* 1996;14:623–640.
12. Naimark D, Krahn MD, Naglie G, Redelmeier DA, Detsky AS. Primer on medical decision analysis: Part 5—Working with Markov processes. *Med Decis Making.* 1997;17:152–159.
13. Ross KS, Carter HB, Pearson JD, Guess HA. Comparative efficiency of prostate-specific antigen screening strategies for prostate cancer detection. *JAMA.* 2000;284:1399–1405.
14. Le Pen C, Maurel F, Breart G, Lopes P, Plouin PF, Allicar MP, Roux C. The long-term effectiveness of preventive strategies for osteoporosis in postmenopausal women: A modeling approach. *Osteoporos Int.* 2000;11:524–532.
15. Thomson R, Parkin D, Eccles M, Sudlow M, Robinson A. Decision analysis and guidelines for anticoagulant therapy to prevent stroke in patients with atrial fibrillation. *Lancet.* 2000;355:956–962.
16. Aoki N, Kajiyama T, Beck JR, Cone RW, Soma K, Fukui T. Decision analysis of prophylactic treatment for patients with high-risk esophageal varices. *Gastrointest Endosc.* 2000;52:707–714.
17. Ng AK, Weeks JC, Mauch PM, Kuntz KM. Decision analysis on alternative treatment strategies for favorable-prognosis, early-stage Hodgkin's disease. *J Clin Oncol.* 1999;17:3577–3585.
18. Crawley F, Bevan D, Wren D. Management of intracranial bleeding associated with anticoagulation: Balancing the risk of further bleeding against thromboembolism from prosthetic heart valves. *J Neurol Neurosurg Psychiatry.* 2000;69:396–398.

19. Robinson A, Thomson RG. The potential use of decision analysis to support shared decision making in the face of uncertainty: The example of atrial fibrillation and warfarin anticoagulation. *Qual Health Care*. 2000;9:238–244.
20. Grossfeld GD, Tigrani VS, Nudell D, Roach M 3rd, Weinberg VK, Presti JC JR, Small EJ, Carroll PR. Management of a positive surgical margin after radical prostatectomy: Decision analysis. *J Urol*. 2000;164:93–99.
21. McConnell LM, Goldstein MK. The application of medical decision analysis to genetic testing: An introduction. *Genet Test*. 1999;3:65–70.
22. Chalfin DB. Decision analysis in critical care medicine. *Crit Care Clin*. 1999;15:647–661.
23. Powe NR, Danese MD, Ladenson PW. Decision analysis in endocrinology and metabolism. *Endocrinol Metab Clin North Am*. 1997;26:89–111.

11

Diagnosis

C onsider a 48-year-old woman presenting to the office with a complaint of chest pain. The immediate concern is angina pectoris. Why? Because the condition is both common and dangerous. Our minds are immediately triggered by considerations of **probability** and **risk**.

The history is conducted as a sequence of hypothesis tests. The answer to each question either raises or lowers the probability that the chest pain is angina. To the extent that answers lower the probability of angina, they of necessity must suggest alternative diagnoses. Clearly the pain must be angina if there are no alternative diagnoses. When answers suggest alternatives, additional hypotheses generated from these alternatives are posed and tested by further questioning. The sequential testing of our history is an effort to elucidate a correspondence between the characteristics of this individual patient and others in whom a diagnosis of angina or some alternative cause of chest pain, such as esophageal spasm, was ultimately secured. When the correspondence is very strong, a diagnosis is made. When the correspondence is less strong, as is often the case, a differential diagnosis list results. Each entry on the list corresponds more or less well with the patient under investigation. Conditions both uncommon and benign need to correspond quite well with the patient to deserve consideration. Conditions that are either common or dangerous need to correspond only weakly with the patient to deserve placement on the list. Conditions both common and dangerous, such as angina in the US, are automatically on the list and need a good reason (such as clear evidence of an alternative diagnosis) to be taken off.

The particular patient provides the following information. At 48, she is 3 years past natural menopause. The chest pain has been intermittent for 1 month, not clearly associated with activity. She notes that it occurs with stress. She is uncertain about any association with exertion, but notes that she is rather sedentary. The pain, when it occurs, is "twisting" in character, and located slightly to the right of center in the chest without radiation. She has felt palpitations several times, but not consistently. She generally feels breathless when the pain occurs, but has attributed this to anxiety. She denies diaphoresis or nausea.

The patient has no significant past medical history and takes no prescription medications. She takes vitamin C 500 mg daily on general principles. She notes that she was once treated with a prescription medication for heartburn, but more than 5 years ago with no recurrence. Family history is unobtainable; the patient was adopted in early childhood. She has not had a physical exam in approximately 5 years, at which time she changed jobs and insurers. She does not know her cholesterol or blood pressure.

She works as a computer analyst. She has smoked ½ pack per day for 28 years. Her alcohol consumption is moderate, and her diet fairly "typical." The review of systems is notable for increasingly frequent thirst and urination over the past 18 months and occasional blurry vision.

What do we know at this juncture? The patient has certain risk factors for vascular disease that increase the probability of angina, specifically a history of smoking and non-use of hormone replacement several years after menopause. A sedentary lifestyle and typical Western diet increase risk as well. Possibly decreasing the probability of angina is the prior history of heartburn. Knowing the degree to which the current pain mimicked the previous pain of heartburn would be helpful. The suggestion of polyuria and polydipsia raises the possibility of recent onset diabetes mellitus.

As is true of the history, the physical examination is an opportunity to test a sequence of hypotheses. Based on the history, we might expect the patient to be overweight or obese had we not yet seen her. We would be interested in the vital signs, specifically the blood pressure and resting heart rate. We would be interested in the cardiac exam, in examination of the optic fundi, and examination of the peripheral pulses. Other aspects of the exam might or might not be of interest.

The patient is overweight, with a height of 5'5" and a weight of 172 lbs (BMI = 28.75). The blood pressure is 158/94 and the resting heart rate is 88. The PMI seems to be laterally displaced to a minimal degree but is difficult to define. The optic fundi appear normal. Peripheral pulses are normal. The extremities, abdomen, and neurological exams are unremarkable.

Now where do we stand? The physical exam has demonstrated hypertension and nascent obesity, and possibly left ventricular hypertrophy, raising the probability of angina. Still uncertain, we are probably all eager for some lab work. Worth noting at this juncture is that our clinical suspicions and doubts would be difficult to quantify, and such quantitative estimates as we could produce would doubtless vary among us quite considerably. Yet few if any of us would have thus far found sufficient evidence to exclude or confirm angina (or an alternative diagnosis). We all want more information.

Among the tests of interest now would be serum cholesterol and HDL, serum glucose (and possibly a glycosylated hemoglobin), and a resting cardiogram. The ECG is essentially normal. The cholesterol is 252, and the HDL 46. The serum glucose (random) is 160, and the glycosylated hemoglobin is slightly elevated.

We now have evidence that the patient is both hyperlipidemic and diabetic, increasing her risk of coronary disease, and are likely to have adjusted our probability estimate of angina upward. The ECG, however, refutes our impression of LVH and should cause us to revise our estimate downward. It is worth noting that generally we would not quantify the exact degree to which each finding moderates our probability estimate, nor would we seek to know the sensitivity and specificity of each test used thus far to revise our impression.

Are these violations of the principles of clinical epidemiology and evidence-based medicine? Theoretically, perhaps yes. Practically, certainly no. Even if dedicated to rigorous and evidence-based decision making, strict quantification of every clinical consideration is impractical at best, impossible at worst. Similarly, pausing to review the performance characteristics of even the most routine diagnostic studies prior to each use would prove prohibitively inconvenient.

To function under the constraints of clinical medicine, and nonetheless adhere to the basic demands of evidence-based practice requires something of a compromise. An appreciation for the semiquantitative nature of clinical estimates is required so that ultimately, following the application of history, physical, and initial testing, an estimate, or at least a range of estimates, can be generated to define the prior probability of the disease in question. While a strict statistical approach to the diagnostic process would call for a numerical estimate, in many clinical situations a categorical estimate—such as low, moderate, or high probability—is sufficient. In any case, some vaguely quantitative estimate is an essential prerequisite to further testing so that a diagnosis is not made solely on the basis of a test result, but on the basis of the test result, the test performance, and the patient's unique circumstances.

The probability of angina at this point might be considered to be moderate, or even high, and might be quantified at between 60% and 80%. Is this helpful? At the lower limit of this estimate, 60%, angina is still far too likely a consideration to ignore. At the upper limit of the range, 80%, the residual uncertainty is far too great to consider the diagnosis established. You might choose a different range of estimates and subject your range to the same assessment. This process, varying a single parameter and interpreting the clinical implications, is a form of **sensitivity analysis** (see Chapter 10), in which the sensitivity of the work-up to changes in the parameter is established. Working with the range of estimates asserted above, the work-up is relatively insensitive to varying the estimate: across the entire range of values, the need for additional diagnostic studies persists. Thus, attention should now turn to the most useful diagnostic studies and their operating characteristics, their performance in a patient like this one, the potential outcomes associated with each, and the implications of each potential outcome.

Before proceeding with the work-up a brief digression is in order. What if the need to continue the work-up were sensitive to the range of probability estimates? For example, what if the estimates of the probability of angina ranged either from a lower limit at which the diagnosis could be discarded (e.g., <5%) or to an upper limit at which further testing would not be required to confirm the diagnosis (e.g., >95%)? Under such circumstances, the most acute clinical need is to situate the patient accurately within the range of probability estimates. At this point, clinical judgment and experience are insufficient. Evidence is needed. Specifically, the prevalence of angina in patient groups corresponding as closely as possible to the patient under evaluation is needed. This information requires a search of the literature.

We need information on the epidemiology of angina in women. In MEDLINE (see Appendices A.1 and A.2 for discussion of on-line searching), we can enter "angina AND women/epidemiology." Limiting to the past 5 years, this search calls up 247 articles. (The number of references retrieved will likely have changed by the time this is published; the search results are therefore meant to be merely illustrative.) Entering "gender AND risk factors AND angina/epidemiology" and limiting to 5 years pulls up 53 references. A search of "chest pain AND women/epidemiology" brings up 81 references. One of these is: Redberg RF. Coronary artery disease in women: Understanding the diagnostic and management pitfalls.

Medscape Womens Health. 1998;3:1. This article provides general information on the presentations of women with coronary disease and recommendations for the selection of diagnostic studies. It does not help refine the probability estimate for our patient. Using the explode function to call up related articles results in 113 citations, most of which have clear relevance to the question we are posing. Among the references called up is: Chiamvimonvat V, Sternberg L. Coronary artery disease in women. *Can Fam Physician*. 1998;44:2709–2717. This article reviews the literature to provide specific recommendations regarding the diagnosis and management of coronary disease in women. The impact of different risk factors on the probability of coronary disease is discussed and is specifically relevant to our question.

A precise probability estimate for our patient is of course not to be found, but useful information is. We learn, if we did not know previously, that the strongest predictors of cardiac risk in women are diabetes and post-menopausal status without use of hormone replacement, and that atypical and non-exertional pain is more common than in men. This information would likely cause us to move our probability estimate toward the upper limit of the range. In doing so, depending on the range we started with, we would either become convinced of the diagnosis without the need for further testing, or become/remain convinced of the need for further testing. Thus, the gathering of evidence can at best be used to enhance the role of judgment in clinical care, but it can never replace it. An issue worth noting briefly is that to be certain of the reliability of the information garnered from the search, the original studies on which reviews were based would need to be accessed and evaluated. For the pursuit of evidence to be practical and fit within the available time, however, we are often left to rely on the diligence of the authors of a review and on the dual filters of peer review and journal editorial policies to assure us of reliable information. The filtering process is imperfect and apt to vary with the stature of the journal.

Our digression is now over; the literature would suggest that the patient is in fact at substantial risk of having coronary disease, and therefore that the probability of angina accounting for the chest pain is fairly high. The estimate may reasonably be moved to the upper limit of the earlier estimate, namely 80%. What are the implications of such a high prior probability of disease for the remainder of our diagnostic efforts? First, to move the posterior probability of disease up substantially, we will need a test with very high specificity (i.e., a good rule-in test; see Chapters 2 and 4). We also know that we will be very suspicious of a negative test result, and that the negative predictive value of a test will need to be very high to dissuade us of our impression. While the negative predictive value of any test will be limited by the high prior probability, a test with very high sensitivity (i.e., a good "rule-out" test) will be most convincing if negative. We can anticipate that if a fairly specific test is positive we will be satisfied that the diagnosis of angina pectoris has been confirmed, and that if a highly sensitive test is negative we will begin to reconsider the diagnosis of angina, but not abandon it alltogether. A negative test will likely call for additional testing. All of this is essential to consider before we launch into a diagnostic work-up.

As we prepare to do so, the literature again is needed. What are the sensitivity and specificity of various diagnostic tests for confirming or refuting (ruling in or out) the diagnosis of angina in this patient? A MEDLINE search entering "coronary disease AND women AND diagnostic test performance/diagnosis" yields one article: Crouse LJ, Kramer PH. Are there gender differences related to stress or pharmacological echocardiography? *Am J Card Imaging.* 1996;10:65–71. The article reviews the epidemiology of coronary disease in women and, more importantly, discusses the deficiencies of various diagnostic tests from routine to perfusion stress tests. The article argues for the use of stress echocardiography, but acknowledges that the supporting evidence is (or was) preliminary.

Using the explode function to pull up related articles yields 117 articles, many of which are specifically pertinent to our question. A particularly relevant article is: Travin MI, Johnson LL. Assessment of coronary artery disease in women. *Curr Opin Cardiol.* 1997;12:587–594. Another is: Tong AT, Douglas PS. Stress echocardiography in women. *Cardiol Clin.* 1999;17:573–582,ix–x. The references provide an array of options, but they generally indicate that the accuracy of stress echocardiography is particularly good. The aggregate evidence reported suggests that the sensitivity and specificity of myocardial perfusion imaging are approximately 83% and 77%, respectively, while for stress echocardiography, the sensitivity is 78%, and the specificity 86%.

While we could spend more time searching the literature, demands on our time are likely to make that impractical. But the time invested has been well spent. To rule in angina for the patient in question, we need a highly specific test. The reported performance characteristics of stress echocardiography suggest that among the routinely available modalities, it is most specific in women. However, the sensitivity of perfusion imaging is somewhat higher, suggesting that it might be more useful in an effort to rule out disease.

Generally, we have a bias favoring the detection or exclusion of a particular disease. In this case, the 80% prior probability estimate reveals our bias: we are 4 times more inclined to rule disease in than out. This bias has practical value in suggesting the needed test characteristics. The high specificity of stress echocardiography makes a compelling case for its use. Additional information of value in reaching the decision is the availability of the test, the cost and cost-effectiveness of the test, and the skill with which the test is performed locally. These considerations may be directly pursued, but guidance is often derived from prevailing practice patterns.

To bring our diagnostic efforts to a close, the results of stress echocardiography must be factored in. If the patient has a "positive" test, the post-test probability of angina (see Chapter 3) is 96%. Note that despite a high prior probability and the use of the best (or one of the best) available tests, there is still one chance in 25 that the patient has a condition other than angina. While this degree of confidence in the diagnosis is almost certainly sufficient to intervene, the degree of uncertainty is not inconsequential. Were the patient to have a negative test, the probability of angina would be reduced to approximately 51%. While this is substantially lower than the 80% prior probability estimate, it is far too high to exclude the diagnosis with confidence. Further testing would be required to rule out angina. The only alternative would be to revise the prior probability estimate. While subjecting the prior probability estimate to a sensitivity analysis as discussed above is appropriate, post-test revisionism is fraught with hazard. If the results of a test are used to modify the disease probability estimate that was the basis for ordering the test, a tautological loop is created that undermines the role of clinical judgment in the diagnostic process.

Naturally, such intense effort in the course of every work-up would make clinical practice unbearably cumbersome and intolerably slow. Only the occasional work-up would require this level of effort. And, because patients often share characteristics, the benefits of such an exercise conducted for one patient will likely be useful for diagnosing other patients in a practice. Finally, the occasional intense effort to refine a diagnostic strategy would cultivate skills and the application of quantitative principles of general relevance to even relatively "simple" differential diagnoses.

Management

The statistical principles governing the diagnostic process are equally germane to the selection of therapies. Decisions are again predicated on the probabilities of outcomes associated with alternative management plans, and the risks associated with each. Under most circumstances, treatment decisions are bounded by a narrower list of alternatives than are diagnostic decisions. Decisions regarding therapy are largely driven by estimates of the probability of outcomes, both beneficial and adverse.

In choosing among the treatment options for any patient with serious illness, the clinician is instantly at odds with the Hippocratic precept, *primum non nocere*. To do no harm requires that treatment choices be entirely predicated on the absence of risk, yet no treatment choices are devoid of risk. Therefore to truly prioritize the avoidance of harm above the performance of good requires that medical decisions simply not be made at all. Naturally, this lack of decision and attendant lack of action may itself be harmful.

The term **clinical epidemiology** is particularly appropriate to describe considerations of the potential harmful consequences of clinical decisions. While optimal decisions will still expose individual patients to potential harm, and fail to preclude adverse outcomes, they will translate into the most net benefit achievable for the *population* of patients with a particular condition. This net benefit cannot be achieved without risking individual harm. Probability favors, but cannot assure, a positive outcome in any individual patient subject to decisions optimizing group outcomes.

Rather than the avoidance of harm, therefore, the appropriate clinical imperative for both individual patient and patient populations is to maximize the degree to which potential benefit exceeds potential risk. This is achieved by establishing the ratio of anticipated benefit to anticipated risk for the therapeutic options under consideration. The **benefit to risk ratio** is useful in establishing the **therapeutic threshold**, the conditions under which benefit and risk of treatment are equal. The therapeutic threshold is $1/(B:R + 1)$, where B:R is the ratio of benefit to risk.[1]

One of the conditions relevant to the establishment of the therapeutic threshold is **diagnostic certainty**. If the wrong diagnosis is made, treatment for that condition exposes the patient to potential harm without any potential benefit. As there is always some residual uncertainty when a diagnosis is made, a decision must be reached to stop the testing process and begin therapy. In part, this decision should be influenced by the benefit to risk ratio of therapy for the condition in question. If potential for benefit is high and the potential for risk is low, the administration of therapy may be more appropriate than further testing even with substantial residual uncertainty. Conversely, when the benefits of treatment exceed the risks of treatment by a slim margin, and especially when the risks are great, the inclusion of even relatively few incorrectly diagnosed individuals in the treated group is likely to result in net harm rather than net benefit. Near diagnostic certainty would be required under such circumstances.

Return now to considerations of the 48-year-old woman with chest pain (see Chapter 11). Following a positive stress echo, the probability of angina is 96%. This degree of certainty would likely terminate the diagnostic process for most if not all clinicians. The next probable decision would be to send the patient for cardiac catheterization as a means of choosing between revascularization and pharmacotherapy/lifestyle interventions. The decision regarding catheterization, to be complete, should incorporate the 4% residual diagnostic uncertainty; any putative benefits of cardiac catheterization do not pertain to the 4% of patients who do not have symptomatic coronary disease. This group would benefit from the current "gold standard" test excluding a diagnosis they do not have and helping them to avoid unnecessary treatment.

To assess the risks and benefits of catheterization, the probability of adverse outcomes associated with empiric pharmacotherapy and lifestyle modification without catheterization would need to be estimated. The impact catheterization would have on distinguishing among those patients for whom angioplasty, bypass surgery, or lifestyle modification/pharmacotherapy would be preferred, on the rates of cardiac events, and on treatment-related complications would need to be considered. The rate of adverse events due directly to cardiac catheterization would need to be known and weighed against the anticipated benefits.

Whether or not the patient is referred for revascularization, she has multiple cardiac risk factors that require modification. She is diabetic, overweight, sedentary, hypertensive, post-menopausal, and hyperlipidemic. Each of these risk factors for MI provides opportunity for intervention. Assuming the diabetes does not require exogenous insulin, as seems likely, treatment options include diet and medications from several classes including thiazolidinedione, metformin, and sulfonylureas. Each approach offers certain potential benefits and certain potential risks. Diet is perhaps the safest intervention but may also be least likely to be effective.[2] Thus, despite the low risk of dietary therapy, the comparison of benefit:risk ratios might not favor it as the sole approach. Each of the other risk factors offers similar alternatives. As a decision is reached within each category, the potential for drug interactions needs to be considered an added risk of therapy. The potential synergy in risk factor modification needs to be considered a potential benefit.

As was true for diagnosis, a formally quantitative approach to the decisions guiding therapy is unappealing. Generating precise estimates of probable benefit and harm for each possible intervention alone and in combination is generally impractical. In the case of the patient under discussion, a convergence of evidence generally familiar to clinicians treating adults with coronary disease would guide decisions without the need to revisit the putative risks and benefits of every alternative.

But the convergence of evidence is not always sufficient. In light of findings from the Heart and Estrogen/Progestin Replacement Study (HERS)[3,4] and prior study of hormone replacement therapy (HRT),[5] the role of hormone replacement therapy in this patient would be quite uncertain.[6] If the patient had risk factors but had not yet experienced angina, HRT might be less controversial, but considerable uncertainties would persist. Would combination therapy with estrogen and progesterone lower aggregate risk of adverse outcomes more or less than estrogen monotherapy? How would risk reduction with hormones compare to risk reduction with selective estrogen receptor modulators (SERMs), such as raloxifene? Given that statins lower lipids more effectively than hormone replacement,[7] would statin therapy preclude a role for HRT in cardiac risk reduction? Given that the patient's family history is unknown, what is the potential harm of HRT with regard to breast cancer risk in particular? If sufficient information were available in the literature to assign a probability and utility value to each of the various outcomes associated with the decision to perform cardiac catheterization, a decision analysis might be useful in selecting the best therapy for this patient (see Chapter 10).[8]

While familiarity with decision analysis may clarify the process of therapeutic decision making, we in fact compile an array of options and weigh one against the other even without the use of this tool. Without specifying precise probabilities, outcomes, or utilities, we weigh these against one another to reach management decisions. To return to the analogy first provided in the preface, medical decision making might be considered comparable to sailing. Medical information is the sea, and good decisions safe moorings. For much of the routine navigation of clinical practice, familiarity with the local waters (knowledge/prior experience), a general sense of direction (judgment), occasional directions (advice from colleagues), and a basic understanding of sailing itself (principles of clinical epidemiology) will likely be sufficient to see the clinician and patient reliably to their mutual destination. However, when the weather and sea are rough, and/or the waters unfamiliar (i.e., when confronted with a difficult case or clinical dilemma) the more elaborate tools of navigation-chart and compass and GPS (i.e., the tools of clinical epidemiology, such as decision analysis) become extremely useful, if not essential.

※ REFERENCES

1. Kopelman RI, Wong JB, Pauker SG. A little math helps the medicine go down. *N Engl J Med*. 1999;341:435–439.
2. Katz DL. Diet, Diabetes Mellitus, and Insulin Resistance. In Katz DL. *Nutrition in Clinical Practice*. Philadelphia, PA: Lippincott Williams & Wilkins; 2000:92–103.
3. Hulley S, Grady D, Bush T, Furberg C, Herrington D, Riggs B, Vittinghoff E. Randomized trial of estrogen plus progestin for secondary prevention of coronary heart disease in postmenopausal women. Heart and estrogen/progestin replacement study (HERS) research group. *JAMA*. 1998;280:605–613.
4. Herrington DM. The HERS trial results: Paradigms lost? Heart and estrogen/progestin replacement study. *Ann Intern Med*. 1999;131:463–466.
5. Nawaz H, Katz DL. American College of Preventive Medicine Practice Policy Statement: Perimenopausal and postmenopausal hormone replacement therapy. *Am J Prev Med*. 1999;17:250–254.
6. Kuller LH. Hormone replacement therapy and coronary heart disease. A new debate. *Med Clin North Am*. 2000;84:181–198.
7. Darling GM, Johns JA, McCloud PI, Davis SR. Estrogen and progestin compared with simvastatin for hypercholesterolemia in postmenopausal women. *N Engl J Med*. 1997;337:595–601.
8. Petitti DB. *Meta-Analysis, Decision Analysis, and Cost-Effectiveness Analysis. Methods for Quantitative Synthesis in Medicine*. 2nd ed. New York: Oxford University Press; 2000.

APPENDICES

Appendix A

Getting at the Evidence

❋ APPENDIX A.1: ACCESSING THE MEDICAL LITERATURE: HOW TO GET THERE FROM HERE

O nline search engines offer the advantages of up-to-date, tailored information access. The disadvantages of online searching include the potential time lost in futile efforts and the need to weigh the quality of evidence from a diverse array of sources.

Online medical databases are collections of published medical articles from peer-reviewed (and sometimes non peer-reviewed) journals. The National Library of Medicine's (**NLM**) **MEDLINE** is the premier example. For the generalist clinician, **MEDLINE** tends to be the most useful database. It is appropriate for the efficient identification of available answers to most clinical questions. There are numerous searchable databases with more targeted application as well.

NLM Online Databases and Databanks

The National Library of Medicine maintains a computerized database bank, collectively called **MEDLARS**® (**MED**ical **L**iterature **A**nalysis and **R**etrieval **S**ystem). MEDLARS contains several online databases including some 20 million references (and growing). Some of the more important databases maintained by the NLM are listed in Table A1.1. Table A1.2 provides the characteristics of some of the more commonly used NLM databases.

TABLE A1.1	Some Databases Maintained by the National Library of Medicine

AIDSDRUGS	HSDB®
AIDSLINE®	HSRPROJ
AIDSTRIALS®	IRIS
AVLINE	MEDLINE®
BIOETHICSLINE®	MEDLINE*plus*
CancerLit®	MeSH Vocabulary®
CATLINE®	OLDMEDLINE
CCRIS	POPLINE®
ChemID*plus*	PreMEDLINE
DART®	RTECS
DIRLINE®	SDILINE®
DOCLINE	SERLINE®
DOCUSER®	SPACELINE
EMIC	TOXLINE®
ETICBACK	TOXNET
GENE-TOX	TRI
HISTLINE®	TRIFACTS

Source: National Library of Medicine website (http://www.nlm.nih.gov)

MEDLINE

MEDLINE covers many broad areas in the fields of medicine, nursing, dentistry, veterinary medicine, public health, and health care systems, among other clinical and basic sciences. The MEDLINE database consists of citations and abstracts from approximately 4,300 journals as of mid 2000. The majority of journals published in the US are included in MEDLINE along with journals from almost 70 other countries. MEDLINE contains foreign language citations to articles with an English abstract. MEDLINE's ever-expanding pool of citations reached 11 million in 2000, of which about three-quarters provide abstracts. The database, however, is limited to articles published as of 1966 or after. Citations prior to 1966 are available in a database called **OLDMEDLINE**, but do not provide abstracts or MeSH (see below) term indexing.

PreMEDLINE represents a preliminary MEDLINE, providing basic citation information and abstracts before the completed records are prepared and added to MEDLINE. Each record is identified with a **Unique**

TABLE A1.2   Databases Maintained by the NLM and Their Characteristics

Database Name	Subject and Content Area	Coverage	Special Features and Comments	NLM Search Engine to Access
AIDSDRUGS	Substances being tested in AIDS-related clinical trials	English language; potential AIDS-related therapeutics	Dictionary of chemical and biological agents currently being evaluated in AIDS clinical trials	IGM
AIDSLINE® (**AIDS** information on**LINE**)	Acquired immunodeficiency syndrome (AIDS) and related topics	All languages; publications from 1980 to the present	Contains over 156,000 records; includes journal articles, government reports, letters, technical reports, meeting abstracts/papers, monographs, special publications, theses, books and audiovisuals	IGM
AIDSTRIALS (**AIDS** clinical **TRIALS**)	Clinical trials of substances being tested for use against AIDS, HIV infection, and AIDS-related opportunistic diseases	Open and closed trials	Contains over 850 records; each record covers a single trial, and provides information such as title and purpose of the trial, diseases studied, patient eligibility criteria, contact persons, agents being tested, and trial locations	IGM
AVLINE® (**A**udio**V**isuals on**LINE**)	Biomedical audiovisual materials and computer software	Primarily English language items from the US; all audiovisuals and computer software cataloged by NLM since 1975	Contains over 31,000 items including: motion pictures, videocassettes, slide/cassette programs, filmstrip/cassette programs, and computer software special features: clinical educational materials and audiovisual/computer software serials	Locator*plus*

Source: National Library of Medicine website (http://www.nlm.nih.gov)
IGM = Internet Grateful Med (http://igm.nlm.nih.gov)
PubMed (http://www.ncbi.nlm.nih.gov/PubMed/)
Locator*plus* (http://www.nlm.nih.gov/locatorplus/locatorplus.html)
TOXNET (http://toxnet.nlm.nih.gov)
DOCLINE (http://www.nlm.nih.gov/psd/cas/newdocline.html)

TABLE A1.2 (cont.)

BIOETHICS-LINE® (**BIOETHICS** onLINE)	Ethics and related publications in health care and biomedical research	English language; publications from 1973 to the present	Contains over 53,000 records relating to the ethical, legal and public policy issues surrounding health care and biomedical research; journal articles, monographs, analytics (chapters in monographs), newspaper articles, court decisions, bills, laws, audiovisual materials, and unpublished documents	IGM
CATLINE® (**CAT**alog onLINE)	Bibliographic records covering the biomedical sciences	All languages; virtually all of the cataloged titles in the NLM collection, from the fifteenth century to the present	File contains over 786,000 records; NLM's authoritative bibliographic data; it is a useful source of information for ordering printed material, verifying interlibrary loan requests, and providing reference services	Locator*plus*
ChemID*plus* (**CHEM**ical **ID**entification)	Dictionary of chemicals		A chemical dictionary file for over 339,000 compounds of biomedical and regulatory interest; records include CAS registry numbers and other identifying numbers, molecular formulae, generic names, and structures	TOXNET
DIRLINE® (**DIR**ectory of Information Resources onLINE)	Directory of resources providing information services	Primarily the US, with some coverage of international organizations	Contains about 16,000 records on health and biomedical information resources, including organizations, government agencies, information centers, professional societies, volunteer associations, support groups, academic and research institutions, and research facilities	IGM
DOCUSER® (**DOC**ument delivery **USER**)	Directory of libraries and other information-related organizations which use NLM's interlibrary loan (**ILL**) services	Contains records for over 14,000 health-related libraries located in the US, plus about 1,700 foreign libraries	Provides descriptive and administrative information, including institutional identification, interlibrary loan policy data, and participation in the National Network of Libraries of Medicine (**NN/LM**)	DOCLINE

TABLE A1.2 (cont.)

HealthSTAR (**Health** Services, Technology, Administration, and Research)	Clinical (emphasizes the evaluation of patient outcomes and the effectiveness of procedures, programs, products, services, and processes) and non-clinical (emphasizes health care administration and planning) aspects of health care delivery	Primarily English language, but international in scope	Contains about 3.1 million records; journal articles, technical and government reports, meeting papers and abstracts, books and book chapters emphasizing health care administration; combines former **HEALTH** (**Health** Planning and Administration) and **HSTAR** (**H**ealth **S**ervice/**T**echnology **A**ssessment **R**esearch) databases	IGM
HISTLINE® (**HIST**ory of medicine onLINE)	History of medicine and related sciences	All languages; publications from 1964 to the present	File contains about 207,000 records that include iterature about the history of health related professions, sciences, specialties, individuals, institutions, drugs, and diseases in all parts of the world	IGM
HSRPROJ (**H**ealth **S**ervices **R**esearch **PROJ**ects in Progress)	Health services research project descriptions, including health technology assessment and the development and use of clinical practice guidelines	Primarily the US, with increasing coverage of international research	Provides project records for research in progress funded by federal and private grants and contracts; records include project summaries, names of performing and sponsoring agencies, principal investigator, beginning and ending years of the project, and when available, information about study design and methodology	IGM
MEDLINE® (**MED**lars onLINE)	Biomedicine	All languages; publications from 1966 to the present	Contains over 9.2 million records; includes articles from more than 3,800 international biomedical journals	IGM PubMed
MEDLINE-*plus*	Consumer health information		Health information tailored for general public use	IGM

TABLE A1.2 (cont.)

MeSH Browser (MeSH vocabulary file)	Browser to thesaurus of biomedical-related terms		Contains about 19,000 medical subject headings; an online dictionary and thesaurus of current biomedical subject headings, subheadings, and supplementary chemical terms used in indexing and searching several **MEDLARS** databases; can search by vocabulary trees	IGM PubMed
OLD-MEDLINE	Biomedicine	All languages; publications mostly from 1960 through 1965	Contains 771,287 records. Unlike **MEDLINE**, this file contains no abstracts or MeSH headings	IGM
POPLINE® (**POP**ulation information on**LINE**)	Family planning, population law and policy, and primary health care, including maternal/child health in developing countries	Primarily English language items but international in scope; publications from 1970 to the present with selected citations dating back to 1886	Contains over 248,000 records; provides worldwide coverage of population, family planning, and related health issues, including family planning technology and programs, fertility, and population law and policy; in addition, **POPLINE** focuses on developing country issues including demography, AIDS, sexually transmitted diseases, maternal and child health, primary health care communication, and population and environment	IGM
PreMEDLINE	Biomedicine	All languages; all citations currently in process for **MEDLINE**	Provides basic citation information and abstracts before the records are indexed and put into **MEDLINE**. As the indexing is finished, the completed records are added to the weekly **MEDLINE** update and the **PreMEDLINE** record is deleted from the database	IGM
SDILINE® (**S**elective **D**issemination of **I**nformation on**LINE**)	Biomedicine	All languages	Selective monthly updates with about 31,000 new **MEDLINE** citations from previous month	IGM

TABLE A1.2	(cont.)			
SERLINE® (**SER**ials on**LINE**)	Biomedical serial titles	All languages; serials published from 1665 to the present	Contains bibliographic records for all serials cataloged for the NLM collection, titles ordered or being processed for the NLM, and all serial titles indexed for **MEDLINE** and **HealthSTAR**; many records contain locator information which identify major biomedical libraries within the National Network of Libraries of Medicine (NN/LM)	*Locatorplus*
SPACELINE	Space life sciences	All languages; international **MEDLINE** (1966 to the present), plus thousands of citations from 1961 to the present from the NASA SPACELINE Office	Cooperative venture of NLM and the National Aeronautics and Space Administration (NASA)	IGM
TOXLINE® (**TOX**icology information on**LINE**)	Toxicological, pharmacological, biochemical and physiological effects of drugs and other chemicals	Primarily English language items; some international coverage	Journal articles, monographs, technical reports, theses, letters, and meeting abstracts/papers and reports	IGM TOXNET
CCRIS (**C**hemical **C**arcinogenesis **R**esearch **I**nformation **S**ystem)	Chemical carcinogens, mutagens, tumor promoters, and tumor inhibitors		Contains carcinogenicity, tumor promotion, tumor inhibition, and mutagenicity test results derived from the scanning of primary journals, current awareness tools, National Cancer Institute (**NCI**) technical reports, review articles, and International Agency for Research on Cancer (**IARC**) monographs published since 1976	TOXNET
DART® (**D**evelopmental **a**nd **R**eproductive **T**oxicology)	Teratology, developmental and reproductive toxicology	International; publications from 1989–present	Contains references on biological, chemical, and physical agents that may cause birth defects	TOXNET

TABLE A1.2 (cont.)

EMIC and **EMICBACK** (**E**nvironmental **M**utagen **I**nformation **C**enter **BACK**file)	Mutagenicity; genotoxicity	International; publications from 1950–1991	Contains references to chemical, biological, and physical agents that have been tested for genotoxic activity	TOXNET
ETICBACK (**E**nvironmental **T**eratology **I**nformation **C**enter **BACK**file)	Teratology, developmental and reproductive toxicology	International; publications from 1950–1989	Contains references on agents that may cause birth defects	TOXNET
GENE-TOX (**GEN**Etic **TOX**icology)	Chemicals tested for mutagenicity		An online data bank created by the Environmental Protection Agency (**EPA**) to review and evaluate the existing literature in the field of genetic toxicology	TOXNET
HSDB® (**H**azardous **S**ubstances **D**ata **B**ank)	Hazardous chemical toxic effects, environmental fate, safety and handling	Derived from a core set of standard texts, monographs, government documents, technical reports, and the primary journal literature	Organized by chemical record and covers the toxicity and biomedical effects of chemicals	TOXNET

TABLE A1.2 (cont.)

IRIS (Integrated Risk Information System)	Potentially toxic chemicals		Contains chemical-specific Environmental Protection Agency (**EPA**) health risk and regulatory information	TOXNET
RTECS® (Registry of Toxic Effects of Chemical Substances)	Potentially toxic chemicals		Non-bibliographic databank that focuses upon the acute and chronic effects of potentially toxic chemicals; data on skin/eye irritation, carcinogenicity, mutagenicity and reproductive consequences	TOXNET
TRI (Toxic chemical Release Inventory) series	Annual estimated releases of toxic chemicals to the environment, amounts transferred to waste sites, and source reduction and recycling data	Industry submissions reported to EPA for the years 1987–1994	Non-bibliographic files based upon data submitted by industrial facilities around the country to the Environmental Protection Agency (**EPA**) as mandated by Section 313 of the Emergency Planning and Community Right-To-Know Act	TOXNET
TRIFACTS (Toxic chemical Release Inventory **FACT** Sheets)	Health, ecological effects, safety, and handling information for most of the chemicals listed in the **TRI** (Toxic chemical Release Inventory) files		Based largely upon the State of New Jersey's Hazardous Substance Fact Sheets; designed for a lay audience, they present scientifically accepted information in nontechnical language	TOXNET

Identification (UI) number at this stage. Each article is then indexed according to a predetermined indexing system known as **Medical Subject Heading (MeSH) terms**, or "**mesh terms**." Subsequently, indexing for **Publication Type** (e.g., Randomized Controlled Trial, Review, etc.) is added to enhance searchability. Once this process is completed, a citation is added to MEDLINE. As the record is transferred to MEDLINE, it is deleted from PreMEDLINE. More than 8,000 of these citations are transferred every week.

MeSH terminology

The NLM indexes each article with a standardized vocabulary system. The **MeSH** vocabulary contains approximately 17,000 terms. Each MeSH term represents a solitary concept in medicine. New terms are entered as they develop in the medical literature. MeSH is the major means by which a search engine will retrieve articles. Each article published in biomedical journals is indexed with several MeSH terms that represent the overall theme and contents of the article. MeSH terms themselves are grouped under major divisions called trees. For example, *atrial fibrillation* is a MeSH term, but it also is a subcategory of *cardiovascular disease* which itself is a branch of *disease* as illustrated in Figure A1.1. Each MeSH term is linked to other terms in a vocabulary hierarchy.

Diseases (MeSH Category)
Cardiovascular Diseases
Heart Diseases
Arrhythmia

Atrial Fibrillation - Arrhythmia, Sinus - Atrial Flutter - Bradycardia - Cardiac Complexes, Premature - Heart Block - Long QT Syndrome - Parasystole - Pre-Excitation Syndromes - Sick Sinus Syndrome - Tachycardia - Ventricular Fibrillation

---

Figure A1.1. Illustration of a major tree, MeSH term, and MeSH subheading in descending order.

TABLE A1.3   **Listing of Qualifiers Used for MeSH Term** *atrial fibrillation*

blood	nursing
chemically induced	pathology
classification	physiopathology
complications	prevention & control
diagnosis	psychology
drug therapy	radiography
economics	radionuclide imaging
enzymology	surgery
epidemiology	therapy
etiology	ultrasonography
genetics	mortality
metabolism	veterinary

Source: National Library of Medicine website (http://www.nlm.nih.gov)

Major MeSH terms (McSH subheadings) are further categorized into MeSH subtopics to further refine the indexing. A searcher can narrow his or her search by choosing more specific terms down the line, or may expand the search to be more inclusive by choosing terms higher up in the MeSH hierarchy. In the above instance, a search with the more general term *cardiovascular diseases* would yield far more records than a search with the term *atrial fibrillation*.

For most clinicians, the term *atrial fibrillation* is apt to be broader than the goals of a particular search. The addition of **qualifiers** to the MeSH headings or sub-headings results in a narrower search. Qualifiers further dissect a concept into categories such as etiology, pathology, diagnosis, etc. Available qualifiers for "atrial fibrillation" are listed in Table A1.3.

A listing of all (current) qualifiers included in Medline is provided in Table A1.4. Qualifiers are designated by an intervening forward slash (/) character. For instance, the term *atrial fibrillation/etiology* indicates a search targeting articles on the etiology of atrial fibrillation. A search with no qualifiers added will include all of the qualifiers that exist for that term. As shown in Table A1.4, two-letter abbreviations may be used for qualifier terms. Table A1.5 lists "Publication Type" terms for MEDLINE.

TABLE A1.4   Subheadings (Qualifier terms) Used with MeSH Terms in MEDLINE and Their Standard Abbreviations

Abnormalities AB	Embryology EM	Physiopathology PP
Administration and Dosage AD	Enzymology EN	Poisoning PO
Adverse Effects AE	Epidemiology EP	Prevention and Control PC
Agonists AG	Ethnology EH	Psychology PX
Analogs and Derivatives AA	Etiology ET	Radiation Effects RE
Analysis AN	Genetics GE	Radiography RA
Anatomy and Histology AH	Growth and Development GD	Radionuclide Imaging RI
Antagonists and Inhibitors AI	History HI	Radiotherapy RT
Biosynthesis BI	Immunology IM	Rehabilitation RH
Blood Supply BS	Injuries IN	Secondary SC
Blood BL	Innervation IR	Secretion SE
Cerebrospinal Fluid CF	Instrumentation IS	Standards ST
Chemical Synthesis CS	Isolation and Purification IP	Statistics and Numerical Data SN
Chemically Induced CI	Legislation and Jurisprudence LJ	Supply and Distribution SD
Chemistry CH	Manpower MA	Surgery SU
Classification CL	Metabolism ME	Therapeutic Use TU
Complications CO	Methods MT	Therapy TH
Congenital CN	Microbiology MI	Toxicity TO
Contraindications CT	Mortality MO	Transmission TM
Cytology CY	Nursing NU	Transplantation TR
Deficiency DF	Organization and	Trends TD
Diagnosis DI	Administration OG	Ultrasonography US
Diagnostic Use DU	Parasitology PS	Ultrastructure UL
Diet Therapy DH	Pathogenicity PY	Urine UR
Drug Effects DE	Pathology PA	Utilization UT
Drug Therapy DT	Pharmacokinetics PK	Veterinary VE
Economics EC	Pharmacology PD	Virology VI
Education ED	Physiology PH	

Source: National Library of Medicine website (http://www.nlm.nih.gov)

TABLE A1.5   Terms Used for "Publication Type" in MEDLINE

Addresses	Legal Cases [includes law review, legal case study]
Bibliography	Letter [includes letters to editor]
Biography	Meeting Abstract
Classical Article [for republished seminal articles]	Meta-Analysis [quantitative summary combining results
Clinical Conference [for reports of clinical case conferences only]	of independent studies]
Clinical Trial [includes all types and phases of clinical trials]	Multicenter Study
Clinical Trial, Phase I	News [for medical or scientific news]
Clinical Trial, Phase II	Newsletter Article
Clinical Trial, Phase III	Overall [collection of articles; consider Meeting Report]
Clinical Trial, Phase IV	Periodical Index [for cumulated indexes to journals]
Congresses Controlled Clinical Trial	Practice Guideline [for specific health care guidelines]
Randomized Controlled Trial	Published Erratum [consider Corrected and Republished Article]
Comment [for comment on previously published article]	Retracted Publication [article later retracted by author]
Consensus Development Conference	Retraction of Publication [author's statement of retraction]
Consensus Development Conference, NIH	Review [includes all reviews; consider specific types]
Corrected and Republished Article [consider Published Erratum]	Review, Academic [comprehensive, critical, or analytical review]
Dictionary Directory Duplicate Publication [duplication of material	Review, Multicase [review with epidemiological applications]
published elsewhere]	Review of Reported Cases [review of known cases of a disease]
Editorial Festschrift [for commemorative articles]	Review Literature [general review article; consider other reviews]
Guideline [for administrative, procedural guidelines in general]	Review, Tutorial [broad review for nonspecialist or student]
Historical Article [for articles about past events]	Scientific Integrity Review [U.S. Office of Scientific Integrity reports]
Interview	Technical Report
Journal Article [excludes Letter, Editorial, News, etc.]	Twin Study [for studies of twins]
Lectures	

Source: National Library of Medicine web sites (http://www.nlm.nih.gov)

How to obtain access to MEDLINE

MEDLINE is available on CD-ROM and web-based search engines. Some private companies download NLM databases and then market them on CD-ROMs, mostly to colleges and universities (e.g., **Silver Platter**), where closed hospital computer systems may not allow for Internet access.

NLM offers two free web-based programs, PubMed and Internet Grateful Med (IGM) to which many websites link. Most MEDLINE vendors charge for full text retrievals and document deliveries but some (e.g., **OVID**), offer a majority of the articles online as full text.

PubMed and INTERNET GRATEFUL MED (IGM)

PubMed and **Internet Grateful Med (IGM)** are the two main search engines provided by the NLM. Both are web-based, user-friendly, relatively quick, and are offered free of charge without registration. Both allow MEDLINE searches, and IGM has the added feature of allowing searches of most of the other NLM databases (see Table A1.2) by selecting that database on the first page. Both have an automatic MeSH mapping feature. PubMed also provides links to journal sites on the web (when available) which may allow access to the full text. PubMed's "advanced search mode" allows quick searches (by author, date, page number, journal, volume, etc.).

Searching MEDLINE

MEDLINE records can be searched using MeSH terms, title or text words or phrases, author name, journal name, publication type, dates, language, study subjects or any combination of these. As stated above, MeSH terms are a vocabulary of medical and scientific terms assigned to most documents in MEDLINE by the indexers at the NLM. Text terms are strictly word searches for the exact words or phrases found in the title and abstract of a document. Whenever possible, it is advantageous to use MeSH terms over text terms for several reasons:

1. MeSH terms are assigned on the theme subject of the entire document and not just the citation text (title and abstract). Thus, a

search using a MeSH term can find relevant documents even when the exact term in question is not found in the citation. This feature is especially important for documents that do not have abstracts, because titles are very short and often omit important terms.

2. Some MeSH terms are assigned as **Major Topic** terms, meaning that the indexer has determined that these terms represent the major thrust of the document. Using the Major Topic field in MEDLINE searches can help discard documents that are less relevant to your search. These terms are designated in the citation and MEDLINE reports with an asterisk (*).

3. The use of MeSH terms and MeSH subheadings can allow searches that are very narrow and specific, and can help to speed the search process and avoid the retrieval of irrelevant material.

Both PubMed and IGM have links to the NLM's MeSH Browser through which these vocabulary trees can be visualized, and searches focused or expanded. **Automatic MeSH mapping** refers to the process where words or queries entered in the search fields are automatically checked against the NLM's MeSH directory and appropriately replaced in the search. This system is not foolproof, however, and matching to a proper MeSH term is sometimes not achieved.

Searches can be conducted by use of **Boolean operators** (mathematical set language) or **natural language**. Boolean search operators are more exact.

Boolean Search Operators

AND   is used for combining terms or phrases. Only those records that match with **all** the specific terms separated by **AND** are retrieved.

> Atrial fibrillation **AND** etiology **AND** mitral stenosis

The above field will result in retrieval of only those records that contain all these words in the title or the abstract. This is the most commonly used search operator being used (Hint: it happens automatically when you enter several words)

OR   Searches for records containing **either** of the words it separates. Using **OR** will lead to a higher number of articles retrieved than using **AND**.

> Congestive cardiomyopathy **OR** dilated cardiomyopathy

In the above, the preferred search term is unknown, therefore **OR** is used to conduct a search based on the alternatives.

NOT   Searches for records containing the query word preceding it without containing the word following it. That is, it **discards** records containing the terms after the not. For example:

> Congestive cardiomyopathy **NOT** hypertrophic cardiomyopathy

Would retrieve all articles on congestive cardiomyopathy except those pertaining to hypertrophic cardiomyopathy

★   is a wild card operator to match part of a word or phrase. Examples: micro* matches microorganism, microsome, etc. Similarly, by placing * before a word or part of a word will match all words ending with that word (e.g., *itis will match card*itis*, arth*ritis*, encepha*litis*, etc.)

While there are texts available with useful instruction in accessing medical information online,[1,2,3] printed information about accessing the published evidence base on-line will be somewhat dated by the time it is published. The pertinent websites (e.g., links to *Pubmed* or *Internet Grateful Med* off of the National Library of Medicine home page, http://www.nlm.nih.gov) generally provide tutorials and/or guidance, with the advantage of remaining constantly current.

Appendix A.2 requires internet access, and provides step-by-step guidance through several illustrative searches.

※ APPENDIX A2.2: A WALKING TOUR OF MEDLINE

Use of this appendix requires internet access. Log on to the National Library of Medicine (http://nlm.nih.gov) home page, or select some alternative means to access PubMed to proceed through the illustrative searches provided below. Conduct the searches as detailed below, and refer to the screen for the content discussed. Note that the exact number of citations retrieved at each step of the searches will likely have changed over time; this will not interfere with the demonstration of search techniques.

Search 1: Basic PubMed Search

A 30-year-old Brazilian women presents to the emergency room with a one month history of fatigue, and a three day history of left pleuritic chest pain and dull epigastric pain. Examination reveals stable vital signs and is notable only for a slightly enlarged spleen. Laboratory results show liver enzymes to be elevated (AST 400 IU/L, ALT 350 IU/L, total bilirubin 1.8 mg/dL, alkaline phosphatase 333 IU/L, and Prothrombin time 15 s). An abdominal ultrasound confirms splenomegaly and suggests hepatic fibrosis. A nuclear liver-spleen scan demonstrates portal hypertension with colloid shift. The diagnosis of autoimmune hepatitis is strongly suggested by a positive ANA titer (1:2560, homogeneous pattern).

When this information is conveyed to the patient, she asks what the treatment options are. You conduct a search.

Step I: Formulate a question and a search plan

In this case, the question would be

> What therapies are available for the management of autoimmune hepatitis?

And, as a corollary

> What is the current evidence for the effectiveness of alternative therapies?

Initial search terms from these questions might include

Autoimmune hepatitis, therapy, current reviews

Step II: Identify appropriate MeSH terms

1. Log on to the **NLM**'s **Entrez-PubMed** Start Page (http://www.ncbi.nlm.nih.gov/pubMed/).

2. Next, click on the link to the MeSH Browser.

3. Type the search words or phrase into the "search for" field. This is where natural language is transcribed into MeSH terminology. *Autoimmune hepatitis* is not a MeSH term. However, *Hepatitis, Autoimmune* is, and it will be automatically replaced in the search. A brief definition of the term and the year it was introduced are also provided. Note also that the MeSH tree is displayed, that the "Detailed Display" button provides all of the qualifiers for the term, and that the "Add" button allows for the insertion of search operators (*And, Or, Not*).

4. As we are particularly interested in the treatment of autoimmune hepatitis, we select the "detailed display" link to view the qualifers.

5. From the available qualifiers, we select "drug therapy," "therapy," and "restrict to Major Topic headings only." We then select the "Add" button to reformulate the search.
   Notice the shaded area at the top now includes technical information for the appropriate MeSH terms (*hepatitis, autoimmune*) with the appropriate qualifiers (listed as */drug therapy* and */therapy*) as the major topic area ([MAJR]). Select "PubMed Search" to return to the original PubMed screen with the newly adopted search terms incorporated.
   While *autoimmune hepatitis therapy* in natural language pulls up over 400 citations, the use of MeSH terms as detailed above yields approximately 45 articles.

Step III: Setting Limits

At this point, the articles retrieved can be reviewed, or the search can be further refined by applying **limits**. (Note that limits could have been incorporated into the search right from the beginning.) Select the "Limits" button below the search term field.

Assign the following limits to the search: publication type (review), age (all adult: 19+ years), subject type (human), publication dates (1995–2000). *Entrez dates* (5 years) is an alternative to limiting on the basis of publication dates. Conduct the search.

The limited search yields three very relevant articles. Note that the limits applied are listed at the top and that these limits can be applied all at once (as we have done) or one at a time to whittle down the number of articles retrieved.

If at this point search results were not satisfactory (e.g., if the search retrieved no articles), there are several options. The first is to expand some of the stipulated limits (e.g., remove age limits, or expand the acceptable period of publication). Alternatively, were any articles retrieved, select the "related articles" feature to expand the search.

Selecting the "related articles" hyperlink next to the first article of the three retrieved in the above search identifies over 100 related papers.

At this point you can either apply limits to the search as before or continue to retrieve "related articles" to those most pertinent and useful.

Search 2: PubMed Searching with Search Operators

A 65-year-old woman is brought to your office by her daughter for increasing memory loss. History and examination suggest early dementia, probably of the Alzheimer type. After you reveal your suspicion to the daughter, she asks whether her mother should use ginkgo biloba. Since the patient's daughter is a nurse, she wants to know if there is any good evidence that ginkgo biloba really works. You tell her that you are unable to answer a question that specific, but promise to look into the issue and get back to her.

Step I: Formulate a question and a search plan

Does ginkgo biloba improve dementia?

TABLE A2.1	Using Search Operators and Limits to Narrow a MEDLINE Search	
Search Terms Used	*Limits*	*Number of Articles Retrieved*
ginkgo biloba	none	80
ginkgo biloba AND dementia	none	15
ginkgo biloba AND dementia	clinical trial	2
ginkgo biloba AND memory	none	9
ginkgo biloba AND memory	clinical trial	1
ginkgo biloba AND cognition	none	4
ginkgo biloba AND cognition	clinical trial	1

Step II: Find appropriate MeSH terms

>Search terms: Ginkgo biloba, dementia
>Other related terms: cognition, memory

Initial PubMed search of MEDLINE entering just *ginkgo biloba* yields some 80 articles.

Step III: Setting Limits

Dementia, memory and *cognition* are similar, but separate MeSH terms. Using each of the terms with the search operator "AND" is illustrated in Table A2.1. Conduct these searches with and without publication type limited to "clinical trial." As shown in Table A2.1, these constraints result in the retrieval of a few highly relevant articles. (Note again that the actual retrieval may have changed by this time.)

Search 3: Retrieving a Particular Article

Often, a citation in a lecture or discussion will be of interest. Equally often, the information provided, particularly in the context of informal discussion or clinical rounds, will be incomplete. For example, one might hear a comment such as, "Well of course that's true given that famous *actual causes of death* paper..."

When interested in retrieving an article alluded to in such a way, the most expedient method is to use the "Single Citation Matcher" of PubMed. Select the "Single Citation Matcher" along the left side of the PubMed Services on the PubMed homepage (http://www.ncbi.nlm.nih.gov/PubMed/). Use of this feature requires that some specific information about the article be available, e.g., the year, journal and an author.

If the necessary identifying information to use the "Single Citation Matcher" is unavailable, we can limit the search to match **text terms** in the title. Select limits and change the "All Fields" to "Title Text." Search results based on progressive inclusion of more of the terms from the "allusion" above are shown in Table A2.2.

Other known terms listed under "All Fields" can also be used to perform focused searching of partial citations (for example, by author or journal name). PubMed offers specific selections on the start page which allow you to "Enter one or more search terms," "Enter *author names*," or *"Enter journal titles."*

Note that every citation in MEDLINE is labeled with a MEDLINE Unique Identifier (UI) number, generally listed at the end of a citation. Some libraries may require this number, or the PubMed identification number (the **PMID**) to locate the citation. An example of a typical MEDLINE citation providing these identifiers is shown in Figure A2.1.

TABLE A2.2   Progressive Text Term Search by Title Text

Search Terms Added	Limits	Number of Articles Retrieved
Actual	title text	1504
Actual causes	title text	9
Actual causes of death	title text	6
Actual causes of death in the United States	title text	6
94017136	UID*	1

*See Figure A2.1.

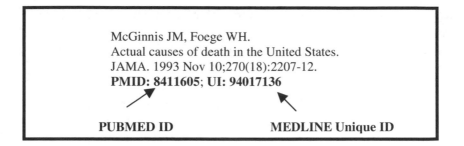

Figure A2.1. Use of MEDLINE UI number and PubMed ID.

By any of several approaches to the search, the article of interest (McGinnis JM, Foege WH. Actual causes of death in the United States. *JAMA.* 1993;270:2207–2212) can be retrieved.

≫ APPENDIX A.3: PUBLICATION BIAS: THE LIMITS OF ACCESSIBLE EVIDENCE

Any search of the literature, however sophisticated, is only as good as the literature it is searching. One of the principal concerns about the quality of the published literature is its susceptibility to **publication bias**. Publication bias is the preferential publication of studies with significantly positive findings, as compared to those with negative (nonsignificant) findings.[4]

There are two interpretations of bias that are germane to this topic. The first, referred to as the use of "bias" in the vernacular, implies preference. It is perhaps understandable that editors and reviewers might prefer studies that demonstrate an association over those that fail to do so. The second interpretation, more related to customary use of "bias" in medicine, is the introduction of a systematic distortion from the truth. The published literature is biased if it distorts reality.

There are two ways in which the literature could distort reality—by describing associations that do not truly exist, or refuting those that do. The first represents false-positive error, the second false-negative error. To some degree, the susceptibility of the literature to systematic distortions resides in the conventional thresholds of tolerance for type I (false-positive) and type II (false-negative) error.

Prevailing convention stipulates that alpha, the threshold for type I error, be set at 0.05, and beta, the threshold for type II error, at 0.2. Thus, when these conventions are honored, there is a 1 in 5 chance that any negative study is misleading, and a 1 in 20 chance that any positive study is misleading. As systematic distortion from the truth requires consideration of what constitutes truth, some conjecture about the "unbiased" medical literature is, at least theoretically, prerequisite to the assessment of publication bias. If all studies performed, regardless of outcome, were equally likely to be submitted for publication, one could posit that the unbiased literature should include 4 positive studies for every negative one, so that the probability of a false conclusion were equal between positive and negative reports.

There are problems with this position, however. Almost certainly, the probability of submission does vary with outcome, so that the journals are less likely to see negative studies.[5,6,7] This distorts the denominator of papers reviewed, and alters the ratio of publication needed to achieve unbiased representation. Further, if 4 positive papers were published for every negative paper (so that the probability of a single misleading report in either category were the same), the weight of published evidence would still favor the positive outcome (i.e., there would be a preponderance of positive papers in the literature, even with no bias). There would, as well, be no way to know which positive outcome were true, and which a fluke.

This problem might be addressed if no paper were published without considering the ratio of positive to negative papers assessing the same outcome or association. One could only be confident of a true positive association when the positive papers outnumbered the negative by more than 4 to 1, and confident of the converse when negative papers occurred more often than 1 for each 4 positive papers. This approach would require systematic submission of all completed studies to a single evaluator who would see "the big picture" and publish the pattern of truth that emerged. However, this approach is not remotely feasible. And, extreme as it is, it is also flawed. Negative studies might be less likely than positive studies to be conducted to completion. Also compounding the situation is actual results that are well beyond the stipulated threshold for tolerable error. For example, p-values much lower than an alpha of 0.05 denote a risk of false-positive much less than 5%.

While publication bias refers to the preferential publication of positive studies, there is a distortion of the literature when studies purport to be negative but are perhaps not. This occurs because many studies, particularly prior to the 1990's, did not address adequately the issue of power. A negative outcome form an under-powered study is not truly negative; rather, it is as if a study were simply not done. When such findings are published, they suggest a conclusion about lack of association that is not justified.[8,9,10,11,12,13]

It is almost certainly true that there are distortions from "the truth" in the published literature. What they are, and how to detect, judge, or measure them is unclear. An appreciation for the limitations of even the most diligent search of the published evidence is useful for, if nothing else, conferring the humility evidence-based practice requires. Even if evidence is available, even if it can be found, even if it can be interpreted, even if it seems conclusive, and even if it pertains to the clinical need at hand, it may not reflect the truth, the whole truth, and nothing but the truth of association. To appreciate and apply evidence is to appreciate and respect its many limitations.

⁂ REFERENCES

1. Bemmel J, Van Bemmel J, Musen MA (eds). *Handbook of Medical Informatics.* Springer Verlag; 1997.
2. Smith RP, Edwards MJA. *The Internet for Physicians (Book with CD-ROM).* Springer Verlag; 1999.
3. Berner ES, Ball MJ (eds). *Clinical Decision Support Systems: Theory and Practice.* Springer Verlag; 1998.
4. Petitti DB. *Meta-Analysis, Decision Analysis, and Cost-Effectiveness Analysis. Methods for Quantitative Synthesis in Medicine.* 2nd ed. New York: Oxford University Press; 2000.
5. Sutton AJ, Duval SJ, Tweedie RL, Abrams KR, Jones DR. Empirical assessment of effect of publication bias on meta-analyses. *BMJ.* 2000;320:1574–1577.
6. Thornton A, Lee P. Publication bias in meta-analysis: Its causes and consequences. *J Clin Epidemiol.* 2000;53:207–216.
7. Vickers A, Goyal N, Harland R, Rees R. Do certain countries produce only positive results? A systematic review of controlled trials. *Control Clin Trials.* 1998;19:159–166.
8. Ottenbacher KJ, Maas F. How to detect effects: Statistical power and evidence-based practice in occupational therapy research. *Am J Occup Ther.* 1999;53:181–188.
9. Mengel MB, Davis AB. The statistical power of family practice research. *Fam Pract Res J.* 1993;13:105–111.
10. Rossi JS. Statistical power of psychological research: What have we gained in 20 years? *J Consult Clin Psychol.* 1990;58:646–656.
11. Mittendorf R, Arun V, Sapugay AM. The problem of the type II statistical error. *Obstet Gynecol.* 1995;86:857–859.
12. Fox N, Mathers N. Empowering research: Statistical power in general practice research. *Fam Pract.* 1997;14:324–329.
13. Williams JL, Hathaway CA, Kloster KL, Layne BH. Low power, type II errors, and other statistical problems in recent cardiovascular research. *Am J Physiol.* 1997;273(1 Pt 2):H487–H493.
14. Lowe HJ, Barnett GO. Understanding and using the medical subject heading (MeSH) vocabulary to perform literature searches. *JAMA.* 1994;271:1103–1108.
   NLM URL: *http://www.nlm.nih.gov*
   Internet URL: *http://www.nlm.nih.gov/pubs/factsheets/factsheets.html*

Appendix B

The Constraint of Resource Limitations

◈ CONSIDERING COST IN CLINICAL PRACTICE

In applying quantitative methods and a population-based perspective to patient care, no factor is more naturally, yet less comfortably, drawn into consideration than **cost**. Cost is an unavoidable element in both clinical practice and public health,[1] and a convenient quantifier of efficiency, and to some degree even quality of care.[2,3] Yet any notion of equating pain and suffering, living and dying, with dollars causes the Hippocratic hairs on a clinician's neck to lift in suspicion and disdain.

One might wish that we were at liberty to ignore cost, that resources were unlimited. If considerations of cost were truly damaging to clinical care, to devotion to quality, then it's elimination from clinical decision making would be a good thing. But is that so?

Consider a situation in which all health care is free. Not just free to a particular consumer or payer, but actually free, due to limitless resources. In such a context, a patient with a poor clinical response could, and perhaps should, be sent to every relevant expert, receive every relevant therapy. Yet what if the probability of a response from each successive referral, each successive treatment, were diminished relative to the last? With unlimited resources, a declining probability of benefit would not, in and of itself, be cause to withhold any service. Perhaps the only reason to do so would be increasing risk from those very services.

But if the disease in question were serious, the risk of nonintervention could be so high that the risk of any intervention might be justified. But what of **effectiveness**?[4] In an environment of unlimited resources, effectiveness, the reliability with which a given intervention produces the intended effect under real-world conditions, would be in the eyes of the beholder. Because it is almost impossible to prove conclusively that something does not work, there is always some small chance, even if it has never worked before, that it could. In situations of clinical desperation, one might be inclined to try something—anything—no matter how nominal the chances of benefit. At some point in this approach to care, unsound interventions will be brought into practice. There will be risk imposed without the justifying concurrence of potential benefit. And the ethical principals underlying medical practice will be violated.

The notion that cost could be the arbiter of medical ethics may seem far-fetched, but some currency, some medium is required so that the relative effectiveness of treatments can be compared.[1] Alternatives to dollars could be considered. Cost could be measured in terms of risk or time or inconvenience, but dollars tend to be a surrogate for these. Benefit could be measured in functional status or survival or quality of life or quality-adjusted life years. But both the "costs" of medical interventions, and the attendant benefits, need to be measured in some way so that the relative merits of alternative interventions are comparable. In the real world, where resources are in fact limited, the dollar costs of procedures and therapies become a convenient, and appropriate, basis for such comparisons.[2]

Once the notion that medical practice standards require a measure of cost becomes acceptable, the distinction between public and private cost arises. Cost is of profound importance to public health, where the impact of resource limitations is felt acutely.[5] In the care of the individual patient, resource limitations are generally an abstraction in the US health care system where money to pay for interventions is the only medium likely to be in short supply. Yet the aggregated costs of individual patient care become the costs of caring for the public, and practice patterns in the aggregate have an enormous impact on expenditures. Ultimately, interventions of great potential benefit, both to individuals and the public, are abandoned due to resource limitations.

〰 COST-BENEFIT ANALYSIS

The simplest and generally least acceptable means of assessing cost trade-offs in clinical practice is **cost-benefit analysis**. The objectionable element in such an approach is the need to measure both cost and benefit in dollars. Thus, if the benefit expected is clinical, such as symptom resolution or extension of life, a translation of the benefit into dollar terms would be required to determine the cost-benefit implications of the intervention. Cost-benefit analysis is used to determine if an intervention will save or cost money.

There are situations in which a cost-benefit analysis makes sense. In an occupational setting, there is likely to be a strong interest in overall profitability. Health-related interventions for employees will be fine up to a point, but beyond a certain point they would be prohibited by cost and the erosion of profit. But if an intervention, such as stress reduction counseling for employees, translated into fewer days missed and greater productivity, the costs of the intervention might be more than offset by the resultant gains. In such a situation, consideration of cost might lead to interventions that would otherwise never be made available.

Another situation in which cost considerations can enhance services is prevention. Clinical preventive services all cost something. But in many instances, the cost of not providing them is higher still. An example is provided by a cost-benefit analysis of influenza vaccination in the occupational setting.[6] When a clinical benefit is associated with an actual and measurable reduction in costs, a compelling argument is advanced for the provision of new services.

〰 COST-EFFECTIVENESS ANALYSIS

Often, dollar savings from an intervention are not expected. A clear example is renal dialysis.[7] The intervention is life prolonging, even life saving, but costly. These costs are sustained and accumulated over time, with little to no economic return on the investment. At the same time, the value of such costly clinical interventions is clear in human terms: reduced suffering, increased survival.

One means of comparing financial cost to clinical benefit is to assess **cost-effectiveness**. Cost-effectiveness considers the cost in dollars per pertinent outcome, such as life saved or illness prevented. Such an analysis is undertaken when the clinical outcome has been established as a social priority. Cost-effectiveness permits comparisons among alternative strategies to determine which achieves the desired outcome at the lowest cost.[8] The greatest generation of pertinent outcomes for each dollar spent, or alternatively the methods leading to the least dollars spent per unit outcome achieved, are considered the most cost-effective. Such an analysis does not require that clinical endpoints be cast in dollar terms, nor that an intervention can produce savings, but merely that its costs be justified by the magnitude of its clinical benefit.

Of note, cost-effectiveness and quality measures often, although not always, correlate well. Poor clinical outcomes and complications of suboptimal care are costly. The efficient achievement of clinical recovery through optimal use of available resources tends to be both desirable professionally and cost-effective. The lowest cost means of achieving a clinical endpoint is apt to be the most direct, most efficient, most reliable means, and as such clinically and financially preferable to the alternatives.

Standards of cost-effectiveness are contextually defined and bound. In the US, interventions with costs in the range of $50,000 per year of life extended are widely supported. Costlier interventions are generally considered unattractive.[9] Programs are adopted by the World Health Organization (WHO) for developing countries only with evidence of dramatically greater cost-effectiveness, in the range of $10 per year of life saved.[10] Obviously the adoption of a global standard of cost-effectiveness in health care delivery would require massive reallocations of resources.

§§ COST-UTILITY ANALYSIS

A variation on the concept of cost-effectiveness is **cost utility**. Whereas cost-effectiveness assumes that the clinical outcome is constant and seeks to demonstrate the least costly means of achieving it, a utility measure permits the outcome side of the formula to vary as well. The prevailing utility measure is a composite of both quality and length of life gained, or **quality adjusted life years (QALY's)**.[3,11] Typically, a year of perfect health is expressed as 1, with reductions in either time or the degree of intact health yielding portions of a quality adjusted life year (QALY). For example, living 10 years with a 50% reduction in quality of life due to a disability would result in a QALY measure of 5. Living 5 years in perfect health would yield the same measure, as would living 20 years with such severe functional limitations that the quality of life were reduced by 75% (to "0.25" the quality of intact health). Dollars spent per QALY gained is a measure of cost utility, allowing variation in both costs and benefits to be considered without specifying a dollar value for those benefits.

🎜 MARGINAL COSTS AND BENEFITS

The relevance of cost considerations to clinical decision making is mediated by the influence of **marginal cost and benefit**, or **utility**. That some additional benefit might result from some additional expenditure is often the case, but once conventional practices have been applied, both the probability and magnitude of additional benefit from additional spending tend to wane. Thus, the benefit at the margin of usual practice, or the marginal benefit, will decline with the extent of the evaluation or treatment. Often it is in just such situations that the costs per additional intervention rise steeply—as the more extravagant the management plan, the more costly its components. As noted above, failure to consider cost at all can result in an inattention to the imbalance between marginal costs and utilities, so that very expensive interventions of little potential value are applied as routinely as low cost interventions of high potential value. In situations where cost and potential benefit rise together, or fall together, considerations of cost-effectiveness are required to determine how to proceed. In situations where costs rise and marginal utilities fall, the intervention is apt to be of questionable merit. But when marginal utility rises as costs fall, there is a clear indication to proceed.

The tension between costs and utilities can be captured in a 2×2 table used to portray "cost-consequence space," as shown in Box B.1.

🎜 OTHER CONSIDERATIONS

Among other important considerations in cost evaluations are perspective, externalities, discounting, and projections. **Perspective** refers to the group (or individual) for whom a particular cost (or benefit) is relevant. For example, society (or a given population) might benefit if a pharmaceutical company made a drug or vaccine available free in a developing

Box B.1

Cost-consequence space. Interventions in cell c are the most favorable, raising utility while lowering cost; interventions in cells a and d require further consideration of cost-effectiveness; interventions in cell b are generally appropriate only in situations of extreme clinical need.

Marginal utility

	+	−
Marginal cost +	*a*	*b*
−	*c*	*d*

Courtesy of: Paltiel D. Lecture; Yale School of Medicine. 1998.

country, while the company (or its consumers) would bear the cost. The trade-offs between cost and benefit would be quite different depending on whose perspective were considered. **Externalities** refer to costs or benefits that occur as an indirect result of a particular intervention, often affecting a different individual or group. For example, if the care of a premature baby in the neonatal intensive care unit requires one or both parents to miss work, the lost productivity is an additional, indirect, or external cost. **Discounting** refers to the erosion of monetary benefits or costs that are postponed until some future time. **Projections** in economic analysis are an effort to anticipate the financial impact of time trends; Markov models (see Chapter 10) are used for this purpose.

Economic analysis in medicine and health care is far too expansive a topic to receive comprehensive treatment here. The intent of this appendix is to highlight the importance of cost considerations in evidence-based practice and to provide examples of application. The reader interested in a thorough discussion of the subject should consult other sources.[12]

≋ REFERENCES

1. Brown GC, Sharma S, Brown MM, Garrett S. Evidence-based medicine and cost-effectiveness. *J Health Care Finance.* 1999;26:14–23.
2. Larson EB. Evidence-based medicine: Is translating evidence into practice a solution to the cost-quality challenges facing medicine? *Jt Comm J Qual Improv.* 1999;25:480–485.
3. Earle CC, Chapman RH, Baker CS, et al. Systematic overview of cost-utility assessments in oncology. *J Clin Oncol.* 2000;18:3302–3317.
4. Shaw LJ, Miller DD. Defining quality health care with outcomes assessment while achieving economic value. *Top Health Inf Manage.* 2000;20:44–54.
5. Berger ML. The once and future application of cost-effectiveness analysis. *Jt Comm J Qual Improv.* 1999;25:455–461.
6. Burckel E, Ashraf T, de Sousa Filho JP, et al. Economic impact of providing workplace influenza vaccination. A model and case study application at a Brazilian pharma-chemical company. *Pharmacoeconomics.* 1999;16(5 Pt 2):563–576.
7. Manns BJ, Taub KJ, Donaldson C. Economic evaluation and end-stage renal disease: From basics to bedside. *Am J Kidney Dis.* 2000;36:12–28.
8. McCabe C, Dixon S. Testing the validity of cost-effectiveness models. *Pharmacoeconomics.* 2000;17:501–513.
9. Newby LK, Eisenstein EL, Califf RM, et al. Cost effectiveness of early discharge after uncomplicated acute myocardial infarction. *N Engl J Med.* 2000;342:749–755.
10. Hinman AR. Economic aspects of vaccines and immunizations. *C R Acad Sci III.* 1999;322:989–994.
11. Vijan S, Hofer TP, Hayward RA. Cost-utility analysis of screening intervals for diabetic retinopathy in patients with type 2 diabetes mellitus. *JAMA.* 2000;283:889–896.
12. Petitti DB. *Meta-Analysis, Decision Analysis, and Cost-Effectiveness Analysis. Methods for Quantitative Synthesis in Medicine.* 2nd ed. New York: Oxford University Press; 2000.

Appendix C

Clinically Useful Measures Derived from the 2 × 2 Contingency Table

		Disease Status	
		+	−
	+	a	b
Test Status			
	−	c	d

$a =$	true-positive cases
$b =$	false-positive cases
$c =$	false-negative cases
$d =$	true-negative cases
$(a + b) =$	all test-positives
$(a + c) =$	all disease-positives
$(b + d) =$	all disease-negatives
$(c + d) =$	all test-negatives
$(a + b + c + d) =$	sample size
$(a + c)/(a + b + c + d) =$	prevalence
$(b + d)/(a + b + c + d) =$	proportion disease free (1 − prevalence)

$a/(a + c) =$ **sensitivity** (the proportion[1] of those with disease correctly detected by the test)

$d/(b + d) =$ **specificity** (the proportion[1] of those without disease correctly identified as disease-free by the test)

$c/(a + c) =$ **false-negative error rate** (the proportion[1] of those with disease with a negative test result; 1 − sensitivity)

$b/(b + d) =$ **false-positive error rate** (the proportion[1] of those truly disease-free with a positive test result; 1 − specificity)

$a/(a + b) =$ **positive predictive value** (PPV) (the proportion[1] of those with a positive test who truly have disease)

$b/(a + b) =$ **proportion misleading positives**[2] (PMP) (the proportion[1] of positive test results that are incorrect; 1 − PPV)

$d/(c + d) =$ **negative predictive value** (NPV) (the proportion[1] of those with a negative test result who are truly disease-free)

$c/(c + d) =$ **proportion misleading negatives**[2] (PMN) (the proportion[1] of negative test results that are incorrect; 1 − NPV)

$b/a =$ **false-positive index**[2] (FPI) (the ratio of false- to true-positives)

$c/d =$ **false-negative index**[2] (FNI) (the ratio of false- to true-negatives)

$(a/c)/(b/d) =$ **odds ratio**

$[a/(a + b)]/[c/(c + d)] =$ **risk ratio (relative risk)**

Measures influenced by prevalence: positive predictive value; negative predictive value; proportion misleading positives; proportion misleading negatives; false positive index; false negative index

---

[1]While identified as a proportion, the measure is typically expressed as a percentage.
[2]Newly established term/measure.

Specific Measures Are More Readily Recalled if the Denominator Is Considered First

Denominator	Measure
disease positives $(a + c)$	sensitivity false-negative error rate
disease negatives $(b + d)$	specificity false-positive error rate
test positives $(a + b)$	positive predictive value proportion misleading positives
test negatives $(c + d)$	negative predictive value proportion misleading negatives

Glossary

accuracy   the tendency for a test to approximate, on average, the truth

ACES   active control equivalence study

Active Control Equivalence Study   a study in which a novel therapy is compared to established therapy with statistical methods adapted to demonstrate lack of difference

Actuarial method   an approach to survival analysis in which time intervals are fixed in advance (see *Kaplan–Meier*)

adherence   the degree to which study subjects comply with the treatments to which they are assigned; compliance

alpha error   false-positive error; also referred to as type I error

alternative hypothesis   in conventional hypothesis testing, the assertion of the association of interest

analyze as randomized   a description applied to intention-to-treat analysis of data from randomized trials; outcome is assessed in groups based on treatment assignment rather than adherence to the assigned treatment

association
the appearance of a meaningful (i.e., cause and effect) relationship between variables

attributable risk
the absolute risk ascribable to a particular exposure or factor; the difference between the risk in the exposed and the risk in the unexposed

attributable risk percent
the attributable risk expressed as a percentage; the difference between the risk in the exposed and the risk in the unexposed, divided by the risk in the exposed, multiplied by 100

benefit-to-risk ratio
a measure of the ratio of probable benefit to potential risk useful in deciding whether or not a particular clinical intervention is advisable; useful in establishing the therapeutic threshold, $1/(B:R+1)$, where B is benefit and R is risk measured in the same units

beta error
false-negative error; also referred to as type II error

bias
systematic distortion from the true

binary data
dichotomous data; data with only two possible values (e.g., yes/no)

bivariate analysis
statistical analysis of the relationship between a single independent and single dependent variable

blinding
concealing treatment status from subject and/or investigator (referred to as double-blinding when concealed from both) in a trial

case report
a detailed description of a single, unusual case

case series
a detailed description of several related cases

case-control study   a study in which groups are assembled on the basis of whether they do (cases) or do not (controls) have the outcome of interest, and are then assessed for differences in exposure

case-finding   use of clinical tests to uncover occult disease or risk factors in individuals undergoing medical care/evaluation (see *screening*)

causality   a cause and effect relationship between independent and dependent variables, the establishment of which requires the satisfaction of Mill's canons or Koch's postulates

Central limit theorem   the assertion that for relatively large samples (i.e., $n > 30$), the distribution of the means of many such samples will be normally distributed even if the distribution for an individual sample is non-normal

cohort study   a study in which groups are assembled on the basis of exposure status and then assessed for differences in outcome

compliance   the degree to which study subjects adhere to assigned treatments; adherence

confidence interval (95%)   a means of conveying not only statistical significance, but the actual range of probable outcome values if a test were to be repeated; the actual outcome measure observed ±1.96 standard errors

confounder   a third variable linked to both putative cause and putative effect that creates the appearance of an association when there is none (positive confounding) or the appearance of no association when there is one (negative confounding)

confounding   the creation, by a third variable linked to both putative cause and effect variables, of the appearance of an association when there is none (positive confounding) or the appearance of no association when there is one (negative confounding)

contingency table   a table that displays the outcome values of one dichotomous or ordinal variable relative to (contingent upon) the outcomes of a second dichotomous or ordinal variable

continuous data   data with values uninterrupted across a given range; e.g., temperature

correlation   an expression of the degree to which movement in one variable influences/predicts movement in a second variable

Cox proportional hazards modeling   a method of multivariable modeling for survival analysis data

critical ratio   the ratio of outcome effect (signal) to variance (noise) in hypothesis testing; the ratio is critical in that it determines the statistical significance

cross-sectional study   a study in which, often by survey, measures of outcome and exposure status are obtained at the same time

cut-off point   the designated value that distinguishes normal from abnormal results of a test, or the presence from the absence of disease

data dredging   an unflattering term applied to the use of a large data set to test for multiple associations without appropriate statistical protection against chance findings

decision analysis   a formalized approach to making complex medical decisions that relies on plotting (in a "tree") the alternatives and rating each in terms of probability and utility

decision tree   the plot of clinical options and the associated probabilities and utilities used in a decision analysis

degrees of freedom   used in various tests of statistical significance, a measure of the number of observations in a data set that contribute to random variation

dependent variable   outcome variable

detection bias   when differential rates of disease or condition detection between groups are attributable to differing levels of investigation or scrutiny between groups

dichotomous   having two possible values (e.g., yes/no)

dichotomous data   data that are expressed with two possible values

double-blind   the concealment of treatment status from both subject and investigator in a trial

ecological fallacy   the inference that an association in a population is an association within individual members of that population when in fact it is not

ecological study   a study in which exposure and outcome variables are assessed at a population rather than individual level, often by use of vital statistics

effect modification   when a third variable, linked to both putative cause and effect variables, changes the relationship between them

effect modifier	the variable that produces effect modification (see above)
effectiveness	the influence of treatment on outcome under real-world circumstances
efficacy	the influence of treatment on outcome under ideal, or near ideal, circumstances
expected value	the distribution of values that would occur by chance under the conditions of the null hypothesis (i.e., lack of association)
external validity	generalizability; the degree to which study outcomes pertain to other individuals or populations
false-negative error rate	the number of negative test results divided by the total number of (truly) positive cases $[c/(a + c)]$
false-negative index	the ratio of false to true negatives (c/d)
false-positive error rate	the number of positive test results divided by the total number of (truly) negative cases $[b/(b + d)]$
false-positive index	the ratio of false- to true-positives (b/a)
frequency distribution	a plot of the values of a particular variable against the frequency of occurrence of each
generalizability	external validity; the degree to which study outcomes pertain to other individuals or populations
hard measure	an outcome measure not considered subjective or open to interpretation
Hawthorne effect	attribution of some or all of the observed outcome to differential levels of contact with the investigators or their associates between groups,

rather than to the specific intervention *per se*; controlled for by establishing comparable levels of "contact" for all study groups

hypothesis　　assertion of an association believed, but not known, to be true

hypothesis testing　　a statistical approach to confirming or refuting a hypothesis

incidence rate　　the number of incident cases during a defined time period, divided by the population at risk at the midpoint of that period

incidence　　the number of new cases of a condition of interest in a defined population during a specified period of time

independent variable　　predictor or causal variable

individualized benefit index　　NNH/NNT when NNH is the larger number (also established by dividing the absolute risk reduction by the absolute risk increase); a measure of the number of patients helped by an intervention for every one harmed

individualized harm index　　NNT over NNH when NNT is the larger number (also established by dividing the absolute risk increase by the absolute risk reduction); a measure of the number of patients harmed by an intervention for every one helped

intention-to-treat analysis　　the analysis of outcomes in the groups derived from a randomization process, regardless of whether subjects in each group actually adhered to the assigned treatment (also referred to as "analyzing as randomized")

internal validity   the degree to which a study reliably measures the association it purports to measure without bias

interval data   ordinal data for which the distance between consecutive values is consistent

intervention trial   a study in which one group of subjects receives a treatment or procedure

Kaplan–Meier method   a method of survival analysis in which intervals of observation are determined by the timing of death (or outcome) as opposed to the fixed intervals of the actuarial method

Koch's postulates   a set of conditions defining causality, most applicable to infectious diseases

lead time bias   the apparent increase in survival time after diagnosis resulting from earlier time of diagnosis rather than later time of death

length bias   the tendency, in a population screening effort, to detect preferentially the longer, more indolent cases of any particular disease

life table methods   analytical methods for survival analysis

likelihood ratio (grand)   the ratio of the likelihood ratio positive to the likelihood ratio negative; equivalent to the odds ratio; a measure of how much more likely it is that a positive test result is true than a negative result false; provides a measure of test reliability that is independent of disease prevalence

likelihood ratio negative   the ratio of the false-negative error rate to specificity; a measure of how likely a false-negative test result is as compared to a true-negative result

likelihood ratio positive   the ratio of sensitivity to the false-positive error rate; a measure of how likely a true-positive test result is as compared to a false-positive result

linear regression   a method of statistical analysis that can be used to determine the amount of movement in a dependent variable expected for a given movement in an independent variable (e.g., the amount of increase in HDL cholesterol for hour of exercise per week)

log-rank test   a method of statistical significance testing for survival analysis

major topic   a heading indicating major divisions within the MeSH language (see *Medical subject heading (MeSH) term*)

mean   the average value of a sample

measurement bias   when differences in the finding of interest between groups are due to systematic differences in methods applied to the measurement of the finding

measures of central tendency   those measures that characterize the clustering of observations in a data set, such as mean, median, and mode

median   the middle value in a set of observations arranged in ascending order

medical subject heading (MeSH) term   designations in a language developed by the National Library of Medicine; used to define the scope of an online search in MEDLINE or related services

meta-analysis   quantitative synthesis of the results of multiple smaller studies into a single analysis

mode   the one or more most frequently occurring values in a data set

multivariate analysis   a term typically used to denote the analysis of multiple predictor variables in relation to a single outcome variable; technically, multivariable analysis denotes multiple predictors and single outcome, while multivariate denotes both multiple predictors and outcome variables

necessary cause   an exposure that must occur if the outcome is to occur; may or may not be sufficient (see *Sufficient cause*)

negative confounding   when a confounding variable obscures a true causal relationship between two other variables

negative predictive value   the proportion of those with negative test results that is truly free of disease $[d/(c + d)]$

nominal data   discontinuous (categorical data) with no implied direction (e.g., blood types)

nonparametric data   data that cannot be characterized by a mean and standard deviation (i.e., parameters)

nonparametric methods   methods of statistical analysis designed for nonparametric data, based largely on ranking the outcome data

null hypothesis   the stipulation of no association that is the conventional basis for hypothesis and significance testing; statistical significance is predicated on finding evidence that allows for the rejection of the null hypothesis with a specified degree of confidence

number needed to harm

the number of patients that need to be exposed to a procedure with a defined risk of a particular adverse effect before, on average, one individual experiences the adverse effect; $1/ARI$, where ARI is absolute risk increase

number needed to treat

the number of patients that need to be exposed to a procedure with a defined probability of a particular beneficial effect before, on average, one individual experiences the beneficial effect; $1/ARR$, where ARR is absolute risk reduction

observational cohort study

a cohort study in which no intervention is performed; subjects with differing exposures are simply observed with regard to outcome

odds ratio

often used as a measure of outcome in case-control studies; the relative odds of exposure in those with to those without the disease/outcome; $[(a/c)/(b/d)]$

one-tailed test

justified when the direction in which an outcome will deviate from the null is predictable based on prior study, an approach to hypothesis testing that places the entire rejection region (or tail) of the hypothetical plot of sample means to one side

operating characteristics

a term often used to denote the performance measures of a diagnostic test, such as sensitivity and specificity

ordinal data

discontinuous (categorical) data with implied direction (e.g., cardiac murmurs graded from I to VI)

parametric data   data for which the frequency distribution is characterizable by mean and standard deviation (parameters)

parametric methods   methods of statistical analysis limited to parametric data

Pearson correlation coefficient   denoted by r, a measure of the degree to which movement in one continuous variable corresponds with movement in a second variable

performance characteristics   see "operating characteristics"

population attributable risk   the degree to which the risk of a particular outcome in a population is ascribable to a particular factor; risk in the population, minus the risk in the unexposed

population attributable risk percent   the percent of total population risk for a particular outcome ascribable to a particular factor; risk in the population, minus risk in the exposed, divided by the risk in the population, then multiplied by 100

positive confounding   when a confounding variable creates the appearance of an association between two variables unassociated in reality

positive predictive value   the proportion of those with a positive test result that truly has the disease; $[a/(a + b)]$

posterior probability   the probability of disease following the performance of a diagnostic test

post-test odds   the odds of disease following the performance of a diagnostic test

post-test probability   see posterior probability

power	the complement of β, the degree of false-negative error $(1 - \beta)$; the probability that an outcome effect will be detected if it exists
precision	the degree to which a test produces the same or similar results when repeated; reproducibility
pretest odds	the odds of disease before the performance of a given diagnostic test
pretest probability	the probability of disease before the performance of a given diagnostic test
prevalence	the number (or proportion) of individuals in a defined population with a condition of interest at a specified time
primum non nocere	first, do no harm
prior probability	the probability of disease before the performance of a given diagnostic test
proportion misleading negatives	the proportion of those with negative test results that truly has disease
proportion misleading positives	the proportion of those with positive test results that is truly disease-free
prospective cohort study	a cohort study in which subjects are followed from the present for a future outcome event
publication bias	the tendency of studies with positive (significant) outcomes to be published preferentially relative to those with negative outcomes; presupposes an appropriate or "unbiased" pattern of publication that has not been clearly defined

publication type   specifies the type of article to be retrieved in a MEDLINE search

qualifiers   terms used to narrow the scope of a MEDLINE search

qualitative meta-analysis   a systematic review of the literature on a give topic without synthesis of the data from the multiple individual trials

quantitative meta-analysis   a systematic review of the literature on a give topic followed by synthesis of the data from the multiple individual trials selected on the basis of formal evaluation and abstraction methods

randomization   the allocation of subjects to treatment/assignments on the basis of chance by use of any of several methods, most commonly a computer algorithm

randomized clinical trial   considered the "gold standard" in the clinical study of humans, a trial in which subjects are randomly assigned to treatment groups, and in which, typically, there is a placebo control arm, and blinding of both subjects and investigators to treatment status (double-blinding)

ratio data   continuous data with a true 0 point for reference (e.g., the Celsius temperature scale)

RCT   the standard abbreviation for randomized clinical trial

recall bias   differential recollection of exposure status as a result of different outcome status among subjects in a case-control study

regression to the mean   see *Statistical regression effect*

rejection region   the portion of the hypothetical distribution of trial outcomes that corresponds to alpha and represents a low enough probability of false positivity to permit rejection of the null hypothesis

relative risk   also known as the risk ratio, and frequently used as a measure of outcome in cohort studies, the ratio of risk of the outcome in those with to those without the exposure; $[\{a/(a+b)\}/\{c/(c+d)\}]$

reliability   the degree to which repeated measures of the same phenomenon correspond; reproducibility; precision

reproducibility   the degree to which repeated measures of the same phenomenon correspond; reliability

responsiveness   the tendency of a test result to vary with changes in the status of the patient

retrospective cohort study   a cohort study in which groups are assembled on the basis of exposure status at some time in the past, then followed through the past for the occurrence of outcome

risk difference   risk in the exposed minus risk in the unexposed

risk ratio   see *Relative risk*

sampling bias   inclusion in a study of subjects not fully representative of the underlying population

screening   efforts directed at detecting occult disease in some at-risk portion of the general population not otherwise actively under medical care or evaluation (as opposed to case finding)

selection bias also known as allocation bias, when there is differential assignment of subjects to treatment groups based on subject characteristics

sensitivity the capacity of a test to detect disease when it is truly present; $[a/(a + c)]$

signal to noise ratio a descriptive characterization of the critical ratio used in hypothesis testing

single-blind the concealment of treatment status from subjects, but not investigators, in an intervention study

soft measure a subjective outcome variable open to interpretation (e.g., level of contentment)

specificity the capacity of a test to exclude disease when it is truly absent; $[d/(b + d)]$

spectrum bias when a test performs differently among patients with differing levels/stages of a disease

standard deviation a measure of the average dispersion of observations in a sample from the sample mean; $\mathrm{Sqrt}\{\sum[(x_i - \bar{x})^2]/(n-1)\}$ where Sqrt is the square root, x_i is the observation value associated with the ith observation, $\bar{x}$ is the mean of the sample, and n is the sample size; the square root of the variance; designated as s

standard error the standard deviation (see above) divided by the square root of the sample size

statistical regression effect (regression to the mean) the tendency, on the basis of random variation, for extreme test values to shift toward the population mean when repeated

statistical significance	the characterization of a study outcome as less probably attributable to chance than the prespecified limit of risk for false-positive error (alpha); typically taken to mean that an apparent association is "real"
sufficient cause	an exposure that will inevitably lead to the outcome; may or may not be necessary (see *necessary cause*)
sum of squares	a measure used to characterize the dispersion of observations about the mean of a sample; $\sum[(x_i - \bar{x})^2$ where x_i is the observation value associated with the ith observation, and $\bar{x}$ is the mean of the sample
survival analysis	a method of analysis applied to studies with a dichotomous outcome measure, such as survival/death, that accounts for differences between groups in the distribution of the outcome over time
therapeutic threshold	the minimal ratio of probable benefit to risk that justifies an intervention; $1/(B:R+1)$, where B is benefit and R is risk measured in the same units
treatment bias	differential care of subjects based on their group assignment other than with regard to the intervention of interest
two-tailed test	the conventional approach to hypothesis testing in which the rejection region of the hypothetical distribution of trial outcomes is divided between the lower and upper tails of the curve
type I error	false-positive error; alpha
type II error	false-negative error; beta

under-powered   a study unlikely (typically due to inadequate sample size) to detect a meaningful outcome effect even when there truly is one

univariate analysis   the initial step in data analysis, the characterization of variables with regard to the range and distribution of values, one at a time

URL   the standard abbreviation for uniform resource locator, the typical designation of an "address" on the World Wide Web

validity   synonymous with accuracy; a measure of the degree to which the results reflect the truth

variance   a measure of the average dispersion of observations in a sample from the sample mean; $\{\sum[(x_i - \bar{x})^2]/(n-1)\}$ where x_i is the observation value associated with the ith observation, $\bar{x}$ is the mean of the sample, and n is the sample size; the square of the standard deviation; designated as s^2

variation   the dispersion of observations in a sample

Z-value   the distance of an observation from the sample mean in units of standard deviations

Text Sources

⚗ BOOKS

Dawson-Saunders B, Trapp RG. *Basic & Clinical Biostatistics.* 2nd ed. Norwalk, CT: Appleton & Lange; 1994.

Eddy DM. *Clinical Decision Making. From Theory to Practice.* Sudbury, MA: Jones and Bartlett Publishers; 1996.

Fletcher RH, Fletcher SW, Wagner EH. *Clinical Epidemiology. The Essentials.* 3rd ed. Baltimore, MD: Williams & Wilkins; 1996.

Friedland DJ (ed). *Evidence-Based Medicine. A Framework for Clinical Practice.* Stamford, CT: Appleton & Lange; 1998.

Friedman LM, Furberg CD, DeMets DL. *Fundamentals of Clinical Trials.* 3rd ed. St. Louis, MO: Mosby; 1996.

Gray JAM. *Evidence-Based Healthcare.* New York: Churchill Linvingstone; 1997.

Hulley SB, Cummings SR, Browner WS, Grady D, Hearst N, Newman TB. *Designing Clinical Research.* 2nd ed. Philadelphia, PA: Lippincott Williams & Wilkins; 2001.

Jekel JF, Elmore JG, Katz DL. *Epidemiology, Biostatistics, and Preventive Medicine.* Philadelphia, PA: Saunders; 1996.

Katz DL. *Epidemiology, Biostatistics, and Preventive Medicine Review.* Philadelphia, PA: Saunders; 1997.

Motulsky H. *Intuitive Biostatistics.* New York: Oxford University Press; 1995.

Petitti DB. *Meta-Analysis, Decision Analysis, and Cost-Effectiveness Analysis. Methods for Quantitative Synthesis in Medicine.* 2nd ed. New York: Oxford University Press; 2000.

Pocock SJ. *Clinical Trials.* Chichester, UK: Wiley; 1993.

Rosser WW, Shafir MS. *Evidence-Based Family Medicine.* Hamilton, Ontario: B.C. Decker Inc; 1998.

Sackett DL, Haynes RB, Guyatt GH, Tugwell P. *Clinical Epidemiology. A Basic Science for Clinical Medicine.* 2nd ed. Boston, MA: Little, Brown and Company; 1991.

Sackett DL, Richardson WS, Rosenberg W, Haynes RB. *Evidence-Based Medicine. How to Practice & Teach EBM.* New York: Churchill Livingstone; 1997.

Speicher CE. *The Right Test.* 3rd ed. Philadelphia, PA: Saunders; 1998.

U.S. Preventive Services Task Force. *Guide to Clinical Preventive Services.* 2nd ed. Alexandria, VA: International Medical Publishing; 1996.

※ UJERJ' GUIDEJ TO THE MEDICAL LITERATURE

Barratt A, Irwig L, Glasziou P, et al. Users' guides to the medical literature: XVII. How to use guidelines and recommendations about screening: Evidence-Based Medicine Working Group. *JAMA.* 1999;281:2029–2034.

Bucher HC, Guyatt GH, Cook DJ, Holbrook A, McAlister FA. Users' guides to the medical literature: XIX. Applying clinical trial results: A. How to use an article measuring the effect of an intervention on surrogate end points: Evidence-Based Medicine Working Group. *JAMA.* 1999;282:771–778.

Dans AL, Dans LF, Guyatt GH, Richardson S. Users' guides to the medical literature: XIV. How to decide on the applicability of clinical trial results to your patient: Evidence-Based Medicine Working Group. *JAMA.* 1998;279:545–549.

Drummond MF, Richardson WS, O'Brien BJ, Levine M, Heyland D. Users' guides to the medical literature: XIII. How to use an article on economic analysis of clinical practice: A. Are the results of the study valid? Evidence-Based Medicine Working Group. *JAMA.* 1997;277:1552–1557.

Giacomini MK, Cook DJ. Users' guides to the medical literature: XXIII. Qualitative research in health care: A. Are the results of the study valid? Evidence-Based Medicine Working Group. *JAMA.* 2000a;284:357–362.

Giacomini MK, Cook DJ. Users' guides to the medical literature: XXIII. Qualitative research in health care: B. What are the results and how do they help me care for my patients? Evidence-Based Medicine Working Group. *JAMA.* 2000b;284:478–482.

Guyatt GH, Haynes RB, Jaeschke RZ, et al. Users' Guides to the Medical Literature: XXV. Evidence-based medicine: Principles for applying the Users' Guides to patient care: Evidence-Based Medicine Working Group. *JAMA.* 2000;284:1290–1296.

Guyatt GH, Naylor CD, Juniper E, Heyland DK, Jaeschke R, Cook DJ. Users' guides to the medical literature: XII. How to use articles about health-related quality of life: Evidence-Based Medicine Working Group. *JAMA.* 1997;277:1232–1237.

Guyatt GH, Sackett DL, Cook DJ. Users' guides to the medical literature: II. How to use an article about therapy or prevention: A. Are the results of the study valid? Evidence-Based Medicine Working Group. *JAMA.* 1993;270:2598–2601.

Guyatt GH, Sackett DL, Cook DJ. Users' guides to the medical literature: II. How to use an article about therapy or prevention: B. What were the results and will they help me in caring for my patients? Evidence-Based Medicine Working Group. *JAMA.* 1994;271:59–63.

Guyatt GH, Sackett DL, Sinclair JC, Hayward R, Cook DJ, Cook RJ. Users' guides to the medical literature: IX. A method for grading health care recommendations: Evidence-Based Medicine Working Group. *JAMA.* 1995;274:1800–1804.

Guyatt GH, Sinclair J, Cook DJ, Glasziou P. Users' guides to the medical literature: XVI. How to use a treatment recommendation: Evidence-Based Medicine Working Group and the Cochrane Applicability Methods Working Group. *JAMA.* 1999;281:1836–1843.

Hayward RS, Wilson MC, Tunis SR, Bass EB, Guyatt G. Users' guides to the medical literature: VIII. How to use clinical practice guidelines: A. Are the recommendations valid? The Evidence-Based Medicine Working Group. *JAMA.* 1995;274:570–574.

Hunt DL, Jaeschke R, McKibbon KA. Users' guides to the medical literature: XXI. Using electronic health information resources in evidence-based practice: Evidence-Based Medicine Working Group. *JAMA.* 2000;283:1875–1879.

Jaeschke R, Guyatt G, Sackett DL. Users' guides to the medical literature: III. How to use an article about a diagnostic test: A. Are the results of the study valid? Evidence-Based Medicine Working Group. *JAMA.* 1994a;271:389–391.

Jaeschke R, Guyatt GH, Sackett DL. Users' guides to the medical literature: III. How to use an article about a diagnostic test: B. What are the results and will they help me in caring for my patients? The Evidence-Based Medicine Working Group. *JAMA*. 1994b;271:703–707.

Laupacis A, Wells G, Richardson WS, Tugwell P. Users' guides to the medical literature: V. How to use an article about prognosis: Evidence-Based Medicine Working Group. *JAMA*. 1994;272:234–237.

Levine M, Walter S, Lee H, Haines T, Holbrook A, Moyer V. Users' guides to the medical literature: IV. How to use an article about harm: Evidence-Based Medicine Working Group. *JAMA*. 1994;271:1615–1619.

McAlister FA, Laupacis A, Wells GA, Sackett DL. Users' Guides to the Medical Literature: XIX. Applying clinical trial results: B. Guidelines for determining whether a drug is exerting (more than) a class effect. *JAMA*. 1999;282(14):1371–1377.

McAlister FA, Straus SE, Guyatt GH, Haynes RB. Users' guides to the medical literature: XX. Integrating research evidence with the care of the individual patient: Evidence-Based Medicine Working Group. *JAMA*. 2000;283:2829–2836.

McGinn TG, Guyatt GH, Wyer PC, Naylor CD, Stiell IG, Richardson WS. Users' guides to the medical literature: XXII. How to use articles about clinical decision rules: Evidence-Based Medicine Working Group. *JAMA*. 2000;284:79–84.

Naylor CD, Guyatt GH. Users' guides to the medical literature: X. How to use an article reporting variations in the outcomes of health services: The Evidence-Based Medicine Working Group. *JAMA*. 1996a;275:554–558.

Naylor CD, Guyatt GH. Users' guides to the medical literature: XI. How to use an article about a clinical utilization review: Evidence-Based Medicine Working Group. *JAMA*. 1996b;275:1435–1439.

O'Brien BJ, Heyland D, Richardson WS, Levine M, Drummond MF. Users' guides to the medical literature: XIII. How to use an article on economic analysis of clinical practice: B. What are the results and will they help me in caring for my patients? Evidence-Based Medicine Working Group. *JAMA*. 1997;277:1802–1806.

Oxman AD, Cook DJ, Guyatt GH. Users' guides to the medical literature: VI. How to use an overview: Evidence-Based Medicine Working Group. *JAMA*. 1994;272:1367–1371.

Oxman AD, Sackett DL, Guyatt GH. Users' guides to the medical literature: I. How to get started: The Evidence-Based Medicine Working Group. *JAMA*. 1993;270:2093–2095.

Randolph AG, Haynes RB, Wyatt JC, Cook DJ, Guyatt GH. Users' Guides to the Medical Literature: XVIII. How to use an article evaluating the clinical impact of a computer-based clinical decision support system: *JAMA*. 1999;282:67–74.

Richardson WS, Detsky AS. Users' guides to the medical literature: VII. How to use a clinical decision analysis: A. Are the results of the study valid? Evidence-Based Medicine Working Group. *JAMA*. 1995a;273:1292–1295.

Richardson WS, Detsky AS. Users' guides to the medical literature: VII. How to use a clinical decision analysis: B. What are the results and will they help me in caring for my patients? Evidence Based Medicine Working Group. *JAMA*. 1995b;273:1610–1613.

Richardson WS, Wilson MC, Guyatt GH, Cook DJ, Nishikawa J. Users' guides to the medical literature: XV. How to use an article about disease probability for differential diagnosis: Evidence-Based Medicine Working Group. *JAMA*. 1999;281:1214–1219.

Richardson WS, Wilson MC, Williams JW Jr, Moyer VA, Naylor CD. Users' guides to the medical literature: XXIV. How to use an article on the clinical manifestations of disease: Evidence-Based Medicine Working Group. *JAMA*. 2000;284:869–875.

Wilson MC, Hayward RS, Tunis SR, Bass EB, Guyatt G. Users' guides to the Medical Literature: VIII. How to use clinical practice guidelines: B. What are the recommendations and will they help you in caring for your patients? The Evidence-Based Medicine Working Group. *JAMA*. 1995;274:1630–1632.

∭ OTHER ARTICLES

Detsky AS, Naglie G, Krahn MD, Naimark D, Redelmeier DA. Primer on medical decision analysis: Part 1—Getting started. *Med Decis Making.* 1997;17:123–125.

Detsky AS, Naglie G, Krahn MD, Redelmeier DA, Naimark D. Primer on medical decision analysis: Part 2—Building a tree. *Med Decis Making.* 1997;17:126–135.

Eiseman B, Jones R, McClatchey M, Borlase B. Cost-effective diagnostic test sequencing. *World J Surg.* 1989;13:272–276.

Eraker SA, Eeckhoudt LR, Vanbutsele RJ, Lebrun TC, Sailly JC. To test or not to test—to treat or not to treat: The decision-threshold approach to patient management. *J Gen Intern Med.* 1986;1:177–182.

Krahn MD, Naglie G, Naimark D, Redelmeier DA, Detsky AS. Primer on medical decision analysis: Part 4—Analyzing the model and interpreting the results. *Med Decis Making.* 1997;17:142–151.

Merz CN, Berman DS. Imaging techniques for coronary artery disease: Current status and future directions. *Clin Cardiol.* 1997;20(6):526–532.

Naglie G, Krahn MD, Naimark D, Redelmeier DA, Detsky AS. Primer on medical decision analysis: Part 3—Estimating probabilities and utilities. *Med Decis Making.* 1997;17:136–141.

Naimark D, Krahn MD, Naglie G, Redelmeier DA, Detsky AS. Primer on medical decision analysis: Part 5—Working with Markov processes. *Med Decis Making.* 1997;17:152–159.

Patterson RE, Churchwell KB, Eisner RL. Diagnosis of coronary artery disease in women: Roles of three dimensional imaging with magnetic resonance or positron emission tomography. *Am J Card Imaging.* 1996;10:78–88.

Patterson RE, Horowitz SF, Eisner RL. Comparison of modalities to diagnose coronary artery disease. *Semin Nucl Med.* 1994;24:286–310.

Rathbun SW, Raskob GE, Whitsett TL. Sensitivity and specificity of helical computed tomography in the diagnosis of pulmonary embolism: A systematic review. *Ann Intern Med.* 2000;132:227–232.

Resnik DB. To test or not to test: A clinical dilemma. *Theor Med.* 1995;16:141–152.

Epilogue

A leading clinician and clinical epidemiologist received the bad news that her 76-year-old father had suffered a large anterior wall myocardial infarction. She rushed to the hospital, where she learned he was hypotensive and in renal failure. She was confronted with desperate options, daunting decisions—intra-aortic balloon pump, emergency bypass surgery, or hemodialysis. Her father had been clear that he never wanted "heroic measures" if and when it came to that. Yet, she thought, that pertained when his condition was truly irreversible. Was it? His cardiac function might improve over time. His kidneys might recover from acute tubular necrosis. Struggling with the possibilities, her own emotions and those of her family, and the weightiness of the decisions to be made, the clinician turned to a trusted friend and colleague for advice.

"But," said the friend, "you're a leading clinical epidemiologist. You know all there is to know about the probabilities of different outcomes with different procedures, the potential risks and benefits involved, the operating characteristics of various tests and procedures. If anyone has the means to make a tough decision like this one, it's you."

"Oh, come on!" replied the clinician, clearly drained and exasperated. "This is *important*!"

With thanks to: David Paltiel, PhD, Yale University School of Medicine, Department of Epidemiology and Public Health.

Index

Absolute risk, 98t, 99
Absolute risk increase (ARI), 93, 98t
Absolute risk reduction (ARR), 98t
Acceptance region, 185
Accuracy, 40-42, 41f, 72
ACES. *See* Active control equivalence studies
Active control equivalence studies (ACES), 163-164
  prominent characteristics of, 178t
Actuarial methods, 141
Adjustment, statistical, 169
Allocation bias, 123, 124t
Alpha (α) errors, 188, 189, 196
Alternative, 3
Alternative hypothesis (H_a), 120, 127, 143
  eliminating, 120-125
Alternative outcomes, 204
Alternatives, 62, 148, 208
Analysis:
  actuarial method of, 141
  as randomized, 172
  bivariate, 119-120, 144
  characterizing associations, 119-120
  constructively deconstructing medical literature, 170-171
  decision, 203-210
  generalizability of results, 123

intention-to-treat, 157, 169, 172
Kaplan-Meir method of, 141
life-table methods of, 141
Markov Analysis or Modeling, 207
meta-analysis, 160-163, 172, 178t
multivariate methods of, 119-120, 144
need to analyze as randomized, 157
nonparametric methods, 134-138, 144
parametric, 118
parametric methods of, 128-134, 143
selection of methods of, 150t
sensitivity, 214
sub-group, 158
survival, 141
univariate, 119-120, 144
Analysis of variance (ANOVA), 132-134, 133f, 144
ANOVA (analysis of variance), 132-134, 133f, 144
Antihypertensive medication, frequency distribution for possible outcome data from example clinical trial of, 129-130, 130f
AR. *See* Attributable risk
ARI. *See* Absolute risk increase
ARR. *See* Absolute risk reduction

EDITOR'S NOTE: Page references followed by n indicate notes. References followed by b, t, or f indicate boxes, tables, or figures, respectively.

Aspirin, example dichotomous
  outcome distribution of myocardial
  infarction with, 134, 135b
Assembly bias, 124t
Assessment of study validity, 167-169
Associations, 110-111
  characterizing, 119-120
  evidence supporting, 110-111
  Koch's postulate of, 108t
Attributable risk (AR), 96, 97, 98t, 99
  population (PAR), 98t, 99
Attributable risk percent (AR%), 97,
  98t
  population (PAR%), 98t, 99
Averaging out, 205-206, 206f, 208

Bayes' theorem, 48-50
  alternative applications, 56-57
  and likelihood ratios, 57-60
  and sequence of testing, 64-65
  application of, 50-56
  approach to NPV, 54
  approach to posterior probability, 51,
    52, 53
  2×2 contingency table and, 50b
  formula for, 48-49
  implications for diagnostic testing,
    60-61
  scenarios, 51-52, 52-53, 53-54, 55-56
Benefits:
  benefit to risk ratio, 220
  individualized benefit index (IBI), 94,
    98t
  of screening, 83, 84t
Beta Blocker Heart Attack trial, 158
Beta (β) errors, 188, 189, 197
Bias, 6, 122-125, 172
  allocation, 123, 124t
  and study design, 153, 154
  assembly, 124t
  detection, 124t, 125, 156
  lead time, 71, 124t, 125
  length, 124t, 125
  measurement, 123-124, 124t, 156
  observer, 124t, 125
  publication, 162, 190
  recall, 124t, 154

representative varieties in hypothesis
    testing, 124t
  sampling, 123, 124t
  selection, 123, 124t
  spectrum, 124t, 125
  susceptibility, 124t
  treatment, 124t, 125
Binary data, 118-119
Biological plausibility, 109
Bivariate analysis, 119-120, 144
Blinding, 169

Calculations:
  power, 197
  sample size, 197
Case-control studies, 151-152, 172
  nested, 152
  prominent characteristics of, 176t
Case reports, 166
Case series, 166
Categorical data:
  nominal, 118
  ordinal, 118
Causality, 109
Central limit theorem, 117
Central tendency measures, 113
Certainty, diagnostic, 220
Chi-square test, 134-138, 135b, 144
CI. See Confidence interval
Ciceron-Arellano I, 89n4
CK. See Creatine kinase
Clinical data. See Data
Clinical dilemmas, 208
Clinical epidemiology, 219
Clinical practice, 201-222
Clinical reasoning:
  principles of, 3-4
  quantitative aspects of, 45-67
  with population-based data, 5-11
Clinical research principles, 105-198
Clinical significance, 196
Clinical studies or trials. See Studies
Cochrane Collaborative, 163
Cohort studies, 155, 172
  observational, 156
  prospective, 156-158, 172, 176t
  retrospective, 155, 172, 176t

Comparability, 163
Conceptual factors, 62-63
Conclusions, 188, 188b
Concurrent testing, 64, 65t
Confidence interval (CI), 140, 144,
    194-195
  95% CI, 194, 197
Confounders, 120-121, 125
Confounding, 120-122, 153, 156
  negative, 121, 154
  positive, 120-121, 154
Consistency, 109
Content validity, 41
Contingency:
  2 × 2 contingency table, 15, 16b,
    50b, 73-74, 74b, 75, 75b
  degrees of freedom for any table, 138
Continuous data, 116-118
  compared between two groups, 193,
    193t
Continuous variables, 116-117
Convenience sampling, 167
Correlation, 141
Costs:
  financial, 83, 84t
  human, 85-87, 86, 86t, 88
  monetary, 79-85
  total program, 88
Cox proportional hazards, 142, 144
Creatine kinase:
  cutoff point > 80 with 50% prior
    probability of MI, 32, 33b
  cutoff point > 150 with 50% prior
    probability of MI, 33b, 34
  cutoff point > 280 with 50% prior
    probability of MI, 34b, 34-35
  troponin or MB fraction of (CKMB),
    31, 32t
Criterion validity, 42
Critical ratio, 116, 127
Crossover trials, 164
Cross product, 140
Cross-sectional studies, 165, 172,
    179t
Cutoff points, 31, 43
  adjusting, 39-40
Data:
  binary, 118-119

  characterization of, 150t
  classes of, 125
  continuous, 116-118
  dichotomous, 118-119, 134, 135b
  interval, 117
  nominal, 118
  ordinal, 118
  ratio, 117
  survival, 141
  "torturing until confession," 149
  types of, 116-118
Data dredging, 149, 158, 168
Dawson-Saunders B, 126n5, 144n2,
    175n138, 197n6
Decision analysis, 203-210
Decision trees, 204, 205f, 208
Degrees of freedom, 115, 138
Detection bias, 124t, 125, 156
Deviation, standard of, 115
Diagnosis, 10, 13-44, 211-217
Diagnostic certainty, 220
Diagnostic studies or tests. *See* Tests
Dichotomous data, 118-119, 134, 135b
Differential diagnosis, 217
Differential error, 123
Dilemmas, clinical, 208
Disease improbability, 56-57
Disease probability, 25-31. *See also*
    Probability
  altering estimates of, 30-31
  scenarios, 25-27, 27-29, 29-30
Dispersion:
  degree of, 130, 130f
  measuring, 114-115
Distribution:
  even, 135-136, 136b, 137b
  Koch's postulate of, 108t
  normal, 117, 117f, 183, 184f
  of dichotomous data, 134, 135b
  rejection region of, 185-186, 186f,
    187f, 196
Doll R, 173n8
Donnelly R, 67n5
Dose-responsiveness, 109
Doyle, Conan, 23n1
Drug effects:
  comparison with placebo effects, 183,
    184f

types of conclusions and errors from statistical tests of, 188, 188b

Ecological fallacy, 166
Ecological studies, 165, 172, 179t
Effectiveness, 169
Effect modification, 122
Effect modifiers, 122, 125
Effects:
    fixed, 162
    random, 162
ELISA, 78
Epidemiology, clinical, 219
Equivalence, 163
Errors:
    differential, 123
    random, 123
    standard, 184
    systematic, 123
    type II or beta (β), 188, 189, 197
    type I or alpha (α), 188, 189, 196
    types of, 188, 188b
Estimates of probability:
    altering, 30-31
    conceptual factors, 62-63
Evidence:
    application in clinical practice, 201-222
    strength of, 169-170
    supporting association, 110-111
Expected values, 136-137
Exposure measures, 150t
External validity, 123, 166

Face validity, 42
Factorial trial designs, 164-165, 165f
False-negative error, 15
False-negative error rate, 43
False-negative index (FNI), 19
False-negative reactions, 78
False-positive error, 15
False-positive error rate, 43, 49
False-positive index (FPI), 22
False-positive reactions, 78
Financial costs, 79-85, 84t
"Fishing expeditions," 149

Fixed effects, 162
FNI. *See* False-negative index
Folsom AR, 100n4
FPI. *See* False-positive index
Frequency distribution, 117, 129-130, 130f
Funnel plots, 162

Generalizability, 123
Gold standard tests, 220
"Goodness of fit" test, 120
Group means, 129, 129f

H_0. *See* Null hypothesis
H_a. *See* Alternative hypothesis
Harm:
    individualized harm index (IHI), 95, 98t
    number needed to harm (NNH), 98t, 99
Hawthorne effect, 57, 169
Heart and Estrogen/Progestin Replacement Study (HERS), 221
Heart beat screening with 99% sensitive and 99% specific test, in adults, 76, 77b
HERS. *See* Heart and Estrogen/ Progestin Replacement Study
HIV testing, 78, 79
Homogeneity test, 161
Human costs, 85-87, 86t, 88
Hypotheses:
    alternative (H_a), 120-125, 127, 143
    asserting, 150t
    multiple, 172
    null, 143
    null (H_0), 127
    revision of, 150t
    testing, 116
Hypothesis testing:
    and stipulation of outcome, 142-143
    bias in, 124t
    key steps in, 109, 110t
    mechanics of, 127-145
    methods of, 141-142
    nonparametric methods, 134-138

parametric methods, 128-134
principles of, 107-126

IBI. *See* Individualized benefit index
IHI. *See* Individualized harm index
"Impending blindess syndrome"
    example screening, 80t, 80-85, 81b,
    82b, 83b
Improbability, 56-57
Incidence, 8-9
Independence, 134, 135, 136b
Individual cross-sectional studies,
    179t
Individualized benefit index (IBI), 94,
    98t
Individualized harm index (IHI), 95,
    98t
Individual patient risk, measuring,
    92-95
Intention-to-treat analysis, 157, 169,
    172
Internal validity, 123, 166
Interval data, 117
Intervention trials, 156-157
Ischemia test examples, 17, 17b, 20b,
    20-21, 22-23, 23b, 23-24, 25-27,
    26b, 28b, 28-29, 29b, 30
Isolation, 108t

Kaplan-Meir method of analysis, 141
Koch's postulates, 108t, 109, 125

Lead time bias, 71, 124t, 125
Length bias, 124t, 125
Life table methods, 141
Life year, quality adjusted, 142
Likelihood ratio (LR), 35-36, 36t,
    38b, 43
  Bayes' theorem and, 57-60
  properties of, 37b
Likelihood ratio negative, 35, 43
Likelihood ratio positive, 35, 43
Linear regression, 141
Line of unity, 39, 162
Literature, medical:

constructively deconstructing,
    170-171
interpreting statistics in, 181-198
statistical significance in, 182-185
*Users' Guides to the Medical
    Literature*, 168
Literature reviews, 160.
    See also Medical literature
Log-rank test, 142
Longitudinal studies, 165
LR. *See* Likelihood ratio

Management, 219-222
Markov Analysis or Modeling, 207,
    208
Matching, 169
Mean, 113-114
  group, 129, 129f
  regression to the, 41
Measurement bias, 123-124, 124t, 156
Measures:
  of exposure, 150t
  of risk, clinically relevant, 98t, 99
  outcome, 150t
  quality of life, 144
Measuring central tendency, 113-114
Measuring dispersion, 114-115
Measuring risk, 91-101
Measuring risk modification, 97-99
Median, 113
Medical literature:
  constructively deconstructing,
    170-171
  interpreting statistics in, 181-198
  statistical significance in, 182-185
  *Users' Guides to the Medical
    Literature*, 168
MEDLINE, 214, 216
Meta-analysis, 160-163, 172
  prominent characteristics of, 178t
  qualitative, 160, 161, 161f
  quantitative, 160
Michels KB, 174n123
Mill JS, 126n1
Mill's canons, 109, 125
Mode, 113
Modeling, Markov, 207

Monetary costs, 79-85, 84t
Multiple hypotheses, 172
Multivariate analysis, 119-120, 142, 144

Necessary cause, 109
Negative confounding, 121, 154
Negative predictive value (NPV), 18, 43, 54, 66
Nested case-control studies, 152
NNH. *See* Number needed to harm
NNT. *See* Number needed to treat
Nominal data, 118
Nomura A, 126n8
Nonparametric analysis, 134-138
Nonparametric tests, 138
Normal distribution, 117
  characteristics of, 117, 117f
  rejection region of, 185-186, 186f, 187f
NPV. *See* Negative predictive value
Null hypothesis (H$_0$), 127, 143
Number needed to harm (NNH), 93, 98t, 99
Number needed to treat (NNT), 93, 98t, 99
Nurses' Health Study, 158

Observational cohort studies, 156
Observer bias, 124t, 125
Odds, 38b, 66
  and probabilities, 57-60
  post-test, 58, 66
Odds ratio, 37b, 96, 144
  calculation of, 139, 140b
  in hypothesis testing, 139-140
Olivares-Sandoval Z, 89n4
One-tailed tests of significance, 185-188, 187f, 197
Open or open-label approach, 169
Ordinal data, 118
Ottenbacher KJ, 198n11
Outcome data:
  continuous, 193, 193t
  proportional, 193, 193t

Outcome effects, 192
  example even distribution relative to uneven distribution of exposed and unexposed subjects, 135-136, 137b
  example even distribution with 1 in 4 experiencing outcome, 135, 136b
  example even distribution with independent treatment and outcome, 135, 136b
  with extreme variation, 112-113, 113f
  without variation, 112, 112f
Outcome measures, 150t
Outcomes:
  dichotomous, 134, 135b
  stipulation of, 142-143

Paired t-tests, 131-132, 143
PAR. *See* Population attributable risk
Parallel tests, 66
Parametric analysis, 118, 128-134, 143
Pearson correlation coefficient (*r*), 141
Perinatal HIV Intervention Research in Developing Countries Workshop participants, 174n17
Placebo effects, 169
  normal distribution of, 183, 184f
  types of conclusions and errors from statistical tests of drugs vs., 188, 188b
Placebo groups:
  example dichotomous outcome distribution with, 134, 135b
  example frequency distribution for possible outcome data with, 129-130, 130f
Plausibility, biological, 109
PMN. *See* Proportion misleading negatives
PMP. *See* Proportion misleading positives
Population attributable risk (PAR), 98t, 99
Population attributable risk percent (PAR%), 98t, 99

Population-based data, 5-11
Positive confounding, 120-121, 154
Positive predictive value (PPV), 19, 43, 49, 66
Posterior probability, 9, 43
  Bayesian approach to, 51, 52, 53
  calculation of, 50
  with concurrent tests, 64, 65t
Post-test odds, 58, 66
Powe NR, 210n23
Power calculations, 197
Power of studies, 189
PPV. *See* Positive predictive value
Precision, 40-42, 41f, 72
Predictive value:
  negative, 18, 43, 54, 66
  positive, 19, 43, 49, 66
Pregnancy screening example with 99% sensitive and 99% specific test, in males, 76, 76b
Prejudice, 6
Prevalence, 8, 11, 14, 49
Primum non nocere (first, do no harm) principle, 189
Prior probability, 9, 11, 46
Probability, 3, 38b
  and diagnosis, 211
  and study design, 147
  disease, 25-31
  estimates of, 62-63
  in decision trees, 204, 208
  odds and, 57-60
  posterior, 9, 43, 50, 51, 52, 53, 64, 65t
  prior, 9, 11, 43, 46
  relative, 3-4
Probability sampling, 167, 169
Prognostication, 91
Proportional outcome data compared between two groups, 193, 193t
Proportion misleading negatives (PMN), 18-19
Proportion misleading positives (PMP), 19, 56-57
Prospective cohort studies, 156-158, 172, 176t
Pruning back, 208

Publication bias, 162, 190
p-values, 190-191, 196

Qualitative meta-analysis, 160, 161, 161f
Quality adjusted life year, 142
Quality of life measures, 144
Quantitative aspects, 45-67.
  See also under Measuring
Quantitative meta-analysis, 160
Questions, research, 150t

r. See Pearson correlation coefficient
Random effects, 162
Random error, 123
Randomization, 169, 172
Randomized clinical trials (RCTs), 157, 158-160, 172, 177t
Random sampling, 167, 169
Ranking, 138
Ratio data, 117
RCTs. *See* Randomized clinical trials
Recall bias, 124t, 154
Receiver operating characteristic (ROC) curves, 36-39, 39f, 43
Regression:
  linear, 141
  statistical regression effect, 41
  to the mean, 41
Rejection region, 185, 196
  for one-tailed tests of significance, 186, 187f
  for two-tailed tests of significance, 185-186, 186f
Relative risk, 92, 98t, 99, 161.
  See also Risk ratio
Relative risk reduction, 92
Reliability, 40-41, 43
Research principles, 105-198
Research protocols, 149, 150t
Research questions, 150t
Responsiveness, 42
Restriction, 169
Results. *See also* Outcomes
  generalizability of, 123

Retrospective cohort studies, 155, 172, 176t
Risk, 3, 62, 91, 99, 204
  absolute, 98t, 99
  absolute risk increase (ARI), 93, 98t
  absolute risk reduction (ARR), 98t
  actual, 92
  and diagnosis, 211
  and study design, 148
  attributable (AR), 96, 97, 98t, 99
  attributable risk percent (AR%), 97, 98t
  benefit to risk ratio, 220
  clinically relevant measures of, 98t, 99
  in clinical investigations, 96
  in decision trees, 208
  measuring and conveying, 91-101
  population attributable (PAR), 98t, 99
  relative, 92, 98t, 99. *See also* Risk ratio
  to individual patients, 92-95
Risk difference, 97, 98t
Risk factors, 96, 99
Risk modification, 97-99
Risk ratio (RR), 96, 139b, 139-140, 144
Risk reduction, absolute (ARR), 98t
ROC curves. *See* Receiver operating characteristic curves
RR. *See* Risk ratio
Rule-in tests, 73, 74-75
Rule-out tests, 73, 79, 88, 216
Ruling in, 10
Ruling out, 10

Sample size, 191-193
  calculations, 197
  formulas, 192, 193t
Sampling, 166-167, 172
  convenience, 167
  probability, 167, 169
  random, 167, 169
Sampling bias, 123, 124t
Screening:
  criteria for, 70-73, 71t
  definition of, 70-71

example financial costs and benefits, 83, 84t
  fundamentals of, 69-89
  heart beat example, 76, 77b
  HIV, 78, 79
  human costs of, 85-87, 88
  "impending blindness syndrome" example, 80t, 80-85, 81b, 82b, 83b
  monetary costs of, 79-85
  objectives of, 73
  pregnancy example, 76, 76b
  pros and cons, 87
  rule-in tests, 88
  scenarios, 80t, 80-85, 81b, 82b, 83b
  sequential testing, 77-79
  SnNout, 73
  SpPin, 75
  statistical considerations for, 73-77
  summary, 88
  tests with high sensitivity, 88
  tests with high specificity, 88
  total program costs, 88
  with 98% sensitivity and 60% specificity with 5% disease prevalence, 73-74, 74b
  with 60% sensitivity and 98% specificity with 5% disease prevalence, 75, 75b
Selection bias, 123, 124t, 156
  and study design, 157
Sensitivity, 13, 43, 48, 49
  in screening, 73
  of studies, 189
Sensitivity analysis, 61, 66, 207, 208, 214
Sequence of testing, 64-65
Sequential testing, 77-79, 88
Serial testing, 66
Signal to noise ratio, 116
Significance, 129
  clinical, 196
  one-tailed tests of, 185-188, 187f, 197
  statistical, 127, 181, 182-185, 196
  two-tailed tests of, 185-188, 186f, 196
SnNout (Sn = sensitive; N = negative result; out = disease ruled out), 73

Specificity, 13-14, 43, 49, 109
Spectrum bias, 124t, 125
SpPin (Sp = specific; P = positive
   result; in = disease ruled in), 75
Squares, sum of, 114, 115f
Standard deviation, 114-115, 183
Standard error, 184
Standardized criteria for clinical
   studies, 160
Standard of deviation, 115
Standards of care, 159
Statistical adjustment, 169
Statistical regression effects, 41
Statistical significance, 127, 181,
   182-185, 196
Statistical tests of drugs vs. placebo,
   188, 188b
Statistics:
  and human costs, 85-87
  and monetary costs, 79-85
  in medical literature, 181-198
  screening considerations, 73-77
Stratification, 169
Strength and causality, 109
Student's t-test, 128-131
Studies:
  active control equivalence studies
    (ACES), 163-164
  case-control, 151-152, 172, 176t
  cohort, 155, 172
  crossover trials, 164
  cross-sectional, 165, 172, 179t
  ecological, 165, 172
  factorial design trials, 164-165, 165f
  longitudinal, 165
  measuring risk in, 96
  observational cohort, 156
  power of, 189
  prospective cohort, 156-158
  randomized clinical trials (RCTs),
    157, 158-160, 172, 177t
  retrospective cohort, 155
  sensitivity of, 189
  standardized criteria for, 160
  types of, 149, 151f, 176t-179t
  under-powered trials, 190
  validity of, 167-169
Study design, 147-179

  factorial, 164-165, 165f
  selection of, 150t
  summary, 172-173
  types of, 149, 151f, 165-166
Sub-group analysis, 158
Sufficient cause, 109
Sum of squares, 114
Survival analysis, 141
Survival data, 141
Susceptibility, 108t
Susceptibility bias, 124t
Systematic error, 123

Technology, 9
Test errors:
  false-negative error, 15
  false-negative index (FNI), 19
  false-positive error, 15
  false-positive index (FPI), 22
Testing, diagnostic
  costs of, 79-85
  implications of Bayes' theorem for,
    60-61
  sequence of, 64-65
  sequential, 77-79, 88
Testing, hypothesis, 107-126
  key steps in, 109, 110t
  mechanics of, 127-145
  methods of, 141-142
  nonparametric tests, 138
  summary, 125-126
Test interpretation, 31-35
Test of homogeneity, 161
Test performance, 13-25
  2 × 2 contingency table and, 15, 16b
  altering, 16-24
  summary, 42-43
Tests, diagnostic
  accuracy of, 40-42
  concurrent, 64, 65t
  cutoff points for, 31
  in parallel, 66
  negative predictive value (NPV) of, 18
  positive predictive value (PPV) of, 19
  precision of, 40-42
  responsiveness of, 42
  serial, 66

true tests of, 40-42
Tests of significance
  one-tailed, 185-188, 187f, 197
  two-tailed, 185-188, 186f, 196
The Alpha-Tocopherol, Beta Carotene
  (ATBC) Cancer Prevention Study
  Group, 175n134
Therapeutic threshold, 220
"Third" variable, 169
Thrombolytic therapy trials, 161,
  161f
Treatment bias, 124t, 125
Trials. *See* Studies
Troponin or MB fraction of
  creatine kinase (CKMB) example
  distribution, 31, 32t
True-positives, 48, 49
T-tests, 143
  paired, 131-132, 143
  student's, 128-131
Two-tailed tests of significance,
  185-188, 186f, 196
Type II or beta (β) errors, 188, 189, 197
Type I or alpha (α) errors, 188, 189, 196

Under-powered trials, 190
Univariate analysis, 119-120, 144
U.S. Preventive Services Task Force
  (USPSTF), 88n1, 169-170, 175n142

*Users' Guides to the Medical
  Literature*, 168
USPSTF. *See* U.S. Preventive Services
  Task Force
Utility, 205

Validity, 41, 43, 172
  construct, 42
  content, 41
  criterion, 42
  external, 123, 166
  face, 42
  internal, 123, 166
  study, 167-169
Variability, 114
Variables:
  continuous, 116-117
  "third," 169
Variance, 115
Variation, 112-113
  extreme, 112-113, 113f
  outcome effects without, 112, 112f
  within-groups, 129, 129f

Wash-out period, 164

Z-score, 193t

About the Author

David L. Katz, MD, MPH, is Associate Clinical Professor of Epidemiology and Public Health & Medicine, and Director of Medical Studies in Public Health at the Yale University School of Medicine. He is board certified in Internal Medicine and Preventive Medicine/Public Health. He earned his BA from Dartmouth College, his MD from the Albert Einstein College of Medicine, and his MPH from the Yale University School of Medicine. He directs courses at the Yale Schools of Medicine and Public Health in biostatistics/clinical epidemiology, public health/epidemiology, preventive medicine, health policy, and nutrition, and has served as clinical preceptor to both medical students and residents. A former preventive medicine residency director, he helped establish a unique, integrated Internal Medicine/Preventive Medicine training program at a Yale affiliated hospital in Derby, CT, and was recognized with the *Rising Star Award* of the American College of Preventive Medicine in 2001. He founded and directs the Yale School of Public Health's CDC-funded Prevention Research Center, where he oversees a staff of 15, and is principal investigator of numerous studies in chronic disease prevention, including both clinical and community-based trials. Dr. Katz has published numerous scientific articles and chapters on topics including chronic disease prevention, nutrition, obesity, clinical epidemiology, and cardiovascular disease. In addition, he has authored several previous books, including *Epidemiology, Biostatistics & Preventive Medicine Review* (W.B. Saunders, 1997) and *Nutrition in Clinical Practice* (Lippincott Williams & Wilkins, 2000).